The Trinity

The Trinity

An Introduction to Catholic Doctrine
on the Triune God

GILLES EMERY, O.P.

Translated by Matthew Levering

The Catholic University of America Press
Washington, D.C.

Originally published as *La Trinité:
Introduction Théologique à la doctrine catholique sur Dieu Trinité*
(Paris: Les Éditions du Cerf, © 2009).

Copyright © 2011
The Catholic University of America Press

Library of Congress Cataloging-in-Publication Data
Emery, Gilles
[Trinité. English]
The trinity : an introduction to Catholic doctrine on the triune
God / Gilles Emery ; translated by Matthew Levering.
p. cm — (Thomistic ressourcement series; v. 1)
Includes bibliographical references and index.
ISBN 978-0-8132-1864-9 (pbk. : alk. paper)   1. Trinity.
2. Catholic Church—Doctrines.   3. Trinity—History
of Doctrines.   I. Title.
BT111.3.E4514 2011
231'.044—dc22
2010053807

Contents

Translator's Foreword

As an introduction to the Trinity, this book presents the origins and development of a Trinitarian Christian culture. Gilles Emery provides the reader with the background not only to appreciate this culture, but also to enter into it. At every stage (biblical, patristic, and systematic) he pays particular attention to doxology and prayer, showing how the historical and contemplative dimensions of Trinitarian doctrine are inseparable. The mark of vibrant Trinitarian culture consists in its ability to appropriate the witness of the Scriptures to the triune God by means of the interweaving of doxological praise, creedal confession, and intellectual precision. Not surprisingly, the early Church developed a vibrant Trinitarian culture.

With particular attention to the Niceno-Constantinopolitan Creed, Emery skillfully presents the patristic doctrine of the Trinity and the lineaments of analogous discourse about God. His discussion of the personal relations of the Father, Son, and Holy Spirit draws especially upon Thomas Aquinas. In Emery's hands, Thomas Aquinas's work of intellectual precision is shown to be a spiritual exercise that fosters the Church's liturgical union with God the Trinity. In order to appreciate the Trinity's creative and salvific acts, the Church must be able to speak about the eternal and transcendent Trinity in its inner life.

Rather than being merely a historical or a systematic introduction, Emery's book is a model of what it means to have a fully cul-

tivated Trinitarian sensibility—biblically, liturgically, dogmatical-
ly. In clear and accessible prose, Emery moves from the witness of
Scripture and faith, to doctrinal formulation of the Trinity in itself,
to the creative and saving act of the Trinity. Each chapter can be
read on its own as an introduction to its subject. Even so, students
would do best to read the book as a whole, starting from the biblical witness to the Trinitarian economy of salvation and returning to
this economy in the final chapter, enriched by the fruits of Trinitarian culture. Read in this way, the book not only teaches about the
doctrine of the Trinity, but also cultivates Trinitarian wisdom in its
readers.

This book first appeared in French. The present English version
contains some new elements. After the publication of the French
version, the author revised and updated the text, and these valuable
emendations have been integrated into this English edition. My
thanks to Gilles Emery and Dominic Legge, O.P., for carefully reading and correcting the translation.

Matthew Levering

Abbreviations and References

CSEL	Corpus Scriptorum Ecclesiasticorum Latinorum, Vienna
CCSL	Corpus Christianorum, Series Latina, Turnhout
PG	Patrologiae Cursus, Series Graeca, Migne, Paris
PL	Patrologiae Cursus, Series Latina, Migne, Paris
SC	Sources Chrétiennes, Paris

a.	article
ch.	chapter
dist.	distinction
q.	question
qla	little question within an article (*quaestiuncula*)

Abbreviations of the biblical books are those of the Revised Standard Version, Catholic edition. Biblical citations are drawn from the Revised Standard Version, Catholic edition (1966; San Francisco: Ignatius Press, 1995). For the Greek text of the New Testament: *The Greek New Testament*, 4th rev. ed., ed. Barbara Aland, Kurt Aland, Johannes Karavidopoulos, Carlo M. Martini, and Bruce M. Metzger (Stuttgart: Deutsche Bibelgesellschaft, 1993).

Citations of the Ecumenical Councils are drawn from *Decrees of the Ecumenical Councils*, vol. 1: *Nicaea I to Lateran V*, ed. Norman P. Tanner (Washington, D.C.: Georgetown University Press, 1990); and vol. 2: *Trent to Vatican II*, ed. Norman P. Tanner (Washington, D.C.: Georgetown University Press, 1990).

Citations of the *Catechism of the Catholic Church* are drawn from *Catechism of the Catholic Church*, 2nd ed. (Vatican City: Libreria Editrice Vaticana, 1997).

For other magisterial texts, when I cite *Enchiridion symbolorum*, my citations are drawn from: Heinrich Denzinger, *Enchiridion symbolorum, definitionum et declarationum de rebus fidei et morum*, 37th ed, ed. Peter Hünermann (Freiburg im Breisgau: Herder, 1991).

Citations of the works of St. Thomas Aquinas refer to Latin editions whose bibliographic details can be found in Jean-Pierre Torrell, *Saint Thomas Aquinas*, vol. 1: *The Person and His Work*, rev. ed., trans. Robert Royal (Washington, D.C.: The Catholic University of America Press, 2005), 330–59 and 424–38. The translations are at times made with the help of available English translations (cited in Jean-Pierre Torrell's work). The references follow the paragraph numbers of the Marietti edition (Turin/Rome).

Introduction

————— : —————

The mystery of the Holy Trinity is "the substance of the New Testament," Pope Leo XIII recalled in his encyclical on the Holy Spirit, *Divinum illud munus* (1897). The Trinity is not one topic of reflection among others, but rather it constitutes the heart of Christian faith. To affirm that the Trinity is "the substance of the New Testament" is to recognize that the Trinity is found at the center of the Gospel, that it is the essential reality of the Gospel, and that it is the very object of faith, hope, and charity. Indeed, the Holy Trinity is "the greatest of all mysteries, since it is the fountain and origin of them all."[1] The Catechism of the Catholic Church likewise affirms:

The mystery of the Most Holy Trinity is the central mystery of Christian faith and life. It is the mystery of God in himself. It is therefore the source of all the other mysteries of faith, the light that enlightens them. It is the most fundamental and essential teaching in the "hierarchy of the truths of faith." The whole history of salvation is identical with the history of the way and the means by which the one true God, Father, Son and Holy Spirit, reveals himself to men "and reconciles and unites with himself those who turn away from sin."[2]

The fundamental task of theology is to render an account of faith and hope. "Always be prepared to make a defense to any one

1. Leo XIII, Encyclical Letter *Divinum illud munus,* no. 3; English translation taken from http://www.vatican.va.
2. *Catechism of the Catholic Church*, 2nd ed. (Vatican City: Libreria Editrice Vaticana, 1997), no. 234; the internal quotation is a citation of the General Catechetical Directory.

who calls you to account for the hope that is in you" (1 Pt 3:15). In this exhortation of St. Peter, "hope" is the equivalent of "faith": it is a matter of rendering an account of faith.[3] Trinitarian theology thus has the task of illuminating the truth of faith in the Trinity. And since the Trinity sheds light on all the other mysteries of faith, theology should show the "connection of the mysteries," that is, the intimate connection of all the other realities of faith with the Trinity. This implies an attentive study of the word of God deposited in the holy Scriptures and transmitted by the tradition: reading the Scriptures thoughtfully as well as studying the Church's teachings (in particular, the teachings of the Councils that expressed the ecclesial faith in the Trinity), considering especially the history of salvation in which God reveals himself in order to unite himself with the human beings whom he saves.

Trinitarian faith is essentially ecclesial. The Trinity is the source of the Church, whose unity participates in the communion of the Father, Son, and Holy Spirit. Faith in the Trinity, love for God the Trinity, and the hope of being united everlastingly to the Trinity form the profound bond by which the Church lives on her journey toward the vision of the Trinity. This ecclesial dimension is found at the center of Trinitarian doctrine. It manifests the gift that God the Father made by sending his Son in the flesh and by pouring forth his Spirit, thereby drawing back toward himself his children whom sin had dispersed. "You gather them into your Church, to be one as you, Father, are one with your Son and the Holy Spirit. You call them to be your people, to praise your wisdom in all your works. You make them the body of Christ and the dwelling-place of the Holy Spirit."[4]

This book offers *a theological introduction to the Catholic doctrine*

3. See Benedict XVI, Encyclical Letter *Spe salvi*, no. 2.
4. *Roman Missal*, 8th preface of Sundays in ordinary time: "ut plebs, de unitate Trinitatis adunata, in tuae laudem sapientiae multiformis Christi corpus templumque Spiritus nosceretur Ecclesia"; *Missale Romanum*, Ex Decreto Sacrosancto Oecumenici Concilii Vaticani II Instauratum, Editio typica tertia (Vatican City: Typis Vaticanis, 2002), 544.

on the triune God. Its intention is to make manifest the meaning and truth of what the triune God has revealed about his own mystery. This approach can be linked with what is commonly called "dogmatic theology." Such an enterprise is both ambitious and humble. Trinitarian theology seeks to obtain a *contemplative understanding* of the faith, that is to say, to display the intelligibility that Trinitarian faith possesses. This intelligibility is the source of the whole Christian life. It is not a matter of an exercise of mathematical sophistication ("three = one") nor of a reflection detached from Christian experience. Rather, Trinitarian theology is an exercise of contemplative wisdom and a work of purification of understanding based upon receiving the revelation of God in faith (it is "faith seeking understanding"). It is inseparable from the purification of the heart by communal and personal prayer.

The search for a better understanding of the faith is sustained by the quest for happiness. "The ultimate end of the whole divine economy is the entry of God's creatures into the perfect unity of the Blessed Trinity."[5] The theological tradition has always understood the purpose of seeking an understanding of the faith in light of our hope for happiness in God. In his work *On the Trinity,* St. Augustine explains: "The fullness of our happiness, beyond which there is none else, is this: to enjoy God the Trinity in whose image we were made."[6] Among other doctors of the Church, St. Thomas Aquinas, echoing St. Augustine, observes at the outset of his reflection on the mystery of the Triune God: "The whole of our life bears fruit and comes to achievement in the knowledge of the Trinity."[7] This "knowledge" is not only conceptual. It is an "experiential" knowledge, a gift of God that prepares us to contemplate him in the joy of

5. *Catechism of the Catholic Church,* no. 260.
6. St. Augustine, *On the Trinity* 1.8.18; the translation (slightly adapted) comes from St. Augustine, *The Trinity,* trans. Edmund Hill, O.P. (Brooklyn: New City Press, 1991), 77. This affirmation sums up the intention of St. Augustine, who has profoundly shaped Catholic theology.
7. St. Thomas Aquinas, *Commentary on the Sentences,* Bk. I, dist. 2, exposition of the text.

heaven. This knowledge comes from faith. And it is precisely of faith that theology aims to speak. In the East, Evagrius of Pontius (fourth century) summarized this aim in a striking formulation: "The kingdom of God is the knowledge of the Holy Trinity."[8]

The hope of contemplating God the Trinity in the blessed life of heaven is nourished by the real gift that God makes today to the Church *in via*. "But even now we are called to be a dwelling for the Most Holy Trinity: 'If a man loves me,' says the Lord, 'he will keep my word, and my Father will love him, and we will come to him, and make our home with him' (Jn 14:23)."[9] Thus, Trinitarian theology is a contemplative exercise oriented toward beatitude, an exercise of wisdom tending toward the blessed vision of God the Trinity in eternal life.

This book is essentially devoted to Trinitarian *doctrine*, that is, to the teaching of the faith concerning the Trinity. The limits of this introductory study do not leave room to present the contributions of the mystics (for example, St. Catherine of Siena, St. John of the Cross, St. Elizabeth of the Trinity), nor the expressions of the Trinity in Christian art,[10] nor certain specialized themes of theological reflection (for example, the place of the Trinity in interreligious dialogue). An introductory book cannot say everything. We will certainly make reference to the liturgy because it occupies such a central place, but one will not find here a thorough exposition of the liturgical expression of Trinitarian faith. In all the domains treated (holy Scripture, the liturgy, the teachings of the Magisterium, the Fathers of the Church, the theological tradition, philosophical resources, dogmatic and moral reflections), our approach is limited to what is most essential. We have especially sought to show the cohesion of these various elements.

8. Evagrius Ponticus, *The Praktikos*, ch. 3 (SC 171:500).

9. *Catechism of the Catholic Church*, no. 260.

10. For an iconographic, theological, and historical presentation of Christian art concerning God the Trinity, see the superb work of François Bœspflug, *Dieu et ses images: Une histoire de l'Éternel dans l'art* (Montrouge: Bayard, 2008); this is, to my knowledge, the best book available on this topic.

Since the principal accent of this introductory work bears on doctrinal *foundations*, we gave up the idea of presenting the most recent theological currents. While the great Trinitarian syntheses of twentieth-century theology, in particular those of Karl Barth and of Hans Urs von Balthasar, continue to inspire many writings today, they present a high level of difficulty that goes beyond the purpose of this book. Given the limits of our enterprise, it would have entailed the risk either of comparing these writings or of juxtaposing them without offering criteria by which one could evaluate each approach.[11] This book therefore does not offer a panorama of the various approaches to Trinitarian theology today.[12] We have certainly wished to take account of recent contributions (many are present in the background of our exposition), but the emphasis of the present work is on traditional sources that offer criteria of discernment for guiding theological reflection.

This work consists of six chapters. The first three set forth the fundamental elements of the Church's teachings. These elements reappear in a more systematic form in the three final chapters. The first chapter constitutes a kind of overture: it offers points of access for entering into the understanding of faith in the Holy Trinity. The teaching of the New Testament on the revelation of the Father, Son, and Holy Spirit comprises the object of the second chapter. The third chapter studies the confessions of faith—that is to say, the reception of revelation in the proclamations of Trinitarian faith, from the New Testament itself up to the *credo* of the first Council of Constantinople. The final three chapters take their starting point in the

11. For a historical overview of ancient and modern contributions to Trinitarian theology, see Roger E. Olson and Christopher A. Hall, *The Trinity* (Grand Rapids, Mich.: Eerdmans, 2002); and Anne Hunt, *What Are They Saying About the Trinity?* (New York: Paulist Press, 1998). For a more systematic approach, see Stephen T. Davis, Daniel Kendall, and Gerald O'Collins, eds., *The Trinity: An Interdisciplinary Symposium on the Trinity* (Oxford: Oxford University Press, 1999).

12. For such a survey, see *The Oxford Handbook of the Trinity*, ed. Gilles Emery and Matthew Levering (Oxford: Oxford University Press, forthcoming); *The Cambridge Companion to the Trinity*, ed. Peter C. Phan (Cambridge: Cambridge University Press, forthcoming).

"Trinitarian Christian culture" that was formed at the end of antiquity, as much in the East as in the West. This culture retains, even today, a decisive importance in orienting our reflection; it also inspired the great medieval syntheses, in particular that of St. Thomas Aquinas, who will serve us as a guide for advancing in understanding of Trinitarian faith. Thus, the fourth chapter sketches the guiding principles of Trinitarian doctrine. It pays special attention to the notion of "person" in order to make clear the Christian affirmation of "three persons who are one single God." On this basis, the fifth chapter provides a synthesis on the Father, Son, and Holy Spirit. This chapter (the longest of the work) presents the "classical" doctrine on the three divine persons, both in the intimate life of the Trinity and in their creative and salvific action. Last, the sixth chapter comes back to the theme of the creative and salvific action of God the Trinity. This is, in a way, a return to the revelation of the three divine persons in their act for us, a return that profits from the clarifications achieved by the dogmatic teaching concerning the Father, Son, and Holy Spirit understood in their distinctive properties. Our journey thus sets out from the revelation of the Trinity in the economy of salvation in order to come back, at the end, to a Trinitarian doctrine of the economy of creation and of grace.

The bibliographical references will be limited. The reader will find at the end of the book a glossary indicating the meaning of the principal terms of the vocabulary of Trinitarian theology.

The Trinity

1

Entering into Trinitarian Faith

Faith in the Trinity rests on God's revelation of himself in the economy of salvation. We do not have access to the Trinity outside what God revealed to us by sending his own Son and giving us his Holy Spirit. This point is crucial. Trinitarian faith is distinct from experiences that begin by observing nature, or studying cultural phenomena, or that start from arguments or human introspection. It rests exclusively on the gift that God makes when he enables believers to know him in faith. The revelation of the Trinity is accomplished by the coming of God himself into human history: God so loved the world that he gave his only Son (Jn 3:16); God's love has been poured into our hearts through the Holy Spirit who has been given to us (Rm 5:5).

The Trinity is a mystery of faith in the strict sense, one of the "mysteries that are hidden in God, which can never be known unless they are revealed by God." To be sure, God has left traces of his Trinitarian being in his work of creation and in his revelation throughout the Old Testament. But his inmost Being as Holy Trinity is a mystery that is inaccessible to reason alone or even to Israel's faith before the incarnation of God's Son and the sending of the Holy Spirit.[1]

---

1. *Catechism of the Catholic Church*, no. 237, 2nd ed. (Vatican City: Libreria Editrice Vaticana, 1997).

Two aspects of this affirmation merit special attention. First, the believer's knowledge of the Trinity rests on the revelation that takes place in the words and in the historical events to which the words are connected. These events are the incarnation of the Son of God and his life in our human condition, as well as the sending of the Holy Spirit to the Church at Pentecost. This manifestation of the Trinity is different from other forms of revelation (for example, the revelation that God can make simply by the interior inspiration of the mind of prophets), because the revelation of the Trinity takes place in events manifested to human eyes. Second, in these events God himself comes. God is not only at the origin of these events, but he also gives himself in them. Thus, in the incarnation, the Son of God in person becomes human and, by his life and his offering on the cross, he obtains salvation through love of his Father and through love of humankind. Similarly, at Pentecost, the Holy Spirit in person is given and comes to dwell in the heart of believers. And when, by the grace of the Holy Spirit, believers receive Jesus as the Son of God, the Father himself comes to dwell in their hearts, as Jesus promised: "If a man loves me, he will keep my word, and my Father will love him, and we will come to him and make our home with him" (Jn 14:23). In the events of salvation, God the Trinity gives not merely "some thing," but rather he gives himself: God the Father sends his Son and pours out his Holy Spirit. These two aspects (God is revealed in historical events, and in them he really gives himself to believers) are at the center of the revelation of the Trinity. They constitute a fundamental and characteristic trait of the evangelical faith that distinguishes it from other forms of knowledge and of religious experience.

THE LITURGY

The liturgy of the Church—in particular the celebration of baptism, confirmation, and the Eucharist—offers the best guide for understanding the depth of Trinitarian faith: in the paschal mystery of

Christ, the Church recognizes and celebrates God the Trinity. The liturgy enables believers to receive the Trinitarian mystery and to live it. Concretely, it is through the liturgy that Christians enter into the mystery of God the Trinity and find the light to live out their lives with God.[2] In the liturgy, the Church proclaims the Word that reveals the mystery of God; she celebrates God and is united to him. The depth of Trinitarian faith can be understood within the home that is the celebration of the Eucharist. Through the Eucharist,

The faithful, united with their bishop, have access to God the Father through the Son, the Word made flesh, who suffered and has been glorified, and so, in the outpouring of the Holy Spirit, they enter into communion with the most holy Trinity, being made "sharers of the divine nature" (2 Pt 1:4).[3]

The Eucharist, which fortifies one's union with Christ, strengthens and nourishes the gift obtained by baptism and confirmation: believers are united to the Father through the Son, in the Holy Spirit. When they commune in the flesh of Christ and receive the Holy Spirit, believers are united to the Father: they are a "new creation" (Gal 6:15). The fruit of the sacraments is not only of the moral order, but rather it concerns first and foremost the *being* of believers. By the coming of the Son of God and the gift of the Holy Spirit, believers are renewed and transformed in their very being. The eternal Son of the Father is born in time in order to give us a share in his own life: "God was made man, so that man might be made God."[4] The sacraments of faith, which unite us to Christ by the gift of the Holy Spirit, obtain for us a *new being* destined to bloom in moral sanctity. "Therefore, if any one is in Christ, he is a new creation"

2. This also directly concerns the enterprise of theologians. Doctrinal reflection on the mystery of God implies the movement by which the theologian himself gives thanks for the gifts of God and tends toward God in the Church. The home of this movement is the liturgy.

3. Vatican II, Decree *Unitatis redintegratio* on Ecumenism, no. 15.

4. St. Augustine, *Sermon* 128 (*PL* 39, col. 1997); St. Thomas Aquinas, *Summa theologiae* III, q. 2, a. 2. On salvation as a participation in God's nature, see Daniel A. Keating, *Deification and Grace* (Naples, Fla.: Sapientia Press, 2007).

(2 Cor 5:17). The Eucharist gives a participation in the very mystery of the Trinity: it is "divinization," in which we become "partakers of the divine nature" (2 Pt 1:4).

Faith in the Trinity is intimately connected to this "new creation" that the sacraments effect. By receiving the Holy Spirit, by communing in Christ, believers enter *into* the divine life. They are led to the Father by the divine power of the Son and Holy Spirit who renew them interiorly. Thus, faith in the divinity of Christ, who is the only-begotten Son of the Father, and in the divinity of the Holy Spirit, who is the Spirit of the Father and the Son, is expressed in an exemplary manner in the sacraments that bring about communion in the divine life. The "stake," so to say, of faith in the Trinity is salvation itself, the participation of the Church in the Trinitarian life. The revelation of the Trinity is ordered to this participation in the Trinitarian mystery that constitutes the Church. The structure or "disposition" of this revelation is well expressed by the collect of the feast of the Holy Trinity:

God the Father, you who by sending into the world the Word of truth and the Spirit of sanctification have manifested to men your admirable mystery, give us in confessing the true faith to recognize the glory of the eternal Trinity, and to adore the Unity in the power of majesty.[5]

The mystery of God has been revealed to us by the Father himself. This revelation is accomplished by the sending of the Son and of the Holy Spirit. By designating the Son as "Word of truth," the prayer of the feast of the Holy Trinity signifies that the Son is sent into the world in order to make known the mystery of God. It belongs to the "Word" as such to make manifest and to reveal the true face of God, by a knowledge that transforms hearts. By designating the Holy Spirit as the "Spirit of sanctification" (cf. Rom 1:4), the Church signifies that the revelation of God is accomplished in

5. We translate here the Latin text of this collect: "Deus Pater, qui, Verbum veritatis et Spiritum sanctificationis mittens in mundum, admirabile mysterium tuum hominibus declarasti, da nobis, in confessione verae fidei, aeternae gloriam Trinitatis agnoscere, et Unitatem adorare in potentia maiestatis."

the gift of new life that is obtained by the outpouring of the Holy Spirit. The revelatory and sanctifying action of the Son and of the Holy Spirit finds its origin in the Father himself, because the Father is the Source of the sending of the Son and of the Holy Spirit, in such a way that the Son and the Holy Spirit reveal the mystery of the Source itself: the mystery of the Father.

This prayer likewise indicates the two aspects of our understanding of the mystery of God the Trinity in faith: the *relations* of the persons and their *unity of being*. The relations are signified by the theme of mission: the Son and the Holy Spirit come forth from the Father who "sends" them. The unity is especially associated with the divine power. The actions of the Son and of the Holy Spirit manifest their equality in power with the Father. The Son and Holy Spirit reveal, sanctify, and save. They perform actions that God alone can accomplish. Their divinity is revealed particularly in this power: the works of God make visible "his eternal power and deity" (Rom 1:20). The prayer of the feast of the Holy Trinity also signifies that the sending of the Son and of the Holy Spirit, which takes place in time, leads the Church to lift up its gaze toward the mystery of God who is above time, that is to say to recognize "the glory of the eternal Trinity." The word *glory* evokes the transcendent mystery of God the Trinity, in all its "weight," manifested by Christ and by the gift of the Holy Spirit, and recognized by the Church's faith and love. In the teaching of the Fathers of the Church about the Trinity and about Christ, the divine *glory* is associated with manifestation, with light and its rays, with renown, with royalty and power; hence, the word "glory" (*gloria*) has come to designate the divine nature proper to the Father, Son, and Holy Spirit.[6]

The liturgy of the Church especially proclaims the glory of the Trinity in the "doxologies" (from the Greek *doxa*: glory). The doxology constitutes a special form of praise. In the strict sense, one calls "doxologies" the formulas in which the word "glory" is attrib-

6. See Antonius J. Vermeulen, *The Semantic Development of Gloria in Early-Christian Latin* (Nijmegen: Dekker and Van de Vegt, 1956).

uted to God by means of a turn of phrase expressing possession. The doxologies do not regard an action of God, as do other liturgical forms of expression, but rather they are focused directly on the glory of God and his sanctity. They do not express a wish, but rather they declare the reality of God. One finds a good example in Revelation 5:13: "To him who sits upon the throne and to the Lamb be blessing and honor and glory and might for ever and ever!" One observes here three fundamental elements that constitute a doxology. First, the doxology names the one to whom it acknowledges glory: here, God who sits on the throne, and the Lamb. Second, it proclaims that glory belongs to him. Third, it includes a phrase that signifies eternity ("for ever and ever"). One can add a fourth element: the "Amen" pronounced by the four living creatures (Rev 5:14).[7]

The "lesser doxology" ("lesser" on account of its brevity) that concludes the liturgical prayer of the psalms offers a familiar example: "Glory to the Father, and to the Son, and to the Holy Spirit."[8] This doxology reflects the baptismal formula conferred "in the name of the Father and of the Son and of the Holy Spirit" (Mt 28:19). In the baptismal formula, the "name" of the Father, Son, and Holy Spirit is much more than a "word." By invoking the "name" of the Father, Son, and Holy Spirit, one signifies the tri-personality of God who manifests himself to human beings, who enables them to enter into a covenantal relationship with him, and to whom one can address oneself. The "name," in the singular, also suggests the unity of the Father, Son, and Holy Spirit. The phrase "in the name of" does not mean "by the mandate of" but rather indicates that, by the action of the Father, Son, and Holy Spirit, the baptized pass from the domination

7. Today, theologians often employ the word "doxology" in a very broad sense. For the authentic and more precise sense that I adopt, see Reinhard Messner, "Was ist eine Doxologie?" in *Liturgie und Trinität*, edited by Bert Groen and Benedikt Kranemann, 129–60 (Freiburg im Breisgau: Herder, 2008).

8. The practice of concluding the prayer of the psalms by this doxology is ancient. It is attested, in the fifth century, in John Cassian, *Institutes of the Coenobia* 2.8 (*SC* 109:72); see also Nicholas Ayo, *Gloria Patri: The History and Theology of the Lesser Doxology* (Notre Dame, Ind.: University of Notre Dame Press, 2007).

of sin to the sovereignty of the triune God whom they can invoke in a personal relationship, in view of the communion with the Son in the Kingdom of his Father, through the Holy Spirit. In reference to the baptismal formula, the Trinitarian doxology expresses the equal greatness of the Father, Son, and Holy Spirit. They are not three glories, nor three portions of glory shared among three persons, but it is the same undivided glory that one proclaims in the Three. To acknowledge in the Son and Holy Spirit the same glory as in the Father, is to confess their equal divinity. At the same time, the doxology signifies the personal distinctiveness of the Father, Son, and Holy Spirit: they have the same glory but they are not blended.

The *Gloria*, the "greater doxology" chanted in the Mass, likewise expresses this shared dignity of the Son and Holy Spirit with the Father, in their distinction: "You alone are the Most High: Jesus Christ, with the Holy Spirit, in the glory of the Father. Amen." And the doxology that concludes the eucharistic prayers renders glory to the Father through the Son, Christ Jesus, in the Holy Spirit. The doxologies, either in the form of a "co-ordinate" address (Glory to the Father, *and* to the Son, *and* to the Holy Spirit) or following a "mediatorial" pattern (Glory to the Father, *through* the Son, *in* the Holy Spirit), are a central expression of Trinitarian faith. The former ("co-ordinate" address) ranks the three persons together as equal, while the latter ("mediatorial" pattern) makes clear the order of the divine persons in the economy of salvation.

Let us listen to the witness of an ancient Christian writing, the *Martyrdom of St. Polycarp,* which presents a beautiful Trinitarian doxology. In this writing, the holy martyr addresses this prayer to God the Father: "For this, and for all else besides, I praise thee, I bless thee, I glorify thee; through our eternal High Priest in Heaven, thy beloved Son Jesus Christ, by whom and with whom be glory to thee and the Holy Spirit, now and for all ages to come. Amen."[9]

9. *The Martyrdom of Polycarp* 14.3, in *Early Christian Writings: The Apostolic Fathers,* trans. Maxwell Staniforth, rev. Andrew Louth (New York: Penguin Books, 1987), 129; cf. *SC* 10 bis, 1998:228 (see the explanation given on 202–7).

Other ancient writings present such Trinitarian doxologies. Thus, for example, the *Apostolic Tradition* of Hippolytus of Rome: "To you be glory, to the Father and to the Son with the Holy Spirit in the holy Church, both now and for ever and into all the ages of ages."[10] In this doxology, the Father, Son, and Holy Spirit are "enumerated," so to say, each in his place but on the same level. This means that the Three have the same dignity and belong to the same order: that of divine persons. Sometimes also, in the doxology, the Father, Son, and Spirit are united under the name "Trinity." An example is found in this antiphon of the first vespers of the feast of the Holy Trinity: "Glory to you, equal Trinity, one Deity, from before all ages, and now and forever more."[11] Trinitarian doctrine—the exposition of faith in the Trinity—makes explicit what the doxologies express under a liturgical form that always remains primary.

At times one finds opposed to Trinitarian faith a rather superficial argument: the word "Trinity" is absent from the Bible; the Trinity is therefore unscriptural. Certainly, the word *Trinity* only appears later, in Greek (*trias*) from the second century and in Latin (*trinitas*) toward the beginning of the third century, in Christian authors. But the *reality* signified by the word "Trinity" is exactly that which the baptismal formula and the doxologies—themselves found in Scripture—express: the Father, Son, and Holy Spirit are "co-numbered" or "numbered together," they are mentioned or "counted one with the other" (the Father, *and* the Son, *and* the Holy Spirit) because they belong to the same order of reality.[12] The creed

10. Hippolytus of Rome, *On the Apostolic Tradition*, trans. Alistair Stewart-Sykes (Crestwood, N.Y.: St. Vladimir's Seminary Press, 2001), no. 6:78; cf. no. 21; see also *SC* 11 bis, 2nd rev. ed., 54 and 88.

11. "Gloria tibi, Trinitas aequalis, una Deitas, et ante omnia saecula, et nunc et in perpetuum."

12. In his treatise on the Holy Spirit, St. Basil of Caesarea shows that the Son is not "sub-numbered" to the Father (he is not "numbered under" or "counted below" the Father, because he is not inferior to the Father), but he is "co-numbered" with the Father. In the same way, the Holy Spirit is not "sub-numbered" but is "co-numbered together with the Father and the Son"; see St. Basil of Caesarea, *On the Holy Spirit* 6.13 and 17 (*SC* 17 bis:286–88 and 392–400).

likewise repeats this baptismal and doxological order of the divine persons. The Church professes her *faith* in the same way that she renders *glory:* "We believe in the Father, and in the Son, and in the Holy Spirit." The *Catechism of the Catholic Church* explains:

From the beginning, the revealed truth of the Holy Trinity has been at the very root of the Church's living faith, principally by means of Baptism. It finds its expression in the rule of baptismal faith, formulated in the preaching, catechesis and prayer of the Church. Such formulations are already found in the apostolic writings, such as this salutation taken up in the Eucharistic liturgy: "The grace of the Lord Jesus Christ and the love of God and the fellowship of the Holy Spirit be with you all" (2 Cor 13:13; cf. 1 Cor 12:4–6; Ep 4:4–6).[13]

In the Holy Spirit that they receive, the baptized are conformed to the Son and they become children of the Father. The baptismal formula (which animates preaching, the confession of faith, catechesis, and prayer), like the doxologies, does not express solely the equal divine dignity of the Father, Son, and Holy Spirit. It also indicates that this divinity belongs to the Three according to an order: the Father, and the Son, and the Holy Spirit. This order means that the Three are distinct. The Father is the Source of the Son and of the Holy Spirit. In the same way that the Father has sent his Son and his Holy Spirit in the economy of salvation, the Father begets his Son from all eternity and eternally "breathes" the Holy Spirit. Thus, the baptismal formula and the doxologies express the divine unity of the Three and their personal distinction, according to an order. This order is well-signified by the final doxology of the eucharistic prayers: "Through him, with him, in him, in the unity of the Holy Spirit, all glory and honor is yours, almighty Father, for ever and ever. Amen." Here, it is necessary to pay attention to the interaction of prepositions and conjunctions. In the baptismal formula, the conjunctions "and"—"and" emphasize the equal dignity of the Father, Son, and Holy Spirit ("co-ordinate" mention of the three per-

---

13. *Catechism of the Catholic Church*, no. 249.

sons). In the doxology of the eucharistic prayers, the prepositions "through"— "in" signify the same order of the Three, but by indicating more precisely the distinct place of the Father, Son, and Holy Spirit in the economy of salvation ("mediatorial pattern"): glory is rendered to the Father "through the Son" and "in the Holy Spirit." Christian liturgical prayer is thus addressed to the Father, through the Son, and in the Holy Spirit. The explanation of St. Basil of Caesarea (fourth century) is illuminating:

If we are illumined by divine power, and fix our eyes on the beauty of the Image of the invisible God, and through the Image are led up to the indescribable beauty of its Source, it is because we have been inseparably joined to the Spirit of knowledge. He gives those who love the vision of truth the power which enables them to see the Image, and this power is Himself. He does not reveal it to them from outside sources, but leads them to knowledge personally, "No one knows the Father except the Son" (Mt 11:27), and "No one can say *Jesus is Lord* except in the Holy Spirit" (1 Cor 12:3).[14]

The Holy Spirit sanctifies the baptized by his "illuminating power" in procuring for them the gift of living faith. This illumination enables one to know the radiance of the majesty of the Son, through whom one attains to contemplation of the Father. The transforming illumination of faith is received *in* the Holy Spirit. It is "from within" the Spirit that the baptized know the Son, through whom they are led to the Father. St. Irenaeus of Lyons (second century) already explained this in similar terms: "Here is, according to the presbyters, the disciples of the apostles, the gradation and arrangement of those who are saved, and the steps by which they advance: they ascend through the Spirit to the Son, and through the Son to the Father."[15] St. Basil of Caesarea summarizes his account by noting two ways to consider the mystery of the Trinity:

14. St. Basil of Caesarea, *On the Holy Spirit* 18.47, tr. David Anderson (Crestwood, N.Y.: St. Vladimir's Seminary Press, 1980), 74; the "Image" here refers to the Son, and the "Source" (the "Archetype") refers to the Father.
15. St. Irenaeus of Lyons, *Against Heresies* 5.36.2 (cf. SC 153:458–60); English translation from http://www.newadvent.org.

The way to divine knowledge ascends from one Spirit through the one Son to the one Father. Likewise, natural goodness, inherent holiness and royal dignity reaches from the Father through the Only-Begotten to the Spirit.[16]

St. Basil sums up here the twofold path of our approach to the Trinitarian mystery. The first path is that of *our experience.* This path begins with the Holy Spirit and, in the Son, leads to the Father. "For our mind, enlightened by the Spirit, looks upon the Son, and in Him, as in the Image, beholds the Father."[17] Under this aspect, the Holy Spirit is in a certain way "the closest to us,"[18] the one who is most intimate to believers because he is poured forth in their hearts. The Holy Spirit is Gift in person: it is *in him* that believers are able to know the Son and to have access to the Father. In baptism, believers are consecrated to the Father through the Son, in the Holy Spirit who accomplishes interiorly their regeneration.[19] The second path is that of the order of the divine life at the heart of the Trinity. This is *the order of origin in God himself.* This path begins from the Father. The Father is the Source who communicates the fullness of divinity to the Son (this is the eternal begetting) and to the Holy Spirit (this is the eternal "spiration" of the Holy Spirit). The one divine nature is possessed by the Three according to an order: Father, and Son, and Holy Spirit. The action of the Trinity in our world reflects this same order: "The Father does all things *through* the Word *in* the Holy Spirit."[20] We likewise find here the order of sending: the Father sends his Son and his Spirit.

16. St. Basil of Caesarea, *On the Holy Spirit* 18.47:74–75.
17. St. Basil of Caesarea, *Letter* 226.3; Greek text (with French translation) in Saint Basile, *Lettres,* ed. Yves Courtonne, vol. 3 (Paris: Les Belles Lettres, 1966), 27; English translation: Saint Basil, *Letters,* vol. 2 (186–368), trans. Sister Agnes Clare Way (Washington, D.C.: The Catholic University of America Press, 1969), 146.
18. St. Thomas Aquinas, *Commentary on the Sentences,* Bk. III, dist. 2, q. 2, a. 2, quaestiuncula 2, ad 3: "The Holy Spirit is the closest to us (*propinquior nobis*), because it is through him that all gifts are given."
19. St. Thomas Aquinas, *Commentary on the Gospel of St. Matthew* 28:19, no. 2465.
20. St. Athanasius of Alexandria, *Letter to Serapion* 1.28 in *The Letters of Saint Athanasius Concerning the Holy Spirit,* trans. C. R. B. Shapland (London: The Epworth Press, 1951), 135; emphasis mine; see also 1.24:127.

The Father who is the Source in the eternal Trinity (this is the order of the reality in God himself, which the order of sending reflects) is also the end to which the Holy Spirit and the Son lead believers (this is the order of experience and of baptismal grace).

In the New Testament, the manifestation of the Father, Son, and Holy Spirit is directly connected to the gift of new life by grace: when the New Testament speaks of the Trinity, it speaks of the salvation of human beings; and when it speaks of salvation, it speaks of the Trinity. We will present certain aspects of the teaching of the New Testament in the following chapter. It is necessary here, however, to recall this: to explore the witness of the revelation of the Trinity in the New Testament does not consist in a simple inventory of biblical verses. It is necessary first and foremost to survey the profound movement of revelation, understood as a whole in its various harmonies. The New Testament offers many complementary "paths" for understanding the revelation of the Trinity. We will briefly consider two of them here.

The first path begins with the human life of Jesus in order to lead us to his passion and his glorious exaltation that reveal the Trinity to us. This path shows that the Trinity is fully manifested at the end of the events of the human life of Jesus. Revelation finds its culminating point in the paschal mystery of Christ that reveals the Trinity. The discourse of the apostle Peter at Pentecost offers us an example (Acts 2:14–36). This apostolic preaching is addressed to the Jews of Jerusalem. St. Peter explains that "Jesus of Nazareth, a man attested to you by God with mighty works and wonders and signs which God did through him in your midst . . . God raised him up, having loosed the pangs of death" (Acts 2:22–24); and a little further on: "This Jesus God raised up, and of that we are all witnesses. *Being therefore exalted at the right hand of God, and having received from the Father the Holy Spirit who was promised, he has poured out this which you see and hear"* (Acts 2:32–33). St. Peter concludes: "Let all the house of Israel therefore know assuredly that *God has made him both Lord and Christ, this Jesus whom you crucified*" (Acts 2:36).

In this preaching, St. Peter begins with the *man* Jesus ("this Jesus") and with what Jesus accomplished, then he recalls his death on the cross, in order to lead to the proclamation of his glorious resurrection. The life of Jesus culminates in his exaltation. St. Peter underscores the newness that this exaltation brings. The resurrection is an event in which three agents act: Jesus, God (*ho Theos*, identified as the Father), and the Holy Spirit. The Three are named in their distinction. The paschal exaltation of Jesus places in full view his vivifying power and his unity with the Father: "God has made him both Lord and Christ." To say that Jesus is Lord (*Kurios*) is to acknowledge in him a dignity comparable to that of God. This name "Lord," which is connected to the worship that Christians render to Christ, expresses the faith of Easter. In his sovereignty, Jesus possesses the prerogatives of God; he shares in the divine condition of his Father: "The Lord said to my Lord, Sit at my right hand" (Acts 2:34). This citation of Psalm 110:1 shows that the glorified Jesus occupies a unique place: he is with the Father in the most profound divine intimacy.[21] St. Paul expresses this in a comparable manner when he explains having received the mission of announcing the Gospel of God "concerning his Son, who was descended from David according to the flesh and designated Son of God in power according to the Spirit of holiness by his resurrection from the dead, Jesus Christ our Lord" (Rom 1:3–4). His glorious resurrection manifests Jesus as Son in the power of the Holy Spirit. The name "Son" expresses here the most profound unity of Jesus with his Father, a properly divine unity that the exaltation of Jesus brings into broad daylight.[22]

In the first discourse of St. Peter on Pentecost, the Father is pres-

21. See Martin Hengel, "'Sit at My Right Hand!' The Enthronement of Christ at the Right Hand of God and Psalm 110:1," in *Studies in Early Christology*, 119–225 (Edinburgh: T. and T. Clark, 1995).
22. See Martin Hengel, *The Son of God* (Philadelphia: Fortress Press, 1976).

ent under the name of "God." The Father has acted through Jesus, he has delivered Jesus from death and exalted him to his right hand. As regards the Holy Spirit, he appears as the paschal Gift par excellence. The Holy Spirit is poured out by the exalted Jesus: the giving of the Spirit is the fruit of the exaltation of Jesus. Put otherwise: the glorious exaltation shows Jesus as the Giver of the Holy Spirit (he "poured out" the Holy Spirit) because, having received the fullness of the Holy Spirit, he is in the glorified state in virtue of which he abundantly pours out this same Spirit. And it is *in* the Spirit of Pentecost that St. Peter proclaims the exaltation of Christ Jesus and his unity with the Father.

One can understand this teaching in the following way. It is God who pours out the Spirit. To pour out the Spirit is a divine privilege. God is in heaven; in order to pour out the Spirit, it is necessary to be where God is, and this is precisely what the paschal exaltation confers on the humanity of Jesus: the exalted Jesus is in heaven and, in his glorified humanity at the right hand of the Father, he exercises the divine prerogative that consists in pouring out the Spirit. The ascension of Christ manifests his filial divinity and enables his humanity to rejoin the throne that his divinity never left, and from where the Spirit is now poured out in abundance. The exaltation of Christ procures us salvation inasmuch as "being established in his heavenly seat as God and Lord, he sends down divine gifts upon men."[23] This reveals an essential trait of Jesus as Christ, Lord, and Son of God: he pours out the Holy Spirit. The vision that St. Stephen receives at the moment of his martyrdom offers us an icon of this: "He, *full of the Holy Spirit,* gazed into heaven and saw the *glory of God,* and *Jesus standing at the right hand of God*" (Acts 7:55). The glorious resurrection of Jesus thus manifests the Trinity: it shows the intimacy (unity) and the distinction of the Three in their saving action. Raised up by the Father, Jesus pours out the Spirit. And in the Spirit, believers are led to contemplation of the exalted Son beside his Father.

23. St. Thomas Aquinas, *Summa theologiae* III, q. 57, a. 6.

The events of Easter (passion, resurrection, ascension, Pentecost) thus provide a fundamental light for understanding the profound identity of Jesus and for discovering, in Jesus, the mystery of the Trinity. Under this aspect, the exaltation of Jesus and the paschal outpouring of the Holy Spirit constitute the center of the revelation of the Trinity. "The sending of the person of the Spirit after Jesus' glorification (cf. Jn 7:39) reveals in its fullness the mystery of the Holy Trinity."[24]

In this first approach, we have focused our attention on the Pasch of Jesus. But the New Testament equally shows that the Holy Spirit is superabundantly present in Jesus from the beginning. The Gospels display in particular the active presence of the Holy Spirit at the baptism of Jesus. When Jesus is baptized, the Holy Spirit descends upon Jesus, he "remains" on him (Jn 1:32), and the Father declares that Jesus is his "beloved Son" (Mk 1:11; Mt 3:17). The Gospels' witness to the baptism of Jesus present certain differences, but they converge on a fundamental affirmation: the kingdom of God comes through Jesus and in Jesus, by virtue of the relation of sonship that Jesus has with God his Father, in the power of the Holy Spirit. The baptism of Jesus, which has profoundly inspired Christian iconography, is a manifestation of the Trinity. However, since the first centuries of Christianity, the episode of Jesus' baptism has suggested to certain misguided readers that Jesus became the Son at the moment of his baptism, or that he only received the Holy Spirit when the Spirit descended upon him "like a dove." For this reason, the best theological tradition insisted that the humanity of Jesus was completely filled with the Holy Spirit from the first instant of his conception.[25] This is the teaching of the Church: "From his conception, Christ's humanity is filled with the Holy Spirit, for God 'gives him the Spirit without measure' (Jn 3:34)."[26]

---

24. *Catechism of the Catholic Church*, no. 244.

25. See St. Thomas Aquinas, *Summa theologiae* III, q. 34, a. 1; q. 39, a. 2; see also q. 7, a. 9, ad 2.

26. *Catechism of the Catholic Church*, no. 504.

In light of this teaching, it is necessary to understand that the fullness of the Holy Spirit was *manifested* at the baptism of Jesus for the reason that "it is from this moment that he began to pour out his grace on others"[27] by his ministry of salvation. Put otherwise, at the baptism of Jesus, the Holy Spirit descends upon Jesus "for us and for our salvation," that is to say in order to show that Jesus, the Son of the Father, has been sent to us as Savior.[28] The baptism of Jesus takes place at the beginning of his ministry. It manifests the fullness of the Holy Spirit with which the humanity of Jesus was filled from his conception. The words of the Father and the sign of the Spirit thus reveal Jesus as Messiah at the beginning of his public activity. The baptism of Jesus is a manifestation, an epiphany. The liturgy of the Church signifies this very well by associating the baptism of Jesus with his epiphany and with the sign of Cana: "Three mysteries mark this holy day: today the star leads the Magi to the infant Christ; today water is changed into wine for the wedding feast; today Christ wills to be baptized by John in the river Jordan to bring us salvation" (antiphon of the *Magnificat* at the second vespers of the feast of Epiphany).[29] Similarly, at the very beginning of the human existence of Jesus, the action of the Holy Spirit (who forms the body of Christ in the womb of the Virgin Mary) reveals that Jesus is the true Son of God, come in a human nature like ours: "The Holy Spirit will come upon you, and the power of the Most High will overshadow you; therefore the child to be born will be called holy, the Son of God" (Lk 1:35). The conception of Jesus by the Holy Spirit shows that Jesus is truly the Son of God.[30]

The passages of the New Testament that start from the filial di-

27. St. Thomas Aquinas, *Commentary on the Sentences*, Bk. I, dist. 16, q. 1, a. 3.

28. St. Thomas Aquinas, *Commentary on the Gospel of St. John* 1:32–33 (nos. 270 and 274).

29. The antiphon of the *Benedictus*, at Lauds of Epiphany, offers a similar association: "Today the Bridegroom claims his bride, the Church, since Christ has washed her sins away in Jordan's waters; the Magi hasten with their gifts to the royal wedding; and the wedding guests rejoice, for Christ has changed water into wine."

30. *Catechism of the Catholic Church*, no. 496; cf. St. Thomas Aquinas, *Summa theologiae* III, q. 32, a. 1.

vinity of Jesus and from his preexistence offer a second "point of entry" for understanding the revelation of the Trinity. Christ Jesus, who exists in the "condition of God" (Phil 2:6), humbled himself for us in the incarnation and in obedience unto death. St. John designates Christ Jesus as the "Word" who "was with God" and "was God" from the beginning (Jn 1:1–2), the "only begotten Son, who is in the bosom of the Father" (Jn 1:18) and who was "sent" by the Father into our world (Jn 3:17). Jesus "comes" into the world, he is sent here by his Father. The theme of coming and of sending indicates the preexistence of Jesus who comes from on high. "Before Abraham was, I am" (Jn 8:58). Jesus enters into the world by a voluntary action that he exercises with his Father. Following this second "point of entry," the New Testament makes clear that the divinity of Jesus, from which the Holy Spirit is inseparable, is found at the root of all that Jesus does and says. Jesus is not only an admirable prophet, but rather he is the incarnate Son of God, sent by his Father; it is in him and through him that the Holy Spirit is poured out. The Trinity does not appear only at the resurrection of Jesus. It is the source that, from the beginning, enlightens the origin of the human life of Jesus, then his ministry, his salvific passion, and his glorious resurrection. The mystery of the divine identity of Jesus, in his relation to the Father and to the Spirit, unveils the profound meaning of Christmas and of Easter. The one who is born of the Virgin Mary, through the action of the Holy Spirit, is the Son of God in person. The one who dies on the cross is the Son of God come to save humankind by his offering to the Father. From the paschal mystery of Christ, that is to say from the glorious unity of the Son with his Father, flows the Holy Spirit who is poured out in the Church. Thus, through the incarnate Son, who died, rose, and is glorified, in the outpouring of the Holy Spirit, believers enter into communion with the Father. *This is the faith in the Trinity that enables one to understand the meaning of the events of the New Testament:* "When the time had fully come, God sent forth his Son" (Gal 4:4); "God has sent the Spirit of his Son into our hearts, crying, 'Abba! Father!'" (Gal 4:6).

Whatever the manner of approaching the Trinitarian faith, the gift of the Holy Spirit furnishes the *key*. It is the Holy Spirit who gives entrance into the mystery of the Son and his Father. The experience of the gift of the Spirit is especially highlighted by St. Paul. St. Paul presents the Christian life as a participation in Christ, a life with Christ. By baptism, believers are "buried" with Christ, in order to live with him in a new life, "as Christ was raised from the dead by the glory of the Father" (cf. Rom 6:1–11). This union with Christ who died and is risen is procured by the Holy Spirit: the Spirit of God comes to "dwell" in believers; by receiving this Spirit, believers belong to Christ and are conformed to him. The new life "in Christ" is a life "in the Spirit" and "by the Spirit" (cf. Rom 8:1–17): as St. Paul says, "be filled with the Spirit" (Eph 5:18). The Spirit unites believers to Christ, he enables them to become children of God, and he thereby leads them to the Father: "You have received the spirit of sonship. When we cry, 'Abba! Father!' it is the Spirit himself bearing witness with our spirit that we are children of God" (Rom 8:15–16). We find here the path of life of the baptized that we have sketched above with St. Irenaeus of Lyons and St. Basil of Caesarea. The gift of the Spirit obtains union with Christ and leads human beings to the Father. "Through him [Christ] we both have access in one Spirit to the Father" (Eph 2:18). It is *in the Holy Spirit* that faith in the Trinity is received, and it is in the Holy Spirit that this faith models Christian existence.

Let us summarize these first elements we have discussed. On the one hand, at the end of the earthly life of Jesus, the events of Easter manifest the Trinity in a magnificent way. In the Spirit poured out after the resurrection of Jesus, believers proclaim the divine glory of the Son with his Father. On the other hand, from the beginning, it is faith in the Trinity that enables one to understand the profound meaning of the incarnation, and then of Easter and of Pentecost: the Father sends his Son and he sends his Spirit. Between these two approaches, there is not a rupture but rather a continuity: they form, as it were, a circle. The loftiest teaching on the Trinity receives its light from faith in the resurrection of Jesus; and faith in the Trinity illumines in its turn the identity of Jesus, his life among human beings, his death, and his resurrection, as well as the action that Jesus continues to accomplish today in his Church.

The teaching of Scripture concerning the Trinity is, at the same time, simple and difficult. It is simple, because it shows the Father, Son, and Holy Spirit in their unity and in the relations revealed by their action of salvation on behalf of humankind. The Trinity is a mystery of communion. "You see the Trinity if you see charity."[31] But this teaching is also difficult. It demands an attentive listening and it calls for an understanding in faith. It invites a contemplation of the Trinity that goes beyond what we can comprehend. St. Augustine observed on the subject of holy Scripture:

> The very style in which Scripture is composed is accessible to all, though very few can enter deeply into it. Like a close friend, it speaks without pretense those clear ideas it contains to the heart of the unlearned and of the learned. It does not exalt those things that it conceals in mysteries with a proud language to which the sluggish and untrained mind dares not approach, as a poor man dares not approach a rich one, but invites all with its lowly language. And it not only feeds them with the evident truth but also exercises them with the hidden truth, though it has the same truth in clear matters as in hidden ones. But so that obvious truths do not become boring, the same truths are again desired as concealed, and as desired are in a sense refreshed, and as refreshed they are taught with sweetness. By these, evil minds are salutarily corrected, little minds are fed, and great minds are delighted.[32]

Scripture's manner of speaking is accessible to all: it is not esoteric. But to grasp its profundity is difficult. St. Augustine notes two

---

31. St. Augustine, *On the Trinity* 8.8.12; the translation (slightly adapted) comes from St. Augustine, *The Trinity*, trans. Edmund Hill, O.P. (Brooklyn: New City Press, 1991), 253. For the numbering of the text, I follow the Latin edition: Sanctus Aurelius Augustinus, *De Trinitate libri XV*, ed. W.J. Mountain, 2 vol., *CCSL* (Turnhout: Brepols, 1968).

32. St. Augustine, Letter 137.18, *To Volusian*, in *The Works of St. Augustine*, part 2, *Letters*, vol. 2: *Letters 100–155*, trans. Roland J. Teske, 223 (Hyde Park, N.Y.: New City Press, 2003) (translation slightly adapted).

aspects. On the one hand, Scripture "nourishes" the faith of all believers by words in which the mystery is expressed in a clear and manifest way. On the other hand, by its more difficult words, Scripture "exercises" the understanding of more advanced believers; they refine their mind in the study of the truth. To be sure, all that is necessary for salvation is expressed somewhere in a clear and manifest manner. In any case, the mystery remains beyond the mastery of our intelligence: it offers itself to a contemplation practiced in humility. Trinitarian theology is a spiritual exercise.

2

The Revelation of the Father, Son, and Holy Spirit

In the preceding chapter, we indicated some biblical paths for entering into Trinitarian faith. It is now necessary for us to examine more closely the New Testament teaching concerning the Father, Son, and Holy Spirit. This teaching can be approached in many ways. One can consider the Gospel texts, for example, under the aspect of what they proclaim. In speaking about the Kingdom of God, they show the paternity of God and the filiation of Jesus, with whom the Holy Spirit is indissociably connected, as is particularly visible in their accounts of Jesus' baptism. Under various titles, the writings of the New Testament concerning the Pasch of Jesus, his Parousia, and his preexistence show the relationship of Jesus with his Father, in which the Holy Spirit is present. One can also consider the teaching of the New Testament in light of diverse genres of expression. These include narrations (the announcement of the Kingdom, the infancy of Jesus, the accounts of Easter, to which one can add the discourses of Jesus in the Gospel according to St. John), passages concerning the practice of the faith (baptism, ecclesial communion, confession of faith, doxology, prayers, and liturgical hymns), or more developed teachings under the form of doctrinal reflection (particularly in St. Paul).

In what follows, without offering a synthesis of biblical theology, we aim simply to pay attention to the words of Scripture that show the *unity* and the *relations* of Jesus, his Father, and the Holy Spirit.[1] Trinitarian faith consists in the recognition of the unity without confusion of the Three. The Trinity revealed himself *in his action for us*. "Being a work at once common and personal, the whole divine economy makes known both what is proper to the divine persons, and their one divine nature."[2] The center of this revelation resides in the actions and words of Jesus, as well as in the action of the Holy Spirit—that is to say in the "mission" of the Son and of the Holy Spirit, of which the Father is the Source. It is in the act of the Father, Son, and Holy Spirit that we discover their unity and the features proper to each person (their "properties").[3]

GOD THE FATHER OF JESUS

In the New Testament, the name Father, attributed to God, is characterized by the union of two aspects: (1) the name Father is understood in reference to the one God of the Jewish faith; (2) the Father is the Father of Jesus. This expresses the continuity of the Christian faith in relation to the Old Testament (first aspect), as well as the newness of the Christian faith (second aspect). The newness brought by Jesus will lead, however, to a deepening of the first aspect; we will return to this at the end of this chapter.

According to the first aspect, the name *Father* integrates all the attributes that the Old Testament gave to the Lord God. He is the creator and savior of his people, the creator of the world, the per-

---

1. The confessions of Trinitarian faith will be studied in the following chapter.

2. *Catechism of the Catholic Church*, 2nd ed. (Vatican City: Libreria Editrice Vaticana, 1997), no. 259.

3. On what follows, see Ben Witherington and Laura M. Ice, *The Shadow of the Almighty: Father, Son, and Spirit in Biblical Perspective* (Grand Rapids, Mich.: Eerdmans, 2002); Arthur W. Wainwright, *The Trinity in the New Testament* (London: S.P.C.K., 1962); Matthew Levering, *Scripture and Metaphysics: Aquinas and the Renewal of Trinitarian Theology* (Oxford: Blackwell, 2004).

sonal God, unique and immortal, provident, ruler and Lord, king, judge, the Father who blesses. The preaching of Jesus offers us many examples: "Look at the birds of the air: they neither sow nor reap nor gather into barns, and yet your heavenly Father feeds them" (Mt 6:26). A special accent is placed on the providence and the sovereignty of the Father: "I thank thee, Father, Lord of heaven and earth, that thou hast hidden these things from the wise and understanding and revealed them to babes" (Lk 10:21). The Catechism of the Catholic Church offers the following summary:

> By calling God "Father," the language of faith indicates two main things: that God is the first origin of everything and transcendent authority; and that he is at the same time goodness and loving care for all his children. God's parental tenderness can also be expressed by the image of motherhood (cf. Is 66:13; Ps 131:2), which emphasizes God's immanence, the intimacy between Creator and creature. The language of faith thus draws on the human experience of parents, who are in a way the first representatives of God for man. But this experience also tells us that human parents are fallible and can disfigure the face of fatherhood and motherhood. We ought therefore to recall that God transcends the human distinction between the sexes. He is neither man nor woman: he is God. He also transcends human fatherhood and motherhood (cf. Ps 27:10), although he is their origin and standard (cf. Ep 3:14–15; Is 49:15): no one is father as God is Father.[4]

According to the second aspect that we indicated above, the New Testament makes clear that the Father is not only Father in his beneficent relationship toward his people, toward humankind and the world, but also that he is *first* and *more fundamentally* Father in his unique relationship toward his Son Jesus. It is through his paternity with respect to Jesus that the Father exercises his paternity in favor of humankind and of other creatures. We discover here the specific aspect of Christian faith concerning the paternity of God. This means that the revelation of the Father finds its foundation in the person of Jesus and that it is concentrated in the person of Jesus, the Son, to such a degree that to speak of the Father is to speak

4. *Catechism of the Catholic Church*, no. 239.

of his Son Jesus. The paternity of God is manifested in the person of Jesus as Son. Thus, in the name *Father,* it is the relation of the Father toward Jesus that is primary.

Let us observe the words of Jesus that apply the name "Father" to God. In the ensemble formed by the Gospels according to St. Matthew, St. Mark, and St. Luke, we find in the mouth of Jesus the expressions "my Father," "Father" alone, or "your Father" (without forgetting the teaching of the prayer of the disciples: "our Father"). The words in which Jesus makes reference to the Father never signify that God is the Father of Jesus in the same way that he is the Father of the disciples. The paternity of the Father with regard to Jesus is of another order, superior and transcendent. Joined to the phrase "my Father," the absolute expression "the Father" and its correlative "the Son" (Mt 11:27; Lk 10:22; cf. Mk 13:32) indicates the depth and specificity of the relation of Jesus toward God his Father. This relation is expressed in the prayer of Jesus: "*Abba!*" (Mk 14:36). The unique relationship between Jesus and his Father possesses a twofold aspect. On the one hand, Jesus relates all things to his Father: Jesus is sent by the Father (Mk 9:37; 12:6), he prays to the Father (Mk 14:36; Mt 11:25–26; Lk 22:42; Lk 23:34 and 23:46) and he goes so far as to declare that he does not know the date of the *parousia* that only the Father knows (Mk 13:32; Mt 24:36). On the other hand, the Gospels show us the total freedom and sovereign authority of Jesus: he teaches with authority (Mk 1:22; Mt 7:29), he is master of the sabbath (Mk 2:23–28), he is greater than the Temple (Mt 12:6 and 12:8), he shows his authority concerning the meaning of the Law (Mt 5–7), he forgives sins (Mk 2:1–12; Lk 7:47–49), he cures by a power that "goes forth" from him (Mk 5:30; Lk 6:19), he requires faith in his own power (Mk 9:23–24; Mt 9:28; Lk 8:50), he explains that salvation depends on adhering to his own person (Mk 8:38; Mt 10:32–33; Lk 9:26; Lk 12:8–9), he is the only one who knows the Father and who can reveal him to human beings (Mt 11:27; Lk 10:22). This authority is the expression of the unique relationship of sonship that Jesus has with God his Father.

In St. John, we encounter the double expression "my Father and your Father" (Jn 20:17). The association of these two aspects, "my Father—your Father," can be clarified by the fact that the ascension of which Jesus speaks ("I am ascending to my Father and your Father") will lead to the gift of the Holy Spirit (Jn 20:22) that will make the disciples children of God (cf. Jn 1:12: "to all who received him . . . he gave power to become children of God"). One can explain these words in the following way: "my Father who, through me, is also your Father." Jesus presents himself as the *first* of those who, thanks to him, possess a new relationship with God as Father. This primacy implies that the sonship of Jesus is *superior* to the sonship of those who come after him, and that his sonship is the *source* of the sonship of those who receive it through him (cf. Jn 1:12). Believers have access to the Father through Jesus, the Son of the Father.

The unique character of the relationship of Jesus to his Father is particularly expressed, in St. John, in the use of the absolute expressions "the Father" and "the Son." These expressions emphasize the exclusive aspect of the Father-Son relationship: the Father is Father *insofar as he is Father of this Son who is Jesus.* The names "the Father" and "the Son" will be received by the Church as the names par excellence for signifying the One from whom Jesus comes forth, and Jesus himself.

Having established these foundations, what content is it necessary to give to the word "Father"? The names *Father* and *Son* are based on an analogy drawn from human family life taken in a broad sense. This analogy is in the order of relation and has two principal aspects: an exclusive origin and a close intimacy. These two aspects enable us to make precise the theological content of the name *Father* in reference to Jesus. Out of concern for brevity, we will make reference principally to the fourth Gospel.

The exclusive origin that characterizes paternity is expressed particularly by the theme of *sending:* the Father is the one who sends his Son. This relation of origin, which identifies Jesus in his relationship to the Father, accounts for what Jesus *does* and what he *is.* For the one who sends, the one sent is like another self. The one sent is invested with the powers of the one who sends; he represents him personally. The acts of the one sent engage the one who sends him and from whom he has his power. With this in view Jesus explains: "I have come down from heaven, not to do my own will, but the will of him who sent me" (Jn 6:38); "He who receives any one whom I send receives me; and he who receives me receives him who sent me" (Jn 13:20). This theme of sending thus expresses the identity of the one sent in his relationship to the one who sends him and to whom his action is related. This relationship, insofar as it is the relationship of the *Son* to his *Father,* goes beyond mere representation. The theme of sending makes sense of the reciprocity of faith in Jesus and faith in the Father: the recognition of Jesus as the one sent is intrinsically connected to the recognition of his Father. The Church's mission is an extension of this sending (cf. Jn 17:18; Jn 20:21).

This sending is also expressed in other ways: for example, in the language of Jesus's "descent" and "ascent." "No one has ascended into heaven but he who descended from heaven" (Jn 3:13); "I have come down from heaven, not to do my own will, but the will of him who sent me" (Jn 6:38; cf. Jn 6:33); "I am ascending to my Father and your Father" (Jn 20:17). This language expresses the preexistence of Jesus and his exaltation in reference to the Father. Jesus' sending is likewise expressed in the existential language of origin: Jesus has *come* from the Father (Jn 16:27, 16:28, 16:30); he has *come* from God and he is "going to the Father" (Jn 16:5, 16:10, 16:17, 16:28). It is necessary to note the remarkable use of the vocabulary of "coming" (cf. Jn 8:14), as well as the use of prepositions: Jesus has come "from God" or "from the Father" (Jn 16:27–28); he "came forth from God" (Jn 8:42). Jesus has his origin in the Father. The *end* of the path of Jesus corresponds to the sending and to the origin: "I go to him who sent me" (Jn 7:33; cf. Jn 16:5), "to the Father" (Jn 16:28).

Thus the sending and coming of Jesus determines the Father-Son relation in all its amplitude. The Gospel according to St. John invites believers to look with faith upon the origin and presence of

Jesus in the Father himself. Jesus was with the Father, and he has come into the world. His sending indicates the course of the life of Jesus in its whole expanse and depth: from the Father to the Father. *The Son's origin and his destination are the same.* Jesus is entirely referred to the Father. This sending therefore expresses the deepest identity of Jesus in terms of relation of origin and, correlatively, of destination. It discloses the unique communion of Jesus with his Father in a unity of existence. It is necessary to note the "dogmatic" stakes of this theme of sending. The patristic and medieval tradition will be especially attentive to the correspondence between the sending of the Son into the world and his eternal origin: in the same way that the Son is sent by the Father, he has his existence from the Father. In other words, when Trinitarian doctrine speaks of the divine person in terms of "relation of origin," it is not a speculation detached from the economy of salvation, but rather it proposes a doctrine grounded on the teaching of the Gospels about Jesus, whose existence is always relative to his Father. The *mystery* of the Father and the Son is present and revealed *in the economy.*

The name *Father,* which indicates the exclusive origin of Jesus, signifies also the close intimacy of Jesus with his Father. This intimacy, which is a veritable unity, appears in numerous passages of the Gospels. Without pretending to be complete, one can recognize the following four notes or dimensions:

1. *Reciprocal knowledge and love.* The mutual knowledge attached to the names *Father* and *Son* is well attested in the synoptic Gospels: "No one knows the Son except the Father, and no one knows the Father except the Son and any one to whom the Son chooses to reveal him" (Mt 11:27 and Lk 10:22). Jesus reveals the Father because he is the Son and in the measure by which he is the Son, by virtue of the mutual knowledge implied by the reality that the names *Father* and *Son* signify. This mutual knowledge characterizes Jesus in his being as Son, and it is open to the human beings to whom the Son makes the Father known. The Gospel according to St. John repeatedly emphasizes that Jesus is the revealer of the Father because

he is the Son and the one sent by the Father: "As the Father knows me and I know the Father" (Jn 10:15); "He who has seen me has seen the Father" (Jn 14:9). This teaching is summed up in John 1:18: "No one has ever seen God; the only begotten Son, who is in the bosom of the Father, he has made him known." Jesus is the revelation of the Father in person because he is the Son turned toward the Father. He reveals the Father not only in virtue of a "function" that he exercises, but rather by reason of his being, which is characterized by his divine relation to the Father. It is this, precisely, that the name "Son" makes manifest. When believers know Jesus as Son, they thereby know God his Father. To see the Son is to know the personal mystery of the Father.

The reciprocal knowledge of the Father and the Son implies their mutual love: "The Father loves the Son, and has given all things into his hand" (Jn 3:35); "The Father loves the Son, and shows him all that he himself is doing" (Jn 5:20); "I do as the Father has commanded me, so that the world may know that I love the Father" (Jn 14:31). This love is signified at the baptism in which Jesus is manifested as Son: "This is my beloved Son, with whom I am well pleased" (Mt 3:17); "this is the Chosen One of God" (Jn 1:34). As with the reciprocal knowledge of the Father and Son, their mutual love is open to human beings who are beneficiaries of it; this love is the source of the revelatory and salvific action of Jesus. Knowledge and love, profoundly united, constitute *communion*. The name *Father* thus signifies a relationship of reciprocal communion with the Son, Jesus. This relationship of communion makes manifest simultaneously the Father and the person of Jesus.

2. The relationship of Father and Son is characterized also by their *unity of action and of power*. Jesus accomplishes the works of his Father (Jn 10:37; cf. Jn 5:36; 9:4; 10:25). He does the divine works of the Father: he raises and makes alive (Jn 5:21), he gives eternal life (Jn 10:28; Jn 17:2) because he has life in himself (Jn 5:26), he exercises judgment (Jn 5:22; 5:27), he teaches the doctrine of the Father (Jn 7:16). The works of Jesus are those of the Father. This unity of

action reveals the mutual interiority of the Father and the Son: "The Father is in me and I am in the Father" (Jn 10:38). In the action of Jesus, it is the Father himself who accomplishes his own works (Jn 14:10). Identity of being is manifested by what one does; the works of Jesus manifest that he receives all things from the Father in unity, to such a degree that, in the action of Jesus, it is the Father himself who acts. The unity of power and action is an important aspect of what is signified in the fourth Gospel when Jesus is designated as *Son* in relation to his *Father*.

3. The action of Jesus, his knowledge of the Father and his love of the Father, in a reciprocity that is unique, disclose *the reciprocal immanence of the Father and the Son*. "He who has seen me has seen the Father; how can you say, 'Show us the Father'? Do you not believe that I am in the Father and the Father in me? . . . The Father who dwells in me does his works. Believe me that I am in the Father and the Father in me" (Jn 14:9–11). This mutual *"being in"* is connected to the identity of Jesus as Son and to that of God as Father: "The Father is in me and I am in the Father" (Jn 10:38); "That they may all be one; even as thou, Father, art in me, and I in thee" (Jn 17:21). The *"being in"* of Jesus and the Father is decisive for revelation and salvation: Jesus leads to the Father; he procures the security of faith by the strength of his action. The immanence of the Father and Son is formulated in terms of reciprocity ("me in the Father, the Father in me") that illuminates the divine plan of revelation and of salvation. This *"being in"* designates a community of love, knowledge, and power that goes beyond a merely "functional" unity; it suggests a unity of vital and transcendent existence, a communion of being of the Son and the Father. Jesus and the Father are, so to say, one single reality in their mutual distinct relation.

4. The Johannine teaching on the action and identity of Jesus can be summarized by this verse: "I and the Father are one" (Jn 10:30). Jesus accomplishes the works of his Father, and these works witness to the identity of Jesus. Jesus does what only God can do: he gives eternal life (Jn 10:28). The power that is exercised in

and by Jesus is therefore the power of God the Father himself: "My Father, who has given them to me, is greater than all, and no one is able to snatch them out of the Father's hand" (Jn 10:29). This unity of power and action of the Father and Son shows that Jesus is worthy to receive an unshakable faith on the part of his disciples. Jesus inspires complete security: the salvific power of Jesus is not only similar to that of the Father, but rather it is the salvific power of the Father himself. As with mutual immanence, the unity of power of the Father and Son concerns the integral mystery of Jesus. It enables one to understand the identity of Jesus and his Father in terms of unity and relation. Thus, the community of power and action of the Father and Son, the source of the strength of faith, leads one to recognize the deepest unity of the Father and Son: their unity of being. This unity is not closed in on itself, but rather it is communicative: "That they may be one even as we are one" (Jn 17:22).

In summary: the paternity of the Father designates the exclusive origin of Jesus, both in his action and in his being; it comprises a dimension of reciprocal knowledge and love that the Gospel underscores in light of revelation and salvation; this paternity is likewise manifested by the power and action common to the Father and Son, in reciprocal immanence. Thus, *it is in Jesus that we discover what the name "Father" means.* The paternity of the Father is not illuminated first by studies in psychology or religious sociology (although this affirmation does not exclude the use of the human sciences as auxiliary resources in theology). It is in hearing and contemplating Jesus that the Church discovers who God the Father is. The whole person and action of Jesus are characterized by his relationship to his Father—a relationship available to human beings who welcome him. This teaching acquires a profound echo in the patristic age, when the Church is confronted with heterodox doctrines, according to which the Son is a being inferior to the Father, unlike the Father, a creature. The Church then recalls that the unity of the Father and Son is not only "moral," but concerns their being. The Father and Son are inseparable in their salvific act and in their very being.

THE LORD JESUS, THE SON

In speaking of the Father, we have spoken of the Son because the Father and Son are relative to each other. The revelation of the Son and the revelation of the Father are simultaneous and reciprocal: they are included within each other. Trinitarian faith is born in the recognition of the divinity of Jesus and the Holy Spirit in their distinct relation with the Father. This is why, in undertaking here a study of the teaching of the New Testament about Jesus, it is necessary to draw attention to certain expressions of his divinity.[5]

When the New Testament employs the name "God" (*ho Theos*), it is nearly always the Father who is designated by this name. One finds, however, a few passages in which the word "God" is also applied to the Son.[6] The apostle Thomas addresses Jesus by saying to him: "My Lord and my God!" (Jn 20:28). This is a confession of Easter faith, with a cultic accent, which associates the names "Lord" and "God." Naming Jesus as *God* is directly connected to the recognition of his resurrection and it is in line with the confession of Jesus as *Lord* (which is, so to speak, the "proper name" of God in the Bible). In the light of the resurrection, the apostles "clearly understood that Christ was God, through what he had shown in his passion and resurrection";[7] it is "by their faith in the resurrection" that the apostles "firmly believed that Christ was true God."[8]

The quotation of Psalm 45:7–8 in Hebrews 1:8 offers a similar application of the word "God" to Jesus, recognized here as Son: "Of the Son he says, 'Thy throne, O God, is for ever and ever, the righteous scepter is the scepter of thy kingdom.'" Does the author of the

5. Cf. C. Kavin Rowe, *Early Narrative Christology: The Lord in the Gospel of Luke* (Berlin: Walter de Gruyter, 2006).

6. To the passages that we adduce here, one could add Romans 9:5. Other passages are subject to discussion: John 1:18; Titus 2:13; 2 Peter 1:1; 1 John 5:20. On the name "God" applied to Jesus, see Raymond E. Brown, *An Introduction to New Testament Christology* (New York: Paulist Press, 1994), 171–95; Murray J. Harris, *Jesus As God: The New Testament Use of Theos in Reference to Jesus* (Grand Rapids, Mich.: Eerdmans, 1992).

7. St. Thomas Aquinas, *Commentary on the Gospel of St. John* 2:22 (no. 414).

8. St. Thomas Aquinas, *Commentary on the Gospel of St. John* 16:25 (no. 2151).

Epistle to the Hebrews simply cite this psalm by keeping its termi-
nology, without understanding Jesus to be God in a proper sense, or
does he mean that Jesus is true God? The context (the difference of
the Son and the angels) pleads in favor of an affirmation of the divinity of Jesus. One can hold with great probability the interpretation that finds here an expression of the divinity of Jesus. Finally,
the first verse of the Gospel according to St. John is without am-
biguity: "In the beginning was the Word, and the Word was with
God, and the Word was God." One could translate the third clause
of this passage as: "And God was the Word" (the word *God* is placed
in front in order to draw attention to it). Jesus is not only "divine" or
of a "divine kind," but rather he is simply God.

The name *Word*, with which St. John associates here the word
"God," can be considered as a summit of the teaching of the New
Testament about Jesus. By clarifying the divine identity of Jesus,
this name *Word* especially manifests the work of creation, providence, revelation, and salvation accomplished by Jesus. The actions and words of Jesus narrated in the body of the Gospel according to St. John, particularly the words "I am" (Jn 8:58; cf. Jn 8:24,
8:28; Jn 13:19), are fully illumined by the affirmation of the divine
and preexistent Word who has "become flesh" (Jn 1:14). This name
Word constitutes a privileged theme of Trinitarian doctrine, offering
notably a point of contact with philosophical reflection. We will return to this in chapter 5.

The designation of Jesus as *God* developed rapidly among Christians, as Ignatius of Antioch witnesses at the beginning of the second century. St. Ignatius speaks of "the will of the Father and of Jesus Christ our God."[9] To the faithful, he declares: "Being *imitators of
God*, once you took on new life through *the blood of God* you com-
pleted perfectly the task so natural to you."[10] "For *our God, Jesus the

9. St. Ignatius of Antioch, *Epistle to the Ephesians*, Greeting, in *The Apostolic Fathers:
Greek Texts and English Translations*, trans. Michael W. Holmes, 3rd ed. (Grand Rapids,
Mich.: Baker Academic, 2007), 183; emphasis mine.
10. St. Ignatius of Antioch, *Epistle to the Ephesians* 1.1 (*The Apostolic Fathers*, 183);
emphasis mine.

Christ, was conceived by Mary according to God's plan, both from the seed of David and of the Holy Spirit."[11] "Allow me to be an imitator of *the suffering of my God.*"[12] The recognition of Jesus as God is connected to the reception of his salvific and life-giving action.

Although naming Jesus as "God" is present in the New Testament, it there remains discreet. The manifestation of the divine identity of Jesus is effected in many other manners, and the New Testament expresses it in many ways. By way of illustration (albeit very limited) of our thesis, one can note the following forms. We propose to understand these forms not in an "atomistic" or isolated manner, but rather in their comprehensive convergence.

1. *Jesus accomplishes the works of God.* Jesus is one who *elects* (Mk 3:13; Lk 10:22; Mt 16:18: "*I* will build *my* Church"); he forgives sins (Mk 2:7: "Who can forgive sins but God alone?"; cf. Lk 7:48); he raises the dead (Mk 5:35–43; Jn 11); he saves; he will come to accomplish the judgment of the world (Mt 25:31–46); he gives life; and he executes judgment even now (Jn 5). Jesus in person does things that only the power of God can accomplish. His actions invite a reflection that, guided by the Holy Spirit, leads to the recognition of his divine identity. The divinity of Jesus is an object of faith: it cannot be proven by human reason, but it is *attested* by the words and signs that find their fullest meaning in faith. Inspired by the Holy Spirit, the apostles deepened this gaze of faith on Christ Jesus. They depict Christ preexisting before the world, creating the universe, and leading it to its goal (Jn 1:3; 1 Cor 8:6; Eph 1:22; Col 1:15–20; Rev 22:13).

2. *Jesus is the one sent from the Father.* We have already discussed above the importance of the theme of sending. We should add that the sending receives a particular emphasis when it is associated with the theme of *coming:* "I came to cast fire upon the earth" (Lk 12:49). The "I have come" formulas pronounced by Jesus, according to the

11. St. Ignatius of Antioch, *Epistle to the Ephesians* 18.2 (*The Apostolic Fathers*, 197); emphasis mine.
12. St. Ignatius of Antioch, *Epistle to the Romans* 6.3 (*The Apostolic Fathers*, 233); emphasis mine.

testimony of the Gospels, can be considered as an expression of his preexistence. Existing with the Father from before all time, Jesus has come into the world, showing thereby his unity of will with the Father who sends him.[13]

In obtaining the definitive salvation of the world, Jesus is the fulfillment of the Scriptures. A particular form of expression of this fulfillment consists in the application to Jesus of names that, in the Old Testament, belong to the Lord God. This transfer shows that Jesus shares in the rank and prerogatives of God. This is the case, for example, in the absolute expression "I am" pronounced by Jesus himself (Jn 8:24, 8:28, 8:58; Jn 13:9). One can likewise think of the name "Lord," the Name whose invocation saves (Rom 10:13).

3. *Jesus presents himself as the "son of man."* In reference to Daniel 7:9–14, this name "son of man" signifies that the definitive establishment of the reign of God is accomplished in Jesus, and that Jesus possesses a celestial and transcendent dignity. This title indicates the messianic power of Jesus, his passage through suffering and death, as well as the glory that he will manifest at his second coming. The title "son of man" shows the awareness that Jesus had of his person and mission. It makes clear the authority of Jesus, but also his tribulations up to the humiliation of his passion.

4. *Jesus is the Son of God.* We have already discussed above the absolute name "Son" ("the Son") by which Jesus designates himself (see in particular Mk 13:32 and Mt 24:36; Mk 12:1–12 and parallel passages; cf. Mt 11:27 and Lk 10:22). The title "Son of God" signifies the unity of Jesus with his Father, the unity that the resurrection fully manifested. The confession of Jesus as "Son of God" is especially connected to Easter faith (see, for example, Rom 1:4); it is not limited, however, to the event of the resurrection and glorious exaltation of Jesus, but it designates the profound identity and "origin" of Jesus, illuminating his whole action of revelation and salvation.[14]

---

13. Simon J. Gathercole, *The Preexistent Son: Recovering the Christologies of Matthew, Mark, and Luke* (Grand Rapids, Mich.: Eerdmans, 2006).

14. It is necessary to distinguish in order to unite: (1) the brilliant *manifestation of*

The title "Son of God" should be placed in relation with the name "Father" and with the absolute expression "the Son," and also with the action of Jesus, with his teaching and prayer (Mk 14:36: *Abba!*). The confession of Jesus' divine sonship by St. Peter is presented as a *revelation* (Mt 16:16–17).[15]

5. *Jesus is the object of worship.* The disciples worship Jesus (Mt 28:17; cf. Mt 4:10). Jesus is associated with the worship that Christians render to God the Father. One can find a good example in the doxology formulated in Rev 5:13: "To him who sits upon the throne and to the Lamb be blessing and honor and glory and might for ever and ever!" Glory is also rendered to the Father *through* the Son: "To the only wise God be glory for evermore through Jesus Christ! Amen" (Rom 16:27); "We utter the Amen through him [the Son of God, Christ Jesus], to the glory of God" (2 Cor 1:20; see also Jude 25). Certain doxologies are addressed directly to Christ: "Grow in the grace and knowledge of our Lord and Savior Jesus Christ. To him be the glory both now and to the day of eternity. Amen" (2 Pt 3:18; cf. Rom 9:5; 2 Tim 4:18; Rev 1:6). In the same way, Christian prayer is addressed principally to the Father, but some prayers are also addressed to Jesus: "Lord Jesus, receive my spirit" (Acts 7:59). This prayer of St. Stephen applies to the risen Jesus the verse of Psalm 31:6 that invokes the Lord God. It is a good example of the invocation of the Name of the Lord. In this invocation, what the Old Testament says of the Lord God is transferred to Jesus himself. Moreover, the New Testament concludes with an acclamation that is addressed to Jesus: "Amen. Come, Lord Jesus!" (Rev 22:20).

The cultic dimension is especially present in the name "Lord" (*Kurios*) that believers attribute to Jesus: "God has highly exalted him and bestowed on him the name which is above every name,

---

Jesus as "Son of God" by the newness that his glorious exaltation produces; (2) *the reality* implied in this divine Sonship, which concerns the eternal being and "origin" of Jesus, his personal identity.

15. See Gerald O'Collins, *The Tripersonal God: Understanding and Interpreting the Trinity* (London: Paulist Press, 1999), 42–46.

that at the name of Jesus every knee should bow, in heaven and on earth and under the earth, and every tongue confess that Jesus Christ is Lord, to the glory of God the Father" (Phil 2:9–11). This name expresses the transcendent glory, the dignity and beneficent power of the risen Jesus (Acts 2:36; Jn 20:28; Rom 10:9: "If you confess with your lips that Jesus is Lord and believe in your heart that God raised him from the dead, you will be saved"). It signifies that, in his glory, Jesus shares in the prerogatives of God himself (Phil 2:10–11; cf. Is 45:23–24). However, even if the name *Lord* connotes the glorious exaltation of Jesus, the New Testament shows that this lordly dignity qualifies the person of Jesus in his deepest being from the beginning. In the first chapter of the Gospel according to St. Luke, Elizabeth calls Mary "the mother of my Lord" (Lk 1:43). The name *Lord* becomes from then on a characteristic appellation of Jesus by Christians. This appellation is likewise encountered in Trinitarian context: the same Spirit, the same Lord, the same God (1 Cor 12:4–6).

In summary, Christian worship, doxologies, prayers, and benedictions constitute a central expression of the divine dignity of Jesus. From its origins, the distinctive trait of Christian faith is especially expressed in confession of faith and in worship, which are two fundamental "loci" of Trinitarian faith. We will return to this aspect in the next chapter, in reference to St. Basil of Caesarea and to the Creed of Constantinople.

THE GIFT OF THE HOLY SPIRIT

The manifestation of the Holy Spirit is at the heart of the revelation of the Father and Son. The study of the Holy Spirit does not constitute a chapter separated from what has gone before. For the purposes of exposition, we have begun by focusing our attention on the Father and Son, but we must remember that the Holy Spirit is precisely the communion of the Father and Son: he is at the center of the revelation of the Trinity as mystery of communion. We here discuss the teaching of the New Testament on this subject.[16]

In the Gospels according to St. Matthew, St. Mark, and St. Luke, the Holy Spirit appears as the agent of the salvation that is accomplished in Jesus and by Jesus. It is by the Holy Spirit that the Virgin Mary conceives Jesus (Mt 1:18, 1:20; Lk 1:35); the action of the Spirit accounts for the fact that the one who is born of Mary is the Son of God in person. The Holy Spirit is characterized here by his prophetic action (Lk 1: the Spirit who comes upon Mary also inspires Elizabeth and Zechariah) and by his formative action (Mary is with child by the action of the Holy Spirit). At the baptism (Mk 1:9–11), the Spirit shows that Jesus is the Messiah come to bring salvation. Jesus is presented as the beneficiary of the Spirit. The presence of the Holy Spirit indicates the prophetic, priestly, and royal dignity of Jesus. The Spirit leads Jesus to the desert (Mk 1:12–13): he is the source of Jesus' faithfulness. The anointing of Jesus by the Holy Spirit concerns the entirety of Jesus' salvific action—not only his baptism but his whole life, his preaching, and all his acts of salvation up to his offering on the cross. The Holy Spirit is promised to the disciples as empowering faithfulness to Jesus and witness to Jesus (Mk 13:11; Mt 10:19–20; Lk 12:11–12).

The Acts of the Apostles show the *continuity* between Jesus and the Church under the sign of the Holy Spirit. The Spirit procures the expansion of the Church. Poured out by the exalted Jesus at the right hand of the Father (Acts 2:33), the Holy Spirit is the new law (cf. Acts 2:1–4). The gift of the Holy Spirit is normally connected to

16. See Yves Congar, *I Believe in the Holy Spirit*, vol. 1, *The Holy Spirit in the "Economy": Revelation and Experience of the Spirit*, trans. David Smith (New York: Seabury Press; /London: Geoffrey Chapman, 1983), 15–62; in French, Max-Alain Chevallier, *Souffle de Dieu: Le Saint-Esprit dans le Nouveau Testament*, 3 vol. (Paris: Beauchesne, 1978, 1990, and 1991). I also used the important article "Saint Esprit," by Henri Cazelles, et al, in *Supplément au Dictionnaire de la Bible*, vol. 11 (Paris: Letouzey and Ané, 1991), col. 126–398; see also Gordon D. Fee, *God's Empowering Presence: The Holy Spirit in the Letters of Paul* (Peabody, Mass.: Hendrickson, 1994).

water baptism (Acts 2:38). The Holy Spirit, who guides the ministry of the apostles, builds up the Church by being the principle of personal sanctification of believers, by animating their actions through charity, and by inspiring their witness. St. Luke shows that the Holy Spirit is directly connected to Christ: the Spirit animates the human action of Jesus, and the risen Jesus pours him out. The gift of the Spirit accounts for the continuity between the terrestrial life of Jesus, the foundation of the Church, and the continuation of the life of the Church. The Holy Spirit exercises his action by reference to Jesus. This aspect is especially important for our reflection today: the gift of the Holy Spirit always implies a relation to Jesus.

According to this teaching, Jesus is the *beneficiary* of the Spirit (he receives the fullness of the Spirit) and he is also his *giver* (he pours out the Spirit through his paschal mystery). This twofold aspect will receive particular attention in dogmatic reflection about Jesus. Jesus is true God and true man. In his humanity, he receives the Holy Spirit, thereby preparing *in himself* the reception of the Holy Spirit by the Church. "This Spirit descended upon the Son of God made the Son of man, becoming accustomed in fellowship with Him to dwell in the human race, to rest with human beings, and to dwell in the workmanship of God."[17] And by his divine action, with the active concurrence of his human action, Jesus communicates the Holy Spirit. We will return to this point in the last chapter of the book.

The teaching of St. Paul on the Holy Spirit is particularly rich. The Spirit associates believers with the risen Jesus (Rom 8:9–11). The action of the Spirit is intimately connected to the resurrection of Jesus (cf. Rom 1:3–4; Rom 8:11). The Spirit is given by God the Father (Rom 8:11; 1 Thess 4:8; 1 Cor 6:19; 2 Cor 1:22; 2 Cor 5:5; Gal 3:5; Gal 4:6) and his action is relative to Jesus. His principal work is the confession of faith in Jesus the Lord (1 Cor 12:3). He is the Spirit

---

17. St. Irenaeus of Lyons, *Against Heresies* 3.17.1 (*SC* 211:330); English translation from http://www.newadvent.org.

of Christ: "Any one who does not have *the Spirit of Christ* does not belong to him" (Rom 8:9); "God has sent the Spirit *of his Son* into our hearts, crying 'Abba! Father!'" (Gal 4:6); "The help of the Spirit *of Jesus Christ*" (Phil 1:19). The origin of the sending is God the Father, but in this sending Christ occupies a place such that the Spirit is characterized by the relation that he has with Christ. The Spirit is relative to Christ. Thus, in St. Paul, the phrases "in Christ" and "in the Spirit" are very close and are at times employed interchangeably.[18] The "agents" that are Christ and the Holy Spirit are distinct: they are not conflated. Christ acts by the Spirit (cf. Rom 15:18–19), but not inversely. Christ's mode of acting and that of the Spirit are distinct, but their effects are similar. The Spirit enables believers to receive Christ; he applies and inscribes the work of Christ in believers. His action is situated in the relation of the Father and Christ Jesus, as well as in the personal relationship that believers have with the Father through Jesus. The Spirit acts in community of action with the Father and Son (cf. 1 Cor 12:4–6), and he is placed at the same level as the Father and Son (cf. 2 Cor 13:13). This leads to the recognition that he exists according to the mode of what we call a "person," like the Father and Son.

St. Paul places a special emphasis on *life in the Spirit.* The Holy Spirit is the principle of a new life in which he is the law (Rom 8); he is the principle of freedom (Rom 8:2; Gal 5:18; cf. 2 Cor 3:17), the principle of moral and theologal life (Gal 5:13–25); he is the pledge and the guarantee of the inheritance promised to believers (Eph 1:14; cf. Rom 8:23; 2 Cor 1:22; 2 Cor 5:5). The Holy Spirit is given in person to the faithful in whom he dwells (Rom 8:9, 8:11), being at the same time transcendent and present in believers. The Holy Spirit is at the starting point and at the center of Christian life: it is *in* the Spirit that believers share in Christ, *through* whom they obtain free access *to* the Father (cf. Eph 2:18). The mode of action of the Holy Spirit is especially manifested by the role that belongs

18. Congar, *I Believe in the Holy Spirit,* vol. 1, 37–39.

to him in the adoption of believers. "God has sent the Spirit of his Son into our hearts, crying, 'Abba! Father!'" (Gal 4:6). Thanks to the Spirit, believers are established in a new relationship with God, a relationship fundamentally different from that of the slave toward his master, because he is the Spirit of filial adoption (Rom 8:15), the Spirit of the Son himself (Gal 4:6). The Spirit unites believers to the Son and thereby enables them to participate in the filial being of Jesus, in order to turn them, in the image of Jesus, toward his Father. It is by the Spirit that the gifts are distributed to the faithful (1 Cor 12:4–11), particularly charity, which is the most excellent gift (1 Cor 13:13), and which comes from the personal presence of the Holy Spirit: "God's love has been poured into our hearts through the Holy Spirit who has been given to us" (Rom 5:5; cf. Rom 13:10). Meditating on this teaching, a large current of Catholic theology will explain that, through what he does, the Spirit reveals who he is: Love, Gift, Communion.

St. Paul shows that the Holy Spirit builds up the Church. The Spirit is the source of the confession of faith (1 Cor 12:3; cf. 1 Cor 2:10) that constitutes the community of believers. He builds up the Christian community in its cultic relationship to God. This Christian community is defined by the presence of the Spirit (1 Cor 3:16; cf. Phil 3:3). The presence of the Spirit is the principle of ecclesial communion (1 Cor 12:13; cf. 2 Cor 13:13; Eph 2:22). The upbuilding of the Church is accomplished through union with Christ: the Holy Spirit produces this union by giving faith, charity, and filial adoption. The upbuilding of the Church is likewise brought about by the particular gifts, ministries, and charisms that the Spirit gives the Church (and first by the preaching of the word of God that gives rise to faith, cf. 1 Thess 1:5–6). These gifts build up the Church in virtue of the one Spirit who is their source and whose action guides toward Christ (cf. 1 Cor 12). Theology accounts for this teaching by regarding the Holy Spirit as Gift in person, by whom all the gifts are given: the Spirit is the Gift of the Father and Son.

The Gospel according to St. John similarly offers a profound teaching on the Holy Spirit. It shows especially the relationship that the Holy Spirit has with the person of Jesus as Son and as sent from the Father. The "christic" dimension of the work of the Holy Spirit is of the first importance. The fourth Gospel also enables one to understand the "personality" of the Holy Spirit. As Pope John Paul II observed: "It is a characteristic of the text of John that the Father, the Son and the Holy Spirit are clearly called Persons, the first distinct from the second and the third, and each of them from one another."[19]

The Son gives the Spirit. This is an important emphasis of the Johannine pneumatology ("doctrine on the Holy Spirit"). The Spirit remains on Jesus (Jn 1:32–33). Jesus possesses the Spirit in his fullness (cf. Jn 3:34–35) and pours him out upon believers (Jn 7:38–39). The Son does not "depend" on the Spirit: the Son gives him. Jesus promises the coming of the Spirit, the "Paraclete" (Jn 14:16); he "gives up" the Spirit on the Cross (Jn 19:30; cf. Jn 19:34), and he breathes the Spirit on the apostles for their ministry after his resurrection (Jn 20:22).

The Spirit is the *Paraclete* (Jn 14:16–17; 14:26; 15:26; 16:7), that is to say: the protector, the advocate, the intercessor, the consoler, and the interior teacher of doctrine. The Paraclete makes the work of Christ active in the believers whom he teaches, helps, and protects in fidelity to Jesus. He is the *Spirit of truth* (Jn 14:17; 15:26; 16:13). The Paraclete is the subject of actions that refer to Christ: he abides in the disciples of Jesus (Jn 14:17), he teaches and calls to mind the teaching of Jesus (Jn 14:26), he bears witness to Jesus (Jn 15:26), he comes and establishes the sinfulness of the world (Jn 16:7–11), he leads into the whole truth (Jn 16:13), he glorifies Jesus (Jn 16:14), he reveals what belongs to Jesus (Jn 16:14–15). One can observe a strict parallelism between the action of the Paraclete and that of Jesus.[20] The mission of the Spirit/Paraclete, Pope John Paul II explained, "draws

---

19. John Paul II, *Lord and Giver of Life: Encyclical Letter Dominum et Vivificantem*, no. 8 (Washington, D.C.: Office of Publishing and Promotion Services, United States Catholic Conference, 1986), 15.

20. See the detail in Congar, *I Believe in the Holy Spirit*, vol. 1, 55–56; see also

from the mission of Christ, consolidating and developing in history its salvific results."[21] The object of the mission of the Paraclete is the mystery of the Son: the mission of the Paraclete concerns the thoroughgoing reception of the Son who leads to the Father.

The fourth Gospel shows the *relations* that the Spirit has with the Father and the Son. We observe first of all his relationship with the Father. The Father gives, sends the Paraclete (Jn 14:16, 14:26). The Paraclete reveals what is the Son's and what is also the Father's (Jn 16:14–15). The Paraclete "comes forth" from the Father, from where the Son has also come forth. "When the Counsellor [Paraclete] comes, whom I shall send to you from the Father, the Spirit of truth, who proceeds from the Father, he will bear witness to me" (Jn 15:26). One can hold the three following aspects. First, the Father is the Source of the sending of the Paraclete; second, the mission of the Son and that of the Spirit are interiorly connected; third, the Son participates actively in the sending of the Spirit by the Father.

The Gospel according to St. John emphasizes the relation that the Spirit/Paraclete has with the Son, Jesus. The Spirit is "another Paraclete" (Jn 14:16); this expression indicates the otherness but also the continuity between Jesus and the Spirit. The Paraclete works in total reference to Jesus: he teaches and recalls what Jesus taught; he bears witness to Jesus; he glorifies Jesus (Jn 14:26; 15:26; 16:14); he is given through the prayer of Jesus and he is sent in the name of Jesus (Jn 14:16 and 14:26). The exalted Son will himself send the Paraclete from the Father (Jn 15:26; 16:7). The sending of the Paraclete has for its origin, conjointly, the Father and Jesus. The work of the Paraclete is based precisely on the mystery of this origin, that is, on his relation to the Father and the Son. The relation of the Spirit with Jesus is essential: it shows the nature and value of the action of the Paraclete in reference to Jesus; it makes apparent

---

Edouard Cothenet, "Le Saint Esprit dans le corpus johannique," in *Supplément au Dictionnaire de la Bible*, vol. 11 (Paris, Letouzey et Ané, 1991), col. 367.

21. John Paul II, *Lord and Giver of Life: Encyclical Letter Dominum et Vivificantem*, no. 7:14.

the continuity between the work of Jesus and that of the Paraclete. Catholic doctrine makes explicit this teaching by affirming that the eternal origin of the Holy Spirit is revealed in his temporal mission: the Spirit/Paraclete, who is sent by the Father and Son, has his being from the Father and the Son.[22]

In summary: the fourth Gospel presents the Holy Spirit in reference to Jesus, whose work the Spirit deepens and interiorizes in the disciples. His action is the permanent actualization of the very mission of Jesus. His distinction from the Father and the Son is neatly marked. He is "another Paraclete." The origin of the Holy Spirit, who is sent by the Father and the Son, constitutes the basis of his work in believers. His personal character is suggested in a significant manner by the actions that he accomplishes, particularly by his community of action with the Father and Son, which furnishes an important way of understanding his "divine personality." The Scripture does not say explicitly: "The Holy Spirit is God." But it shows that, in relation to the Father and the Son, the Holy Spirit carries out the same work as the Father and the Son. The same thing goes for the existence of the Holy Spirit as "person." The New Testament does not say: "The Holy Spirit is a person." However, as St. Thomas observed, "sacred Scripture speaks of the Holy Spirit as of a subsisting divine person."[23] An important current of the Catholic tradition (St. Augustine, St. Thomas Aquinas) will understand the Spirit as the Love and Gift of the Father and the Son: this doctrinal approach connects the teaching of the fourth Gospel with that of St. Paul.

ONE SINGLE GOD: FATHER, SON, AND HOLY SPIRIT

A reading of the New Testament shows that Trinitarian faith does not come from a theoretical reflection on the one and the many, nor from a speculation on the triadic structure of things. Rather, Trin-

---

22. See the *Catechism of the Catholic Church,* no. 244.
23. St. Thomas Aquinas, *Summa contra Gentiles,* Bk. IV, ch. 18 (no. 3553).

itarian faith is based exclusively on the recognition of the divine lordship of Jesus, the Son of God, Word and Image of the Father, as well as on the recognition of the equal divinity of the Holy Spirit. Before being the object of a doctrinal reflection, the Trinity causes faith, thanksgiving, and the believers' praise of God.

The New Testament leads one to recognize that *Jesus and the Holy Spirit are included in the identity of the one God.*[24] To speak of "inclusion" is to affirm that Jesus and the Holy Spirit are not added to God as from the exterior, but rather God is Father, Son, and Holy Spirit. Faith in the Father, Son, and Holy Spirit *is* faith in the one God. To speak of "identity" is to say that Jesus and the Holy Spirit are not functions or modalities of divine action, but rather their existence concerns the very reality of God, what God is (the Son and Spirit are, with the Father, what we call "divine persons").

This Trinitarian faith is "prepared" in numerous ways in the Old Testament. The Old Testament offers resources that enable Christians to express their Trinitarian faith. These resources particularly include attributes of divine action (wisdom, word, spirit) as well as mediations of the activity of God (the angels).[25] Fundamentally, beyond any particular theme, the preparation of Trinitarian faith in the Old Testament occurs by the revelation of God as transcendent Mystery who is revealed by his action in history. In order to understand this better, we recall first of all our affirmation that in confessing the Father, Son, and Holy Spirit, Christians of the New Testament saw no contradiction with biblical monotheism. At the same time that they confess the Son and Holy Spirit with the Father, the witnesses of apostolic faith affirm the unity of God. In the New Testament, moreover, expressions of Trinitarian faith are often accompanied by the affirmation of the unity of God. This is what we have

24. See Richard Bauckham, *God Crucified: Monotheism and Christology in the New Testament* (Carlisle: Paternoster, 1998); Bauckham, *Jesus and the God of Israel: "God Crucified" and other Studies on the New Testament's Christology of Divine Identity* (Carlisle: Paternoster, 2008).

25. See Larry W. Hurtado, *One God, One Lord: Early Christian Devotion and Ancient Jewish Monotheism,* 2nd ed. (Edinburgh: T. and T. Clark, 1998).

sought to express by speaking of the "inclusion of the Son and the Holy Spirit in the identity of the one God."

On this basis, we now examine the "preparation" of Trinitarian faith in the Old Testament. God manifests himself to Israel as transcendent mystery whose personality escapes human grasp. God is the Living One who, in a supereminent way, enjoys all the perfections of life. The revelation of such a God brings a "depth" that enables Christians of the New Testament to recognize that the Son and Holy Spirit are associated with the Father at the very heart of the divine life. The Living God acts in history; he intervenes in favor of his people and he reveals himself in this action. To Moses, God reveals himself as "I am who am" (Ex 3:14). The Lord manifests himself as the God who acts and who will reveal himself in his intervention in favor of his people. *God reveals "who he is" by his life-giving action in history.* The New Testament shows that the one God has definitively revealed "who he is" by the sending of his own Son and by the gift of his Holy Spirit: God is Father, Son, and Holy Spirit, one single Creator and Savior God, eternally blessed.

Only the faith of the New Testament enables one to discern the Trinity in the Old Testament, but this latter step becomes obvious once one recognizes that the one God is the Father, Son, and Holy Spirit. Recall the revelation of God to Moses at the burning bush. God there reveals himself as "I am who am" (Ex 3:14). An important current of patristic exegesis discovered here the manifestation of the Son who, in the Gospel according to St. John, says of himself: "I am." According to St. Basil of Caesarea, for example, the words of Exodus 3:14 are spoken by the Son, and they reveal that the Son possesses the fullness of being and eternity proper to God.[26] Already, in the second century, St. Justin explained that he who declared "I am He who is, the God of Abraham, and the God of Isaac, and the God of Jacob," was the Son of God himself.[27] In the second half of the second century, Melito of Sardis's homily *On the Passover*

---

26. St. Basil of Caesarea, *Against Eunomius* 2.18 (*SC* 305:70–74).

27. St. Justin, *Apology* 1.63 (*SC* 507: 296–98); English translation, St. Justin Martyr,

presents a striking Christological catechesis. Melito rereads all the work of God in light of faith in Christ, the Son of God.[28] Because the Father, Son, and Holy Spirit are the one God, Christians discover the traits of the Son and of the Holy Spirit, with the Father, in what the Old Testament says of the one God and his action.

One can understand this deepening as follows. In the New Covenant, the revelation of the Trinity is addressed first to Jewish believers formed by the Old Testament. The identity of Jesus is thus expressed starting from the faith professed by the Old Testament, that is, with reference to the God of Israel's faith: "*God* sent forth *his Son*" (Gal 4:4); there is "one God, the Father" and "one Lord, Jesus Christ" (1 Cor 8:6). Yet such words also reveal a profound newness. The revelation of the divinity of Jesus and of the divinity of the Holy Spirit brings a new light: not only that God *has* a Son and breathes forth his Holy Spirit, but that God *is* Father, Son, and Holy Spirit.[29] The one God is the Trinity. The newness brought by Trinitarian faith invites a reappropriation and deepening of what the Old Testament says of God.

One can distinguish two levels of reading the Old Testament. According to the first level (which corresponds to the history of revelation before the coming of Jesus), in the divine works recorded by the Old Testament, it is the Father who reveals himself; not that he was already known as Father of his eternal Son, but rather as Father of Israel, creator of the world, the provident and saving God: "Thou, O Lord [YHWH], art our Father" (Is 63:16). According to the second level of reading, which corresponds to the Trinitarian revelation of the New Testament, Christian faith uncovers the traits of the Trinity in all the actions by which God manifests himself. The

The First and Second Apologies, trans. Leslie William Barnard, Ancient Christian Writers 56 (New York and Mahwah, N.J.: Paulist Press, 1997), 68–69.

28. Melito of Sardis, *On Pascha* 66–86 (*SC* 123:96–110); English translation, Melito of Sardis, *On Pascha and Fragments: Texts and Translations,* edited by Stuart George Hall, Oxford Early Christian Texts (Oxford: Clarendon Press, 1979), 35–49.

29. Jean-Hervé Nicolas, *Synthèse dogmatique: De la Trinité à la Trinité* (Fribourg: Editions Universitaires; Paris: Beauchesne, 1985), 57–59.

God whose works are described in the Old Testament, the one God that one should worship, is not only the Father of Jesus, but is the Father, Son, and Holy Spirit: God the Trinity. It is thus that St. Augustine, for example, discerns the active presence of the Trinity in the first verses of the book of Genesis.[30] The one God, Creator and Savior, the Lord, is the Trinity.

This invites us to reflect on the meaning of the word *God*. If one absolutely identified "God" and "the Father of Jesus" by asserting the exclusive coinciding of what the two names mean, it would not be possible to confess that Jesus is "God" in a manner conformed to Trinitarian monotheism, because Jesus is not his Father. Put otherwise, if one affirmed the complete equivalence of the names "God" and "Father," one would hold that the one God is the Father of Jesus and, "beside" this one God or "below" him, the Son and Holy Spirit would somehow be "added" to God, in such a way that they could hardly be recognized as truly God. And if the Son and Holy Spirit were not true God, what hope could Christians have, since Christians recognize themselves to be saved by the Son come in the flesh and by the gift of the Holy Spirit poured out in their hearts? To conclude this chapter, we will therefore reflect briefly on the word "God." St. Thomas Aquinas will be our guide.

THE NAME "GOD"

Benefiting from clarifications provided by many Fathers of the Church, and applying an analytical method common in his time, St. Thomas distinguishes, on the one hand, what a name signifies, and, on the other hand, the reality or realities that this name designates (that is to say the realities to which this name is applied).[31] On

---

30. St. Augustine, *The Literal Meaning of Genesis* 1.6,12 (*CSEL* vol. 28/1:10); and 2.6.10–2.8.19 (*CSEL* vol. 28/1:39–45); English: St. Augustine, part 1, *Books*, vol. 13, *On Genesis*, trans. Edmund Hill, O.P., The Works of Saint Augustine (New York: New City Press, 2002), 173, 196–201.

31. We thus explain, in a somewhat simplified way, the distinction that St. Thomas makes between "*significare*" and "*supponere.*"

the one hand, a name presents a conceptual content: this is what it signifies formally. On the other hand, a name is often employed, in our statements, in order to "represent" or designate a particular reality. For example, the name "man" signifies human nature in a particular individual. The name "man" signifies one who has a human nature. But when we say that "some men are deprived of liberty," the word "men," in this proposition, designates or is referred to these persons who are captive. The second aspect (the designation, the application of a name to a concrete reality) is attached to the first aspect (the signification), because it is in virtue of what a name signifies that it can have such reference in our statements.

The name *God,* in its proper conceptual content (and not through an accommodation of language), can designate the person of the Father, the person of the Son, or the person of the Holy Spirit; it can likewise be applied to the three together. The word "God" is an appellative name. In order not to extend our exposition, we will limit ourselves to some examples that concern the Father and the Son, understanding that the same reflection applies to the Holy Spirit. "God begets the Son from all eternity, and he sends him into the world for our salvation": in this proposition, the name *God* designates the Father in a distinct way (cf. Gal 4:4: "God sent forth his Son"). Let us take another example, drawn from the *credo:* the Son is "God from God." Here, the first name God distinctly designates the Son, while the second clearly designates the Father. Consider two other examples: "God is Father, Son, and Holy Spirit"; "Be with us, one God almighty, Father, Son, and Holy Spirit."[32] Here, the word *God* is applied to the whole Trinity.

Language has importance. The object of faith is expressed in statements whose value must be measured. In his study of the vocabulary of faith, St. Thomas Aquinas explains that "this name *God* signifies the divine essence as in Him who has it."[33] The name *God*

32. "Adesto, unus Deus omnipotens, Pater, Filius et Spiritus Sanctus" (antiphon of the Office of Readings of the feast of the Holy Trinity).
33. St. Thomas Aquinas, *Summa theologiae* I, q. 39, a. 4.

"signifies Him who has divine nature" (these explanations come from St. John Damascene, who summarized the results of the Eastern patristic reflection).[34] Hence it is that the name "God," in virtue of what it *signifies*, can be *applied* distinctly to the Father, or to the Son, or to the Holy Spirit, just as it can designate the three together. Commenting on the first verse of the Gospel according to St. John, St. Thomas uses this analysis of language in order to show that, where it is written that "the Word was with God," the word *God* distinctly designates the Father. And when St. Thomas reads in the same place that "God was the Word," he notes that the word *God* (which appears here in Greek without article: *theos*) distinctly designates the person of the Word who is the Son: this word *God* can take the place of the three persons or of one of them in particular.[35] The same explanations can be applied to other biblical passages that attribute the name "God" to Christ, for example the confession of faith of the apostle Thomas addressing himself to Jesus: "My Lord and my God (*ho theos mou*)!" (Jn 20:28). In addition, if one remembers that the divinity of Jesus was manifested in reference to his Father, starting from the faith in the one God professed by the Old Testament, one can also better understand that, in the New Testament, the appellative name "God" (*ho Theos*) is applied in a privileged way to the Father, without excluding the true divinity of the Son and Holy Spirit.

A final remark concerning vocabulary is in order. To express the divine unity of the Father, Son, and Holy Spirit, one usually speaks of "monotheism." We follow this common usage, but we should note that the term "monotheism," which was coined relatively late in Western culture, can sometimes be ambiguous. Notably, the undifferentiated use of this word can lead to presenting "the monotheisms" (religious or philosophical) as univocal realities, simply iden-

34. St. Thomas Aquinas, *Summa theologiae* III, q. 4, a. 3; cf. St. John of Damascus, *Exposition of the Orthodox Faith*, Bk. III, ch. 11 [55]; Greek text in *Die Schriften des Johannes von Damaskos*, ed. Bonifatius Kotter, vol. 2, *Expositio fidei* (Berlin: Walter de Gruyter, 1973), 133.

35. St. Thomas Aquinas, *Commentary on the Gospel of St. John* 1:1 (nos. 44 and 53–59).

tical. But it is not enough to affirm the existence of one God. It is also necessary to consider the *unity* of God, and to see *how* God is one. Furthermore, it is necessary to observe the relations that this "one" God has with the world and with human beings. This latter aspect bears a central importance: it is necessary to consider the religious and cultural implications of the assertion of God's oneness, in particular the understanding of the relations between God and the world (from the Christian point of view: creation, providence, the incarnation, Pentecost), as well as the relations that faith in one God gives rise to among human beings. On the one hand, God is "one," not only by relation to other things, but first and foremost in himself: God is *simple*. We will return to this point in chapter 4. On the other hand, for Christian faith, God is "one" in three persons: Father, Son, and Holy Spirit. Finally, the Father, Son, and Holy Spirit are known by us in faith because the Father "so loved the world that he gave his only Son" (Jn 3:16) and because he "sent the Spirit of his Son into our hearts, crying, 'Abba! Father!'" (Gal 4:6). It is in this sense that we speak of "Trinitarian monotheism."

In sum, the revelation of the divinity of Jesus and of the Holy Spirit is not made by a sort of "addition" that would break the divine unity (three gods, or two gods inferior to the first), but by an *inclusion of Jesus and of the Holy Spirit in the identity of the one God*. This inclusion expresses the continuity of the New Testament in relation to the Old Testament, as well as the newness of faith in Christ and in the Holy Spirit. Accordingly, this inclusion has led Christians to reflect more profoundly on the meaning of the word "God" and on the use of this word in designating the Father, Son, and Holy Spirit. *It is faith in Jesus and in the Holy Spirit that enables one to apprehend the richness of the word "God." God is Trinity: Father, Son, and Holy Spirit.*

3

The Confessions of Trinitarian Faith

Confessions of faith in the Triune God were developed according to a variety of circumstances and occasions: the liturgy (particularly baptism), catechesis, the preaching of the faith, and the defense of the faith, as well as exorcisms and healings (because healings are an occasion to proclaim the faith). Among the functions of the formulas of faith, the principal are the teaching of the faith and the liturgy. In this chapter, we propose to examine these confessions of faith, from the New Testament up to the First Council of Constantinople in A.D. 381.

CONFESSIONS OF FAITH IN
THE NEW TESTAMENT

The New Testament contains various confessions of faith. Their central content is the salvific action of God in Christ, understood as a new creation by the Holy Spirit. Under this aspect, one can connect them with prayers and hymns. They focus their attention on the event of salvation as well as on the "agents" of this salvation: the Father, the Lord Jesus, and the Holy Spirit. The mystery of God the Father in his relation to Jesus and the mystery of Jesus himself in his relation to the Father, as well as the action of the Holy Spirit in his

relation to the Father and the Son, are here signified as the central
reality of the definitive salvation, illuminating all things. The confessions of faith, with the liturgical prayers, chants, and hymns, furnish the foundation of preaching (1 Tim 3:16), of catechesis (2 Cor
5), of doctrinal argumentation (1 Cor 15:3–5), and of exhortations
to the Christian life (2 Cor 8:9; Phil 2). They also reflect the central "movement" of the liturgy itself: from the Father, in the Spirit,
through Christ Jesus, to the Father (cf. Eph 2:18; Phil 2:6–11).[1]

The value of the *confession* of faith corresponds to the central
place of *faith* itself in the New Testament: "If you confess with your
lips that Jesus is Lord and believe in your heart that God raised him
from the dead, you will be saved" (Rom 10:9). This confession is
rooted in baptism and in the mission of teaching that Christ confided to his apostles: "All authority in heaven and on earth has been
given to me. Go therefore and make disciples of all nations, baptizing them in the name of the Father and of the Son and of the Holy
Spirit, teaching them to observe all that I have commanded you;
and lo, I am with you always, to the close of the age" (Mt 28:18–
20). One can arrange the confessions of faith according to genres or
"models." We note four types of formulations of faith.[2]

1. The first type consists in the name of Jesus with a "title." For
example: "Jesus is Lord" (Rom 10:9); "Jesus is the Son of God" (1
Jn 4:15). These formulations constitute the core of the *credo.*

2. The developed "kerygmatic" formulations constitute a second
type of confession of faith. These formulations present the object of
the preaching of the faith (the "kerygma"), generally under a narrative form that proclaims the central events of the life of Christ Jesus.
For example: "That Christ died for our sins in accordance with the
scriptures, that he was buried, that he was raised on the third day

1. Geoffrey Wainwright, *Doxology: The Praise of God in Worship, Doctrine and Life,
A Systematic Theology* (Oxford: Oxford University Press, 1981); Pierre Grelot, *La liturgie
dans le Nouveau Testament* (Paris: Desclée, 1991).

2. In this chapter, my exposition borrows many elements from Bernard Sesboüé
and Joseph Wolinski, *Histoire des dogmes*, vol. 1, *Le Dieu du salut* (Paris: Desclée, 1994),
69–280; J. N. D. Kelly, *Early Christian Creeds*, 3rd ed. (New York: Longman, 1995).

in accordance with the scriptures, and that he appeared to Cephas, then to the twelve" (1 Cor 15:3–5).

3. A third kind consists in two-part formulae. They contain mention of the Father and the Son. One finds them, for example, at the beginning of the letters of St. Paul: "Paul an apostle . . . through Jesus Christ and God the Father who raised him from the dead" (Gal 1:1). One finds likewise a good example in the Christological hymn of the epistle to the Philippians: "Jesus Christ is Lord, to the glory of God the Father" (Phil 2:11). The Father and the Son are frequently connected with a title or a work that characterizes them. For example, lordship is attributed to the Son and the action of raising Jesus is attributed to the Father. These two-part formulae often offer praise of the Father and the Son, recognized in their unity and in their distinction, in reference to their work for us. One encounters this in the earliest expressions of Christian faith: "To us who believe in him that raised from the dead Jesus our Lord" (Rom 4:24). Christian preachers use such bipartite formulations for announcing Christ Jesus to Jewish believers, and also for presenting the faith to pagans, as St. Irenaeus explains: to the Jews, the apostles and their disciples proclaimed that Jesus is the Son of God, and that he received from his Father an eternal kingdom; "To the Greeks they preached one God, who made all things, and Jesus Christ his Son."[3] These binary formulations are not, in themselves, anterior to Trinitarian formulations. Formulations of one, two, or three members flourished in the same writings of the New Testament.[4]

4. Lastly, less numerous than two-part formulae, the formulations with three parts mention the Father, the Son (Christ, the Lord Jesus), and the Holy Spirit. One can discern, on the one hand, Trinitarian formulae properly so-called, for instance: "Go therefore and make disciples of all nations, baptizing them in the name of the Father and of the Son and of the Holy Spirit" (Mt 28:19); "The grace

---

3. St. Irenaeus of Lyons, *Against Heresies* 3.12.13 (*SC* 211:238); English translation from http://www.newadvent.org.

4. Kelly, *Early Christian Creeds*, 24–25.

of the Lord Jesus Christ and the love of God and the fellowship of the Holy Spirit be with you all" (2 Cor 13:13).[5] One can observe, on the other hand, some ternary formulations in which an idea about Christian life is expressed according to a Trinitarian structure, for example: "Now there are varieties of gifts, but the same Spirit; and there are varieties of service, but the same Lord; and there are varieties of working, but it is the same God who inspires them all in every one" (1 Cor 12:4–6).[6] These formulations are always connected to the action of Father, Son, and Holy Spirit for us. Each of the Three is designated by a *name* (Father-God, Son-Lord-Jesus-Christ, Spirit-Holy Spirit) with which one connects a *work*. This is already the structure of later creeds of the Church that take shape here. Among these tripartite formulations, many involve an apostolic teaching that is the basis for a practical need (to conform one's life to the revelation of God).

In certain tripartite formulations, one observes the sequence "Spirit, Son, Father" (for example, in 1 Cor 12:4–6, cited above). This sequence starts from the ecclesial and personal experience of the gift of the Spirit, and rises through the Son to the Father: this is the order of Christian experience of the Trinity, the order of the believer's knowledge. Other tripartite formulations present the sequence "Father, Son, Spirit." This is the case of the baptismal formula and also of other biblical passages; for example: "It is God who establishes us with you in Christ, and has commissioned us; he has put his seal upon us and given us his Spirit in our hearts as a guarantee" (2 Cor 1:21–22). This sequence "Father-Son-Spirit" expresses the order of divine action, so to say, the order from the side of God himself. It occupies a determining place in the liturgy and doxology. One observes finally that, from both sides, the bipartite or tripartite formulations emphasize the divine unity and the unity of each of the Three: "For us there is one God, the Father, from whom

5. With this Trinitarian formula, of liturgical origin, one can connect the greeting at the beginning of the book of Revelation (Rev 1:4–6).

6. See also, for instance, Gal 4:6; Rom 8:11; Rom 15:15–16; and Eph 2:18.

are all things and for whom we exist, and one Lord, Jesus Christ, through whom are all things and through whom we exist" (1 Cor 8:6); "There is one body and one Spirit, just as you were called to the one hope that belongs to your call, one Lord, one faith, one baptism, one God and Father of us all, who is above all and through all and in all" (Eph 4:4–6). Such formulations underscore the monotheistic nature of Trinitarian faith.

TOWARD THE CHURCH'S CREEDS

From the first patristic expressions of the faith, the "kerygmatic" formulations that regard Christ Jesus are associated with Trinitarian formulations. On the one hand, these confessions of faith tend with increasing precision to grant the Father, Son, and Holy Spirit an equal status, and to distinguish them from the ensemble of creatures.[7] On the other hand, the articulation of faith in Christ and faith in the Trinity occurs in two principal ways.[8] According to a first way, the Christological confession is added to the Trinitarian formulation (it follows it), as one can see in the following text from St. Irenaeus:

The Church, indeed, though disseminated throughout the world, even to the ends of the earth, received from the apostles and their disciples the faith *in one God the Father Almighty,* the Creator of heaven and earth and the seas and all things that are in them; and *in the one Christ Jesus, the Son of God,* who was enfleshed for our salvation; and *in the Holy Spirit,* who through the prophets preached the economies, the coming, the birth from a Virgin, the passion, the resurrection from the dead, and the bodily ascension into heaven of the beloved Son, Christ Jesus our Lord, and his coming from heaven in the glory of the Father to recapitulate all things, and to raise up all flesh of the whole human race.[9]

7. Basil Studer, *Trinity and Incarnation: The Faith of the Early Church* (Edinburgh: T. and T. Clark, 1993), 29.

8. Sesboüé, *Le Dieu du salut,* 78, 84–92.

9. St. Irenaeus of Lyons, *Against Heresies* 1.10.1–2 (*SC* 264:154–56) in St. Irenaeus of Lyons, *Against the Heresies,* vol. 1, *Book 1,* trans. Dominic J. Unger with further revisions by John J. Dillon (New York: Paulist Press, 1992), 48–49; emphasis mine.

In this text, St. Irenaeus professes first the faith in one God the Father, in one Christ Jesus, and in the Holy Spirit. He then confesses the mysteries of the life of Christ that are connected to the mention of the Holy Spirit: the birth of Christ, his passion, his resurrection, and his parousia. At the end of antiquity, the Creed *Quicumque* (at times called the "Athanasian Creed") possesses a similar structure: it professes first the faith in the Trinity who is the one God, then it confesses the incarnate Son in the mysteries of his flesh.[10] The hymn Te Deum likewise comprises a Trinitarian formulation followed by a Christological sequence.

A second way of uniting Trinitarian faith and faith in Christ consists in inserting the expression of faith in Christ in the second member of the Trinitarian confession (which regards the Son). In this case, the Christological sequence is, so to say, "grafted" onto the name of the Son and is then integrated into a Trinitarian structure. One sees this, for example, in the following text of St. Justin:

> We are not atheists, since we worship the Maker of the universe, and declare, as we have been taught, that He has no need of blood and libations and incense, whom we praise to the utmost of our power through the word of prayer and thanksgiving for all things that we receive. . . . We present before Him petitions that we may live again in incorruption through faith in Him. Our teacher of these things is Jesus Christ, who was also born for this purpose, and was crucified under Pontius Pilate, procurator of Judaea in the time of Tiberius Caesar; and we will show that we worship Him rationally, having learned that He is the Son of the True God Himself, and holding Him in the second place, and the prophetic Spirit in the third rank.[11]

Christians confess their faith in the Creator God, in Jesus Christ, and in the Spirit. In this extract from St. Justin, the Chris-

---

10. Heinrich Denzinger, *Enchiridion symbolorum, definitionum et declarationum de rebus fidei et morum*, 37th ed, ed. Peter Hünermann (Freiburg im Breisgau: Herder, 1991), nos. 75–76.

11. St. Justin, *Apology* 1.13 (*SC* 507:158–60), in St. Justin Martyr, *The First and Second Apologies*, trans. Leslie William Barnard, Ancient Christian Writers 56 (New York and Mahwah, N.J.: Paulist Press, 1997), 30–31.

tological sequence is limited to two mysteries of the life of Christ (his birth and his passion), which are integrated into the Trinitarian profession of faith. St. Justin likewise mentions here the order of the Father, Son, and Spirit. This order does not imply inequality, but rather it signifies the place that the Son and Spirit occupy in the formulations of liturgical prayer, in the doxology, and in the confession of faith: the Son is recognized at the second "place" and the Spirit at the third "rank." One finds likewise a good example of the integration of the Christological sequence at the heart of the Trinitarian confession in the following passage from St. Irenaeus:

And this is the order of our faith, the foundation of the edifice and the support of our conduct: God, the Father, uncreated, uncontainable, invisible, one God, the Creator of all: this is the first article of our faith. And the second article: the Word of God, the Son of God, Christ Jesus our Lord, who was revealed by the prophets according to the character of their prophecy and according to the nature of the economies of the Father, by whom all things were made, and who, in the last times, to recapitulate all things, became a man amongst men, visible and palpable, in order to abolish death, to demonstrate life, and to effect communion between God and man. And the third article: the Holy Spirit, through whom the prophets prophesied and the patriarchs learnt the things of God and the righteous were led in the path of righteousness, and who, in the last times, was poured out in a new fashion upon the human race renewing man, throughout the world, to God. For this reason the baptism of our regeneration takes place through these three articles, granting us regeneration unto God the Father through His Son by the Holy Spirit: for those who bear the Spirit of God are led to the Word, that is to the Son, while the Son presents them to the Father, and the Father furnishes incorruptibility. Thus, without the Spirit it is not possible to see the Word of God, and without the Son one is not able to approach the Father.[12]

In this passage from St. Irenaeus, we should briefly call attention to the following elements. First, the rule of faith possesses a Trinitarian structure (Father, Word-Son-Lord, Holy Spirit). Second, the sequence regarding the Word (the Son) enumerates many mys-

---

12. St. Irenaeus of Lyons, *On the Apostolic Preaching* 6–7, trans. John Behr (Crestwood, N.Y.: St. Vladimir's Seminary Press, 1997), 43–44; cf. *SC* 406:90–92.

teries: creation through the Word, his manifestation to the prophets, his incarnation, his passion, and his resurrection. The mysteries of the Son in his flesh are ordered to the "recapitulation" of all things. The Word is made visible and palpable (incarnation); he becomes man in order to destroy death (by his own death) and in order to demonstrate life (by his resurrection). The Christological sequence is integrated into a Trinitarian structure. Third, St. Irenaeus describes as an "article" or "chapter" each of the three unities or sequences of the rule of faith; this word will enter into the habitual language of the Church (the "articles of faith"). Fourth, this rule of faith is baptismal. It is connected to the catechesis of baptism: "the baptism of our regeneration takes place through these three articles." Fifth, the Trinitarian dynamism of Christian existence is signified in a very expressive way: "those who bear the Spirit of God are led to the Word, that is to the Son, while the Son presents them to the Father, and the Father furnishes incorruptibility." The Christian life is by nature Trinitarian. By the Spirit, believers go to the Son, and through the Son to the Father. The credo confesses the life-giving Trinity who shapes and models Christian existence.

In order to describe the *creed*, one can equally speak of the *symbol of the faith*. In this context, the Greek word "*symbolon*" means half of a broken object (for example, a seal) presented as a token of recognition. "The symbol of faith, then, is a sign of recognition and communion between believers." It offers "a summary of the principal truths of the faith."[13] In the third century, a correspondent of St. Cyprian speaks of the "symbol of the Trinity" (*symbolum Trinitatis*) in order to describe the Christian creed, in the context of baptism.[14] The Trinity is the very object of the Christian faith and the center of the new existence that this faith causes.

13. *Catechism of the Catholic Church*, 2nd ed. (Vatican City: Libreria Editrice Vaticana, 1997), no. 188.

14. St. Cyprian, *Letter* 75.11 (Letter of Firmilian to Cyprian), in Saint Cyprian, *Letters (1–81)*, trans. Sister Rose Bernard Donna (Washington, D.C.: The Catholic University of America Press, 1964), 303.

THE CHALLENGE OF HERESIES

In their teaching function, the creeds pay special attention to the true expression of the faith by avoiding the errors that disfigure it. These errors, which furnished the Fathers of the Church with the occasion for deeper reflection on the Trinity, led the Church to make precise the formulations of her faith.[15] This aspect does not regard only the past, but also our own meditation today. Consideration of an error enables one to discover the depth of the truth, and a more profound knowledge of the truth helps one to discern the root of the error that opposes it. In order to understand the terms of the credo of Nicea and Constantinople, it is necessary to note at least four heterodox currents of thought that, in various ways, led the Church to make precise the expression of her faith.

Adoptionism constitutes a premier, radical form of negation of the Trinity. One calls "adoptionism" a group of heterodox doctrines for which Jesus is simply a man who *was adopted as a son* by God. Jesus would not be the Son of God by nature but rather by "adoption," in a manner comparable to the saints. The Fathers of the Church often present adoptionism in the following way. For the adoptionists, Jesus is a "mere man" (*psilos anthropos, purus homo*) to whom God gives an exceptional grace of sonship. The divine Word came to dwell in the man Jesus by grace, but Jesus is not personally the Word. A famous variant of adoptionism holds that Christ Jesus had been a simple and pure man who, thanks to his virtuous life and by the gift of the Spirit that had been given to him, had merited to become "God" by grace. By denying the true divinity of the Son, adoptionism destroys faith in the Trinity.

A more subtle deformation of the faith, and one more intellectually demanding, is presented by a second group of heterodox currents that can be grouped under the name "unitarian monarchianism." These currents exclude the real distinction of the Father, Son,

15. On the role of heresies in the formation of Catholic thought, see Mark Edwards, *Catholicity and Heresy in the Early Church* (Farnham, UK: Ashgate, 2009).

and Holy Spirit in God. They reproach orthodox Christianity for professing two or three gods. They certainly acknowledge the *names* of Father, Son, and Holy Spirit that Scripture employs, but they see there only *modes* of manifestation of the same one God. The same God manifests himself sometimes as Father, sometimes as Son (in the incarnation), sometimes as Holy Spirit (in the Church). Hence comes the name "modalism" at times given to this current, which is also called "Sabellianism," from the name of Sabellius, one of its representatives. Threefold in his modes of manifestation, God would be only a monad in himself. At the beginning of the third century, Tertullian describes the thought of Praxeas, a representative of this current: "He maintains that there is one only Lord, the Almighty Creator of the world, in order that out of this doctrine of the unity he may fabricate a heresy. He says that the Father Himself came down into the Virgin, was Himself born of her, Himself suffered, indeed was Himself Jesus Christ."[16] Hence comes also the name "patripassianism" (the Father suffered) given at times to this current. This "unitarian monarchianism" is a form of rationalism that levels the Trinitarian economy. Unitarian monarchianism denies that God is in himself such as he has revealed himself to be for us. This error led the doctors of the Church to reflect more profoundly on the relationship between the Trinity and the unity of God (the Trinitarian unity). It likewise requires Christian theologians to make precise the relationship between the Trinity as manifested in the economy and the Trinity in itself (the relationship of the Trinity with history).

For the orthodox faith, the Son who is begotten by the Father is not confused with the Father, but rather he is "distinct in *real number*."[17] The Trinitarian disposition manifested in the economy of salvation exists in the very reality of God. God is "Trinity," as Tertul-

---

16. Tertullian, *Against Praxeas* 1.1 (*CCSL* 2:1159); English translation from http://www.ccel.org.

17. St. Justin Martyr, *Dialogue with Trypho* 128.4, ed. Michael Slusser, trans. Thomas B. Falls, revised by Thomas P. Halton (Washington D.C.: The Catholic University of America Press, 2003), 194; emphasis mine.

lian explains. It is in order to express this real otherness of Father, Son, and Holy Spirit that Tertullian developed the systematic use of the word "person" (*persona*). The Father and the Son are distinct "as regards person, not substance" (*personae, non substantiae*), this substance being one.[18] The word "person" signifies henceforth what is Three in God, while the "substance" designates what is One in God. We owe modalism for having inspired, among Catholics, the use of the word "person" for signifying the Father, Son, and Holy Spirit in their proper and distinct subsistence. In the East the use of the Greek word "hypostasis" (*hupostasis*) was developed, under the influence notably of Origen. "There are three hypostases (*treis hupostaseis*): the Father and the Son and the Holy Spirit."[19] Here again, the opposition to modalism (as well as to gnosticism) contributed to the formation of this dogmatic vocabulary. It is necessary to observe the ontological note of "concrete reality," of proper existence and of subsistence that the word *hypostasis* emphasizes. By its etymology, this term evokes "that which stands in a stable way underneath." The Trinity is not merely a matter of appearance or of manifestation, but rather of being. The very reality of salvation depends on this. We will come back to this point in the next chapter by examining the meaning of the word "person."

A third difficulty was posed to the Church by the thought of Arius and, above all, by the complex developments of certain doctrines that appeared in his wake.[20] Around the years A.D. 318–320, at Alexandria, Arius firmly denied modalism and fell into the opposite error, as it were. He could not accept that the Son is "eternally begotten" by the Father or that the Son is "of the same substance" as

18. Tertullian, *Against Praxeas* 12.6–7 (*CCSL* 2:1173).

19. Origen, *Commentary on the Gospel of John* 2.10.75 (*SC* 120:224).

20. For what follows, see J. Warren Smith, "The Trinity in the Fourth Century Fathers," in *The Oxford Handbook of the Trinity,* edited by Gilles Emery and Matthew Levering (Oxford: Oxford University Press, forthcoming); Smith underlines that the real debate between Pro-Nicenes and Anti-Nicenes in the fourth century was not whether the Son was "divine," but whether he was *true God, equal in divinity with the Father.*

the Father. God is one, "unbegotten," and eternal. Since the Son is
begotten, he cannot be unbegotten; therefore he is not eternal like
God. For Arius, to say that the Son is coeternal with God would be
to affirm that he is unbegotten like God, which is impossible. Moreover, to hold that the Son or Word is begotten of the substance of
the Father would imply, for Arius, a material conception of God and
a change in God. Furthermore, Arius does not acknowledge a rational human soul in Christ, so that the affective passions of Christ described by Scripture (sadness, suffering) must be attributed to the
nature of the Word as such. These passions are incompatible with
the immutability of the divinity. Arius therefore denies the eternity
of the Word or Son. As St. Athanasius reports, Arius said: "God was
not always a Father; once God was alone and not yet a Father, but
afterwards he became a Father. . . . The Son was not always. . . . The
Word of God . . . once was not, and was not before his generation."[21]
Arius confuses the fact of being "without beginning" and the fact of
being "without principle" (according to the Catholic faith, the Son
indeed has a principle, who is the Father, but the Son is eternal, without beginning). Arius holds therefore that the Son is a creature made
from nothing by the will of God: the Son can neither see nor know
the Father perfectly and accurately, but he can reveal the Father only
inasmuch as he is the perfect reflection of the Father's will. The Son
is the highest creature, the one by whom God created the other creatures: the Logos was created by the Father to be his agent of creation.
He is, so to say, "between" God and the other creatures. While God
is immutable, the Logos had to be subject to change in order to enter into a changeable body, suffer, and die on the cross. The Son is
not therefore equal or consubstantial with the Father, but rather he
is subject to change, and ontologically subordinate to the Father. As
regards the Holy Spirit, he is likewise a creature. Arius considers the
Father, Son, and Holy Spirit as three unequal hypostases.

---

21. Arius, "Thalia," in St. Athanasius, *Select Treatises*, trans. John Henry Cardinal
Newman, vol. 1 (New York: Longmans, Green, 1897), 159.

In the final analysis, the Christ of Arius is neither true God nor true man. In the judgment of orthodoxy, the Christ professed by Arius is incapable of procuring salvation. Correlatively, Arius places the name "Father" on the second level. For Arius, the unbegotten God becomes Father when he begets the Son: "God was not always Father, there was a time when God was not Father." The Church was not wrong in determining that this doctrine is no longer Christian. Nevertheless, after the Council of Nicea (in A.D. 325) had rejected the teaching of Arius, the disputes were interminable. Certain theologians admitted a "subordination" of the Son in relation to the Father, as well as a certain inequality between the Father and the Son. St. Athanasius of Alexandria set forth a virulent picture of the heresy, baptized "Arianism."[22] Other theologians held that the Son is of like substance with the Father (*homoiousios*: similar in essence), without, however, going as far as recognizing that he is of the same substance.

The doctrinal crisis arrived at one of its summits with Aetius and Eunomius of Cyzicus, who argued that the Son is absolutely unlike (*anomoios*) the Father in essence (this doctrine is usually called "anomoian"). In the *Apologia* that he wrote around A.D. 360, Eunomius explains that "unbegotten" ("ingenerate") positively names the very substance of God, what God is. He adds that the unbegotten and immutable God cannot beget a Son that would be his equal. He thus conceives the Son as a work coming forth from the activity of God, and whose essence is wholly unlike God's essence. The Son, who is begotten, is a creature of God and the creator of the Holy Spirit.[23] Further on we will revisit the speculative difficulties posed by the heresy of Eunomius, because they had a great impact on the elaboration of the Trinitarian teaching of the Church.

22. See Lewis Ayres, *Nicaea and Its Legacy: An Approach to Fourth-Century Trinitarian Theology* (Oxford: Oxford University Press, 2004), 105–30; after Arius was condemned by the Council of Nicea, his thought by and large ceased to be influential, except as a polemical label that supporters of Nicea attached to their opponents.

23. Eunomius of Cyzicus, *Apology* 26 (SC 305:288–90).

Among the heterodox doctrines that led the Church to make precise her faith in the Trinity, it is necessary to mention, in the fourth place, the negation of the divinity of the Holy Spirit by some believers who acknowledged the divinity of the Son. A first group is known to us by the *Letters to Serapion* of St. Athanasius of Alexandria (written a little before A.D. 360 or around that date). Its followers are called "Tropikoi" by St. Athanasius because, in order to elude the biblical texts brought forth in favor of the divinity of the Holy Spirit, they interpreted them as figures of speech or manners of speaking (in Greek: *tropoi*). According to St. Athanasius, they teach that the Son is God, but the Holy Spirit is a creature; the Holy Spirit is an angel superior to the other angels. He is therefore "of another substance" than the Father and the Son, so that there is no longer a Trinity, adds St. Athanasius, but a "duality" or "dyad!"[24] The difficulty encountered by the deniers of the divinity of the Holy Spirit is not without importance. The notion of "begetting" enables one to account for the divinity of the Son: the Son is "begotten" by the Father. But the Holy Spirit is not begotten. How then could he be God? Can one affirm the existence of a divine person who is neither "begotten" (the Son) nor "unbegotten" (the Father)?

In his response, St. Athanasius appeals to baptism, which is Trinitarian.[25] Athanasius presents an argument that he had already applied to the Son in the controversy against "Arianism": the Holy Spirit procures divine life; he sanctifies and "divinizes" believers. No creature could do this. Only God divinizes.[26] The action of the Holy Spirit (like that of the Son) shows therefore that he is true God.[27]

---

24. Saint Athanasius of Alexandria, *Letter to Serapion* 1.2 and 1.10, in *The Letters of Saint Athanasius Concerning the Holy Spirit,* trans. C. R. B. Shapland (London: Epworth Press, 1951), 63, 85–87.

25. See, for example, Saint Athanasius, *Letter to Serapion* 1.28 and 1.30 (trans. Shapland, 136, 139–42).

26. "Who will unite you to God, if you have not the Spirit of God, but the Spirit which belongs to creation?" (Saint Athanasius, *Letter to Serapion* 1.29; trans. Shapland, 138).

27. See, for example, Saint Athanasius, *Letter to Serapion* 1.22–24; 1.27; 1.29 (trans. Shapland, 120–28, 132–33, 136–38).

St. Athanasius notes likewise that the rejection of the divinity of the Holy Spirit leads directly to denying the divinity of the Son, because "the Spirit bears the same relation to the Son as the Son to the Father."[28] St. Athanasius shows that the confession of the Father, Son, and Holy Spirit forms an indissociable whole. "For we shall find that the Spirit has to the Son the same proper relationship as we have known the Son to have to the Father. And as the Son says, *All that the Father has is mine* (Jn 16:15), so we shall find that through the Son all these things are in the Spirit also."[29]

Shortly after St. Athanasius, St. Basil encounters a similar problem. At Caesarea, during a liturgical celebration, St. Basil concludes the doxology in a twofold way: "Lately while I pray with the people, we sometimes finish the doxology to God the Father with the form 'Glory to the Father with (*meta*) the Son, together with (*sun*) the Holy Spirit,' and at other times we use 'Glory to the Father through (*dia*) the Son in (*en*) the Holy Spirit.'"[30] Some of his listeners reproached him for employing the first phrase "together with the Holy Spirit" (co-ordinate doxology),[31] which they did not accept. In the history of doctrines, one calls them "*pneumatomachoi*," that is to say, "opponents of the Spirit" (the expression is found in St. Basil himself), those who do not wish to accept that the Holy Spirit possesses the same power and the same divinity as the Father and the Son. St. Basil therefore applies himself to show that the phrase "with the Son" properly expresses faith in the dignity of the Son, and that the expression "together with the Holy Spirit" is true, conformed to Scripture and completely traditional.[32] Basil gathers nu-

---

28. Saint Athanasius, *Letter to Serapion* 1.21 (trans. Shapland, 118): "But if, in regard to order and nature, the Spirit bears the same relation to the Son as the Son to the Father, will not he who calls the Spirit a creature necessarily hold the same to be true also of the Son?" This teaching emphasizes the divine consubstantiality of the Son and of the Holy Spirit.

29. Saint Athanasius, *Letter to Serapion* 3.1 (trans. Shapland, 170).

30. St. Basil the Great, *On the Holy Spirit* 1.3 (Crestwood, N.Y.: St. Vladimir's Seminary Press, 1980), 17; cf. *SC* 17 bis, 256–58.

31. St. Basil the Great, *On the Holy Spirit* 1.3: "Some of those present accused us of using strange and mutually contradictory terms."

32. After having shown the biblical foundations of the formula "together with the

merous biblical texts showing that the Holy Spirit exercises properly divine actions: he creates, reveals, saves, sanctifies; in baptism, the Holy Spirit deifies. The phrase "together with the Holy Spirit" means that the Holy Spirit possesses the same power and the same dignity as the Father and Son, and that he receives therefore the same *glory*. We have already noted above the value of prepositions in doxologies. The liturgy is the place par excellence for the proclamation of the faith. When the Church celebrates the sacraments, she confesses the faith received from the apostles. This is an illuminating application of the principle *lex orandi, lex credendi* (the law of prayer is the law of faith).[33]

In order to signify the divinity of the Holy Spirit, St. Basil chooses to speak of the "equality of honor" (*homotimia*) of the Holy Spirit with the Father and Son. The preposition "with," employed in the doxology, signifies precisely this "equality of honor." This is a concrete manner of confessing the consubstantiality of the Holy Spirit with the Father and Son. St. Basil relies especially on the baptismal formula. "The Lord speaks of the Spirit and the Father in exactly the same way: 'In the name of the Father, and of the Son, and of the Holy Spirit' (Mt 28:19). The words of baptism are the same, and they declare that the relation of the Spirit to the Son equals that of the Son with the Father. If the Spirit is ranked with the Son, and the Son with the Father, then the Spirit is obviously ranked with the Father also. Their names are mentioned in one and the same series."[34] "What led me to glorify the Spirit is, in the first place, the honour (*time*) conferred by the Lord in associating Him with Himself and with His Father at baptism; and, secondly, the fact that of each of us is introduced to the knowledge of God by such an initiation."[35] The

Holy Spirit," St. Basil cites many traditional witnesses in its favor: *On the Holy Spirit* 29.72–75 (SC 17 bis, 502–18).

33. On this principle, see the *Catechism of the Catholic Church*, no. 1124 (in reference to Prosper of Aquitaine).

34. St. Basil of Caesarea, *On the Holy Spirit* 17.43 (Crestwood, N.Y.: St. Vladimir's Seminary Press, 1980), 70; cf. SC 17 bis, 388–98. This argument was already put forward by St. Athanasius of Alexandria.

35. St. Basil of Caesarea, *On the Holy Spirit* 29.75 (SC 17 bis, 516).

preposition "together with" employed in the doxology corresponds to the conjunction "and" in the formula of baptism. There is a direct correspondence among these three fundamental realities: (1) the formula of *baptism*; (2) the Trinitarian *creed*; (3) and the *doxology*.

We are adding the explanation of [the doctrine concerning the Holy Spirit] in conformity with the meaning of the Scriptures, that as we are *baptized*, so, also, do we *believe*; as we believe, so, also, do we *give glory*. Therefore, since *baptism* has been given to us by the Savior in the name of the Father and of the Son and of the Holy Spirit, we offer a *confession of faith consistent with our baptism, and also the doxology consistent with our faith, glorifying the Holy Spirit with the Father and the Son* in the conviction that He is not separated from the divine nature. For, that which is different according to its nature would not share the same honors.[36]

St. Basil offers here a criterion that even today retains its decisive value. His explanations are guided by the coherence of Christian faith in its major expressions (baptism, credo, glorification of God). There is a strict homogeneity between the sacraments, the profession of Trinitarian faith, and the praise of the Church.

THE CREED OF NICEA AND CONSTANTINOPLE

The tradition of the Church includes various symbols of faith. Among these, a special place belongs to the Creed of Nicea (A.D. 325) and to its development in the Creed of Constantinople I (A.D. 381), which still today serves as a sign of recognition and communion among Christians. In what follows, we present the "faith" (pistis) of the Council of Constantinople I. This entire profession of faith is a complement to the verb "we believe." This confession has for its object the Father, Son, and Holy Spirit. "The profession of faith summarizes the gifts that God gives man: as the Author of all that is good; as Redeemer; and as Sanctifier. It develops these in the three chapters on

36. St. Basil of Caesarea, *Letter* 159, in Saint Basil, *Letters*, vol. 1 (1–185), trans. Sister Agnes Clare Way (Washington, D.C.: The Catholic University of America Press, 1981), 313; emphasis mine.

our baptismal faith in the one God: the almighty Father, the Creator; his Son Jesus Christ, our Lord and Savior; and the Holy Spirit, the Sanctifier, in the Holy Church."[37] The Creed of Nicea-Constantinople is a creed of bishops. Through its reception in the eucharistic liturgy, it has become the confession of faith of the whole Christian community.

"We believe in one God, the Father almighty, creator of heaven and earth, of all things visible and invisible."[38] In this first article, following the usage of the New Testament and of the liturgy, "God" refers to the Father. In the second article, however, the word *God* also designates the Son: "God from God, true God from true God." Thus the word *God* first designates the Father. This word *God* is then applied to the Son with a precision: the Son is God in reference to the Father from whom he has his origin. The affirmation of the unity of God ("one God") is opposed to polytheism as well as to any dualism.

In the first article, the name "God" is specified by that of "Father." At Nicea and Constantinople, the meaning is clear: it is not only a matter of God as Father of the world or Father of humankind, but Father as *Father of Jesus Christ, his Son.* The name "Father" is taken in its Trinitarian meaning. This name "Father" is professed as the name proper to the first person of the Trinity. The *credo* does not retain the word "Unbegotten," which Arius, and later Eunomius of Cyzicus, used to evade the divinity of the Son.[39] Nicea, followed by Constantinople, places *the name Father in the foreground.*[40] God

37. *Catechism of the Catholic Church*, no. 14.

38. For the Greek text of the Creed of Constantinople I, see Giuseppe Alberigo, ed., *The Oecumenical Councils from Nicaea I to Nicaea II (325–787)*, Corpus Christianorum: Conciliorum Oecumenicorum Generaliumque Decreta, vol. 1 (Turnhout: Brepols, 2006), 57.

39. The term "Unbegotten" retains a perfectly orthodox and important meaning if one understands that the Father is not begotten. It signifies a property of the Father: the Father is without principle. But it receives a heretical interpretation if one holds that, being begotten, the Son "became" in a creaturely manner. We will return to this name "Unbegotten" in chapter 5, in our exposition of the person of the Father.

40. St. Athanasius of Alexandria puts forward this theory in his *First Discourse Against the Arians*, nos. 30–34.

is Father from all eternity, and this is his proper name. This is an essential point of Christian faith against Arianism. The first "person" of the Trinity is God *as Father.*

The Father is confessed as "almighty" (*pantokrator*). In the Greek Bible, this word *pantokrator* translates many expressions (*Sabaot,* for instance, in 2 Sm 5:10, or *Shaddai,* for instance, in Job 5:17). This term appears particularly in the book of Revelation, which many times designates God as *pantokrator.* The Greek word *pantokrator* says more than the Latin *omnipotens* or than our English expression "almighty." The Greek word highlights the activity of God. The Lord *pantokrator* is the one who governs and who effectively sustains the world. It does not mean only a possibility ("to be able to do everything"), but rather the effective exercise of creative and providential power. One could perhaps translate it: "ruler of all," "he who holds all things" (*omnitenens*). The Father *pantokrator* is the Creator and Ruler of all the universe in its totality: heaven and earth (cf. Gen 1:1), "all things visible and invisible" (cf. Col 1:16). This pair "visible/invisible" avoids the error of dualist movements that attribute a different origin to the material world and to the spiritual world.

After the Father, the confession of faith in the Son is formulated in three clauses, each clause comprising in its turn three expressions, loosely in succession. The first clause is the following: "in one Lord Jesus Christ, the Son of God, the only-begotten." The *credo* places the name "Son of God" in the first place, since the Son is said to be "begotten" and because the doctrinal debate against Arius concerns the *begetting* of this Son. The ensemble of the sequence devoted to the Son shows how one must understand this name *Son of God:* not Son by grace or by adoption as a creature, but Son by nature and in virtue of his being begotten "from the substance of the Father" (Nicea). The weak sense of the name *Son,* promoted by Arius and the "Arians," is avoided. The title "Lord" does not refer only to Jesus as risen, but rather it signifies clearly that Jesus, in his most profound original being, is God. The names *Son* and *Lord* are taken here in an exclusive and proper divine sense. Lastly, the description of the Son as "only-begotten" reprises the words of John 1:14 and John 1:18 (cf. Jn 3:16; Jn 3:18; 1 Jn 4:9). Jesus, the Son, is the "only-begotten." This name underscores that Jesus is Son in an absolutely unique and proper way, as the two following clauses go on to make explicit.

In the Creed of Constantinople, the second clause of the faith in the Son declares: "begotten of the Father before all ages, Light from Light, true God from true God." The key for understanding this resides in the expression "begotten of the Father," literally "begotten from the Father" (*ek tou Patros*). The Council of Nicea made this quite precise: "that is to say from the substance of the Father" (*ek tes ousias tou Patros*). This expression formally excludes that the Son could be a creature. Unlike creatures, which the will of God produces "from nothing" (*ex nihilo*), the Son is begotten by nature "from the Father" (*ex Patre*). The expression *ex Patre* (*ek tou Patros*) is precisely opposed to the phrase *ex nihilo*. It signifies that the Son is radically, essentially distinguished from the whole created universe. The Son is not a reality exterior to the Father, but rather he receives the very being of the Father. Thus, to say that Jesus is from the Father (from the "substance" of the Father) is to affirm his properly divine identity. His being (his "substance") is identical to that of the Father who begets him.

In the formulation of the creed, the theme of begetting evokes Psalm 2:7: "Today I have begotten you." This verse from the Psalm is taken up in the New Testament, notably in Acts 13:33, where it is applied to the resurrection of Christ. In the Niceno-Constantinopolitan Creed, however, this begetting designates the eternal birth of the Son. We observe again that the phrase "from the Father" (*ek tou Patros*) evokes the words of Jesus: "I proceeded and came forth from God" (Jn 8:42); "I came from the Father" (Jn 16:28). These biblical passages refer principally to the sending of the Son into our world. But in the *credo*, the phrase "from the Father," connected with the theme of begetting, raises the minds of believers toward the eternal origin of the Son (which is the Trinitarian foundation of his being sent by the Father). It is the Father who sends the Son, because it is the Father who begets the Son from all eternity. From this perspective, the expression "begotten before all ages" ("eternally begotten") evokes the preexistence of Wisdom (Sir 24:9; Prov 8:23), with numerous resonances in the New Testament: "In the beginning was the Word" (Jn 1:1); "thy love for me before the foundation of the world" (Jn 17:24).

In this second clause of the confession of the Son, the begetting is made explicit by two complementary expressions. The first declares that the Son is "Light from Light" (or "Light of Light"). Light (*phos*) is a biblical name connected with God and with his Son: "God is light" (1 Jn 1:5); the Word is "the true light" (Jn 1:9); "I am the light of the world" (Jn 8:12). This biblical theme indicates the fullness of revelation, the source of life, the brightness of holiness, and the radiance of the divine nature that excludes all imperfection. This theme of light is an important Trinitarian image. Already in the second century, St. Justin uses the image of "fires kindled from a fire" in order to show that the begetting of the Son by the Father does not entail a diminution of the Father (the Father loses nothing of himself in begetting his Son), nor any change of the Father: "The enkindled fires are indeed distinct from the original fire which, though it ignites many other fires, still remains the same undiminished fire."[41] In the third century, Origen employs the theme of light in order to show the co-eternity of the Father and Son, beyond time: "John also indicates that *God is Light* (1 Jn 1:5), and Paul also declares that the Son is the *splendor* of everlasting light (Heb 1:3). As light, accordingly, could never exist without splendor, so neither can the Son be understood to exist without the Father; for he is called the express image of his substance, his Word and his Wisdom."[42] The expression

41. St. Justin, *Dialogue with Trypho* 128.4, in St. Justin Martyr, *Dialogue with Trypho*, trans. Thomas B. Falls, revised by Thomas P. Halton (Washington D.C.: The Catholic University of America Press, 2003), 194.
42. Origen, *On First Principles* 4.4.1 (*SC* 268, 402). Origen continues: "How, then, can it be asserted that there once was a time when the Son was not? For that is nothing else than to say that there was once a time when the Truth was not, nor the Wisdom, nor the Life. . . . The statements made regarding Father, Son, and Holy Spirit are to be

"light from light" thus expresses the immutability of the begetting or generation of the Son, his eternity and his divinity.

In the second complementary formulation, the creed makes explicit the generation of the Son by declaring that he is "true God." The expression "true God" is biblical. "This is eternal life, that they know thee the only true God" (Jn 17:3); "We are in him who is true, in his Son Jesus Christ. This is the true God and eternal life" (1 Jn 5:20). At Nicea and Constantinople, this expression excludes the conceptions that attribute to the Son a divinity by participation or a divinity inferior to that of the Father. To call the Son "true God from true God" is to affirm that the Son is God by nature, not in a manner inferior to the Father, but as fully as the Father himself: by begetting, the Father communicates to the Son his true and full divinity.

The third clause of the confession of the Son adds three more expressions: "begotten not made, consubstantial with the Father, through whom all things came to be." These expressions reject the error of Arius under all its forms, from the most radical to the most subtle (that which makes of the Son a created being superior to other creatures, the created instrument of creation). By affirming that the Son is "begotten, not made," one says what he is and what he is not. Arius held that the Son is "begotten," but he connected this begetting to a kind of creation. The phrase "not made" specifies therefore one more time the nature of the begetting of the Son. This should be taken in the strong sense, as excluding any relation based on creation between the Father and the Son.

The expression "consubstantial with the Father" ("of one essence with the Father") signifies the same thing as "begotten of the Father" (that is to say, "of the substance of the Father," according to Nicea). In the course of the fourth century, the word "consubstantial" (*homoousion*) gave rise to some lively debates. The "Arians" rejected it: they found it to be unbiblical and to suggest a subdivision

---

understood as transcending all time, all ages, and all eternity"; English translation from http://www.ccel.org.

or a sharing of the Father's substance in a "materialist" manner that clearly would be unacceptable. Other theologians hesitated to acknowledge the value of this formulation. On the one hand, at Nicea, the term "consubstantial" was chosen so as to repulse Arius, who rejected it. On the other hand, St. Athanasius of Alexandria explained that the council introduced this term to make explicit the meaning of Scripture by avoiding with firmness and precision the error of those who rejected the true divinity of the Son. It was necessary to employ a nonbiblical word in order to proclaim clearly the biblical faith! According to St. Athanasius, "consubstantial" means that the divine reality of the Son is identical to that of the Father. The Father and Son are one in being. It is necessary to avoid any idea of change or division of the Father's substance, because God is simple.

Lastly, the third expression of the third clause affirms that "through him [the Son] all things came to be." Nicea specified: "what is in heaven and what is on earth" (cf. Col 1:16). This wording is taken from John 1:3 ("through him all things came to be"; cf. Heb 1:2: "a Son . . . through whom also he created the world"). This expression is more important than it might at first appear. It says that the action of the Son possesses the same range and depth as the action of the Father *pantokrator*. This is a way of proclaiming the one divinity of the Father and Son by means of their community of action. The Son possesses the same power of action and therefore the same nature as the Father. The Niceno-Constantinopolitan Creed first attributed the creative and providential action to God the Father. It then attributes this same activity to the Son. The Son's creative and providential activity manifests his consubstantiality with the Father (this action of the Son shows that he is true God). That consubstantiality likewise illumines the creative activity of the Son: the Son is not Creator in the manner of an inferior intermediary, as Arius supposed, but rather he is Creator inasmuch as he possesses the very substance of the Father. The preposition "through" ("through whom") has a similar importance. It denotes the creative causality of the Son *in relation to the Father*. The Son creates inasmuch as, through his generation, he receives from the Father the divine essence and the creative power. The Son is Creator inasmuch as he is *God begotten by the Father,* because it is from the Father that the Son has what he is and all that he does.

The continuation of the sequence devoted to the Son concerns the mysteries of his life in the flesh assumed "for us and for our salvation," from his birth of the Virgin Mary to his return in glory for the judgment. In the Creed of Constantinople, the confession of the Son concludes with the phrase "and his kingdom will have no end." This formulation comes from the message of the angel Gabriel to the Virgin Mary in Luke 1:33. In the *credo,* it is directed against a subtle form of Sabellianism according to which, at the end of time, when Christ has subjected all things to his Father and has subjected himself to his Father (cf. 1 Cor 15:27–28), the Word will be reabsorbed in some way into the divine unity.[43] Put otherwise, when the economy of salvation is fully accomplished, the Word and the Spirit will return to a primordial unity. On this view the Trinity will be reabsorbed into an original unity. In order to avoid this position, the clause of the *credo* signifies that the Son eternally subsists in his distinction and that he fully retains his royal humanity forever, without ever fading into an indistinct unity: the kingdom of the Son will have no end.

"And in the Holy Spirit, the Lord, the giver of life, who proceeds from the Father, who with the Father and the Son is worshiped and glorified, who has spoken through the prophets"—the Creed of Constantinople first attributes to the Spirit three titles: *Holy, Lord,* and *Life-giving.* These are three ways of signifying the divinity of the Spirit. They come before three longer formulations that develop the faith in the Holy Spirit.

Following a common usage in the New Testament, the Spirit is called *Holy.* Holiness is specially attributed to the Spirit by reason of

---

43. This error is denounced by various authors: see for example Cyril of Jerusalem, *Catechetical Lectures* 15.27 (*PG* 33, col. 909–13); English translation: *The Works of Saint Cyril of Jerusalem,* vol. 2, trans. Leo McCauley, Fathers of the Church 64 (Washington, D.C.: The Catholic University of America Press, 1970), 72–73.

the power of sanctification that he puts into action. The Spirit is the one through whom the Father and the Son sanctify us. According to St. Basil of Caesarea, the name "holy" has to do with the divinity of the Spirit (holiness belongs to his substance), and it also orients our thought toward the property of the Spirit within the Trinity.[44] The Spirit also receives the title "Lord," like the Son. The attribution of this divine title means that the Spirit is God with the Father and Son. A nuance, however, deserves attention. In the *credo*, the Son is confessed as "one Lord": conforming to the usage of the New Testament, the expression "Lord," in the masculine, designates the Son. For his part, the Holy Spirit is confessed as "Lord" without mention of oneness, and with a neuter article (*to kurion*) that is not easy to render into English. The name "Lord" here assumes the status of an attribute. One could make it explicit thus: "One who is of the category of Lord."[45] The Spirit is neither a creature nor an instrument of God, but rather he is God by nature. Lastly, the Spirit is confessed as "giver of life" or "life-giving." This phrase comes from many passages of the New Testament, notably John 6:63: "It is the spirit that gives life." Without excluding the gift of life in its generic sense, the accent is placed on vivification by grace, that is to say, sanctification. One can see here a form of soteriological argument described above: since the Spirit gives life, he is not on the side of realities that are vivified, but rather he is on the side of God. The Spirit is God who gives life. To say that the Spirit is *life-giving* thus constitutes a way of professing his divinity.

These three titles are augmented by three more developed formulations. The first formulation states that the Holy Spirit "pro-

44. St. Basil of Caesarea, *Letter* 159, in St. Basil, *Letters*, vol. 1 (1–185), trans. Sister Agnes Clare Way (Washington, D.C.: The Catholic University of America Press, 1981), 313: "For, the Spirit of Himself has a natural sanctity not received through grace but joined essentially to Him, whence also He has gained in a special manner the name of 'Holy'"; see also *Letter* 214 in St. Basil, *Letters*, vol. 2 (186–368), trans. Sister Agnes Clare Way (Washington, D.C.: The Catholic University of America Press, 1969), 102: "The hypostasis is perceived in the peculiar property of paternity or sonship or sanctifying power."

45. Ignacio Ortiz de Urbina, *Nicée et Constantinople* (Paris: Editions de l'Orante, 1963), 194.

ceeds from the Father," literally: "proceeding from the Father." This expression comes from John 15:26 ("the Spirit of truth, who proceeds from the Father"), but with two nuances. First, the *credo* employs a different preposition than the Gospel according to St. John, the same one that the council used above for signifying the origin of the Son: just as the Son is begotten "from the Father," the Holy Spirit proceeds "from the Father" (*ek tou Patros*). The Holy Spirit is not drawn from nothing in the manner of creatures (*ex nihilo*). Rather, like the Son, he comes forth from the Father: *ex Patre*. (Another difference with John 15:26 is the use of the participle "proceeding," in accordance with the structure of the phrase: *vivifying, proceeding, co-adored*). Second, in the *credo*, the formula "proceeding from the Father" does not concern primarily the sending of the Holy Spirit to the Church (as in John 15:26); instead it signifies expressly the eternal origin of the Spirit. In the Creed of Constantinople, the goal of this expression is not to determine with precision the mode of origin of the Holy Spirit, but to signify the personal divinity of the Holy Spirit. To affirm that the Holy Spirit proceeds from the Father is to say that he is God.[46] His origin is properly divine, mysterious, and ineffable.

"Together with the Father and the Son," the Holy Spirit is "worshiped and glorified." This second precision repeats the argument that St. Basil of Caesarea made in his treatise *On the Holy Spirit*. The Spirit is adored "together with" the Father and the Son, because he possesses the same creative and salvific power, the same divine dignity as the Father and the Son. With them, he therefore receives the same adoration and the same glory: he is God. We find here, as in St. Basil, the correspondence of the *lex orandi* and the *lex credendi*. Lastly, the creed professes that the Holy Spirit "has spoken through the Prophets." This phrase is already found in other symbols of faith, for example in that of the Church of Jerusalem. The Old Testament, in which

---

46. The council was not concerned to specify the part that the Son takes in the procession of the Holy Spirit. It certainly did not exclude it, but its intention did not bear upon this point of doctrine.

the prophets spoke, comes from the same good God as the New Testament. In the Creed of Constantinople, this phrase offers an additional confirmation of the divinity of the Holy Spirit. St. Athanasius explained that, when the Word comes to the prophets, these prophets speak by the Holy Spirit. The Holy Spirit is therefore not exterior to the Word, but rather he is in the Word.[47] The inseparable action of the Holy Spirit and of the Word in the inspiration of the prophets shows the divinity of the Holy Spirit: exercising one same activity, the Word and Holy Spirit possess the same divinity. The Father gives all goods through the Son in the Holy Spirit.[48]

In the Creed of Constantinople, the Holy Spirit is not explicitly declared "God" or "consubstantial with the Father." St. Athanasius had, however, clearly confessed the Holy Spirit in these terms.[49] And St. Gregory of Nazianzus, who presided for a time over the First Council of Constantinople, expressly held the consubstantiality of the Holy Spirit.[50] Nevertheless, rather than employ terms that had raised so much controversy regarding the Son, the council preferred to adopt the path of St. Basil: it used circumlocutions for expressing the divine consubstantiality of the Holy Spirit. Indeed, all the formulations of the creed with regard to the Holy Spirit signify his divinity. Furthermore, the theme of the "co-glorification" was promoted by important theologians of the time, notably St. Gregory of Nyssa, for expressing the ontological status of equality that the Holy Spirit possesses with the Father and the Son.[51] One can

47. St. Athanasius, *Letter to Serapion* 3.5, in *The Letters of Saint Athanasius Concerning the Holy Spirit*, trans. C. R. B. Shapland (London: Epworth Press, 1951), 175.

48. St. Athanasius, ibid.: "For the Father himself through the Word in the Spirit works and gives all things."

49. See, for example, St. Athanasius, *Letter to Serapion* 1.27 (trans. Shapland, 133): "But because he is one, and, still more, because he is proper to the Word who is one, he is proper to God who is one, and one in essence (*homoousios*) with him."

50. See, for instance, St. Gregory of Nazianzus, *Oration* 31.10 (*SC* 250:292), in St. Gregory of Nazianzus, *On God and Christ: The Five Theological Orations and Two Letters to Cledonius* (Crestwood, New York: St. Vladimir's Seminary Press, 2002), 123: "Is the Spirit God? Certainly. Is he consubstantial? Yes, if he is God"; see also *Oration* 40.41 (*SC* 358:294).

51. Lewis Ayres, *Nicaea and Its Legacy*, 258.

note lastly that the consubstantiality of the Trinity was expressly proclaimed by a synod assembled at Constantinople the following year, in A.D. 382.[52]

In the creed, the confession of faith in the Trinity is followed by the mention of the Church: "We believe in the Church." "It is the whole Church that is to be understood here," explained St. Augustine, not only the part of the Church which sojourns on earth, but also that which is found in heaven.[53] Moreover, it is necessary to observe that the confession of the Church is directly connected to faith in the Trinity. "The correct sequence of the Creed demanded that the Church be subjoined to the Trinity: after the Inhabitant, his House; after God, his Temple; after the Founder, his City."[54] God the Trinity dwells in his Church, and it is within the Church that one confesses the Trinity.

Strictly speaking, "to believe in" (*credere in*) is only applied to the Father, Son, and Holy Spirit who are God. The Church is not an article of faith with the same status as the Holy Trinity. Under this aspect, it would perhaps be more correct to say: I believe *that* the Church exists, *that* she is one, holy, catholic, and apostolic (*credo Ecclesiam*). The phrase "we believe in the Church," which one finds in the text of the Creed of Constantinople, is, however, very rich in meaning. The Church is the object of faith when one apprehends her in her entirety, as "mystery," that is to say, not only according to what in her is human, but also according to what in her is divine: this whole that is the Church, and which is one, is a mystery, an object of faith.[55] Because in the Church, as St. Augustine observed, dwells the Trinity.

Put otherwise, the relationship of the Trinity and the Church, in

---

52. See *Decrees of the Ecumenical Councils*, 1:28: "The uncreated and consubstantial and co-eternal Trinity."

53. St. Augustine, *Enchiridion* 15.56, in St. Augustine, *Faith, Hope and Charity*, trans. Louis A. Arand (New York: Newman Press, 1947), 59 (translation slightly modified); Saint Augustine here comments on a Western symbol of faith.

54. Ibid.

55. See the illuminating explanations of Benoît-Dominique de La Soujeole, *Introduction au mystère de l'Église* (Paris: Parole et Silence, 2006), 298–302.

the act of faith, can be envisioned in two ways that do not exclude each other, but that look at the same reality according to two different perspectives. The first perspective emphasizes that faith in God adheres to the divine economy in which the Trinity (the Holy Spirit) comes to dwell in the Church. It is along these lines that St. Thomas Aquinas, witnessing to the ancient tradition, explained: "When we say: I believe 'in the holy Catholic Church' (*in sanctam Ecclesiam catholicam*), this must be taken in so far as our faith is directed to the Holy Spirit who sanctifies the Church; so that the sense is: *I believe in the Holy Spirit sanctifying the Church.*"[56] This perspective, which starts from God in considering the Church, is objectively first. The second perspective takes things according to the inverse movement. It considers the Church herself, in which the Trinity is present, as an object of properly theologal faith: I believe in the Church, which is a mystery. By reason of the indwelling of the Trinity in the Church (the indwelling of the Holy Spirit), this second perspective emphasizes that, when faith living through charity embraces the mystery of the Church, it attains to God himself. One can say that this second perspective is subjectively primary.

The Church receives from the Trinity its existence, holiness, and unity. The Church is "a people made one with the unity of the Father, the Son and the Holy Spirit." This teaching of the constitution *Lumen Gentium* (no. 4) of the Second Vatican Council repeats a beautiful affirmation of St. Cyprian of Carthage: "The greater sacrifice to God is our peace and fraternal concord and a people united in the unity of the Father, and the Son, and of the Holy Spirit."[57] The unity of the Church participates in the unity of the holy Trinity. The prayer of Jesus teaches us this: "The glory which thou hast given me I have given to them, that they may be one even as we are one, I in

---

56. St. Thomas Aquinas, *Summa theologiae* II-II, q. 1, a. 9, ad 5.

57. St. Cyprian of Carthage, *On the Lord's Prayer* 23 (*CCSL* 3A:105); for this and other texts by St. Cyprian, see Finbarr Clancy, "*Ecclesia de Trinitate* in the Latin Fathers: Inspirational Source for Congar's Ecclesiology," in *The Mystery of the Holy Trinity in the Fathers of the Church*, ed. D. Vincent Twomey and Lewis Ayres (Dublin: Four Courts Press, 2007), 161–93.

them and thou in me" (Jn 17:22–23). In his commentary on John 17:11 ("that they may be one, even as we are one"), St. Thomas Aquinas observed: "There is a twofold unity in God. There is a unity of nature . . . , and a unity of love. . . . Both of these unities are found in us, not in an equal way, but with a certain likeness."[58] This implies that the mysterious reality that is the Church does not only come from an action of the Trinity bringing things into existence or maintaining them in existence. The Church is established by the divinizing presence of the Trinity, who dwells in her and who makes her the instrument of salvation. "There where are the Three, the Father, the Son, the Holy Spirit, there also is the Church."[59]

We should consider the *action* of the Trinity as well as the *presence* (indwelling) of the Trinity in the Church. These two aspects can be understood with special reference to the Holy Spirit: the Father acts through the Son *in* the Holy Spirit, and it is also *in* the Holy Spirit that the Father and the Son are given. First, as Scripture and the creed teach, the action of sanctification is accomplished by the Holy Spirit. The Holy Spirit does not, however, act separately from the Father and the Son. The Father and the Son act with the Holy Spirit and in the Holy Spirit, by one and the same action, because they are the same God and because the Holy Spirit is the very Communion of the Father and the Son. Second, "the Holy Spirit doesn't dwell in anybody without the Father and the Son. . . . They are inseparable in their dwelling, just as they are inseparable in their working."[60] In order to express the sanctifying action and the very presence of the Holy Spirit in the Church, one can describe the Spirit as "the soul" of the Church, recalling however that the Holy Spirit remains by nature transcendent to his creatures and that he is not

58. St. Thomas, *Commentary on the Gospel of St. John* 17:11 (no. 2214).

59. Tertullian, *On Baptism* 6.1 (*SC* 35:74); Saint Irenaeus of Lyons explains this even more explicitly, with reference to the Holy Spirit: "For where the Church is, there is the Spirit of God; and where the Spirit of God is, there is the Church, and every kind of grace" (*Against Heresies* 3.24.1; *SC* 211:472–74).

60. St. Augustine, *Sermon* 71.20.33 (*PL* 38, col. 463), in St. Augustine, *Sermons*, vol. 3, *Sermons 51–94*, trans. Edmund Hill, O.P. (Brooklyn: New City Press, 1991), 266.

mixed with them. "What the soul is to the human body, the Holy Spirit is to the Body of Christ, which is the Church."[61] "The Catholic Church is one body and has different members. And the soul which vivifies this body is the Holy Spirit."[62] In summary: the Holy Spirit enables the Church to share in the divine life and to be the place in which the whole Trinity dwells.

The Councils of Nicea I and Constantinople I furnish a decisive criterion for understanding the faith and for guiding its expression. They also mark a turning point for theology. Thus, in order to safeguard the biblical faith, the Fathers of Nicea had recourse to some expressions that were not found literally in the Bible (*essence* or *substance, consubstantial*). Nicea defended the biblical faith by using a language with philosophical accents. Faced with heterodox currents impregnated with philosophical concepts, the authentic expression of the biblical faith made use of notions inherited from Greek culture, although not without purifying these notions by faith.

Further, because of the challenges that the deformations of Trinitarian faith posed, the Church became aware of the need for a teaching on the Trinity "in itself." The difficulties raised by Arius and by Eunomius of Cyzicus led the Church to understand vividly the radical difference between the Trinity and the created universe. The line marking an essential difference does not pass between the Father and all other realities, but rather lies between the Trinity and creatures. Put otherwise, the dividing line between Creator and creature is that God possesses existence by nature, whereas creatures receive existence by participation. This strict distinction between created and uncreated is required by Trinitarian faith. After Nicea, Trinitarian doctrine will be occupied not only with the economy (the action of the Trinity in the world), but also with the eternal being of Father, Son, and Holy Spirit (the Trinity in its intimate

---

61. St. Augustine, *Sermon* 267.4.4 (*PL* 38, col. 1231), in St. Augustine, *Sermons,* vol. 7, *Sermons 230–272B,* trans. Edmund Hill, O.P. (New Rochelle, New York: New City Press, 1993), 276.

62. St. Thomas Aquinas, *Homilies on the Apostles' Creed,* art. 9 (no. 971).

mystery). In order to account for the creative and salvific acts of the
Trinity, one needs a doctrine manifesting the eternal and transcendent mystery of the Trinity. This aspect is decisive. The divine persons cannot be conceived solely in function of their relationship
with the created world. At Nicea and in the debates that followed
this council, the Church vividly perceived the necessity of a reflection and a discourse on the Trinity in itself, in its inner life, for safeguarding faith in the action of the divine persons for us.

4

Three "Persons" or "Hypostases"

The doctrine of Trinitarian faith shared by the Catholic Church and the Orthodox Churches can be summed up by this declaration of the Second Council of Constantinople, in A.D. 553:

If anyone will not confess that the Father, Son and Holy Spirit have one nature (*phusis, natura*) or substance (*ousia, substantia*), that they have one power (*dunamis, virtus*) and authority (*exousia, potestas*), that there is a consubstantial (*homoousios, consubstantialis*) Trinity, one Deity to be adored in three hypostases (*hupostaseis, subsistentiae*) or persons (*prosopa, personae*): let him be anathema. For there is only one God and Father, from whom all things come, and one Lord, Jesus Christ, through whom all things are, and one Holy Spirit, in whom all things are.[1]

The first sentence of this text proclaims faith in the terms fixed by the Cappadocian Fathers. The Father, Son, and Holy Spirit are one God. Their substance or essence is one, as is their power. The Trinity worshiped by Christians is "consubstantial." The Father, Son, and Holy Spirit are really distinct: they are three hypostases or persons; each exists or subsists in a proper manner. The second sentence, introduced by the conjunction "for," signifies that this dogmatic formulation expresses the biblical faith (cf. 1 Cor 8:6). This second sentence describes the purpose of the dogmatic expression

---

1. Council of Constantinople II, Anathema 1 (*Decrees of the Ecumenical Councils*, 1:114).

of faith: to guarantee the correct understanding of biblical revelation. The economy of creation and grace is accomplished through the Son, in the Holy Spirit. The Son and Holy Spirit procure the divine life and they lead to the Father, because they exist distinctly in a relationship of consubstantiality with the Father.

This expression of faith by the Fifth Ecumenical Council benefits from the long and patient effort of doctrinal reflection undertaken by many Fathers of the Church. Among the Fathers whose contribution was especially important, a special place belongs to the Cappadocian Fathers: St. Basil of Caesarea, St. Gregory of Nazianzus, and St. Gregory of Nyssa.

THE TRINITARIAN DOCTRINE OF
THE CAPPADOCIAN FATHERS

We have already described the heresy of Eunomius of Cyzicus. His radical position identified "Unbegotten" or "Unengendered" ("Ingenerate") with the very substance of God: God is in himself, positively, "Unbegotten substance" (*ousia agennetos*).[2] It follows, for Eunomius, that God cannot communicate his own nature by begetting. Since the essence of God is "unbegotten," the only-begotten Son cannot be of the same essence as the Father. There is no community of essence or substance between the Unbegotten and the Begotten; otherwise there would be two equal Unbegottens. On this view one must therefore renounce any idea of resemblance. The name "Begotten" designates the substance of the Son, which was produced by the decision of God and did not exist before it was produced. As for the name "Father," it refers to an activity (*energeia*) of the Unbegotten, different from his substance. This theory, which excludes a priori any possibility of begetting in God, led St. Basil of Caesarea to develop the first speculative doctrine of relation in Trinitarian theology. This doctrine pays great attention to our language.[3]

2. Eunomius of Cyzicus, *Apology* 8 (SC 305:250).
3. See Stephen M. Hildebrand, *The Trinitarian Theology of Basil of Caesarea* (Wash-

To begin, some names that we use express what things are ("white," "horse"), while other names are negative and designate what things are not. The name "Unbegotten" belongs to this second category: it does not signify the substance of God, but rather it signifies that God the Father is "not begotten." St. Basil therefore removes from the name "Unbegotten" the absolute status given it by Eunomius.

Additionally, among the names that we employ, some signify substances—realities that exist in themselves—while other names signify relations. Thus, for example, the word "man" signifies the reality that is a human person; but the name "friend" signifies this man under the aspect of his relation with another person. In our language about God, the word "substance" (*ousia*) belongs to the first category. It designates the essence of God—what God is. As regards the names *Father* and *Son,* they belong to the second category; they signify a relation toward another, that is, a relative mode of being: these are relational names. To name someone *father* is to name him as father *of someone;* and to apply the name of *Son* to Christ is to describe him in his relation to his Father. In this way, St. Basil of Caesarea explains that the names *Father* and *Son* "just express the relation (*schesis*) of the one to the other. A *father* is one who supplies for another the principle of his being in a nature like his own; a *son* is one who receives from another through generation the principle of his being."[4] "Unbegotten" and "begotten" do not denote different essences, but are different "modes of being," describing relationship (*schesis*) between the persons who are really distinct within the eternal Godhead. The use of the notion of relation enables one to show that the generation of the Son and the procession of the Holy Spirit imply no change in the spiritual nature of God.[5]

---

ington, D.C.: The Catholic University of America Press, 2007); see also Bernard Sesboüé, *Saint Basile et la Trinité: Un acte théologique au IVe siècle* (Paris: Desclée, 1998). My exposition is much indebted to Sesboüé.

4. St. Basil of Caesarea, *Against Eunomius* 2.22 (*SC* 305:92).

5. Still more, the doctrine of relation allows one to show that faith in the *generation* of the Son, who is of the *same essence* as the Father, is not in contradiction with the

There are therefore two kinds of names serving to signify God: substantial names and relative names. St. Basil of Caesarea explains that our grasp of the mystery of the triune God requires the "combination" of the two following aspects: first, what is *common* to the Father, Son, and Spirit (their operation, power, nature, essence, divinity); second, what is *proper* to each of them in a distinct way (the distinctive property of the Father, Son, and Holy Spirit, which involves a relational mode of being).[6]

The property that characterizes the Father is *paternity;* specifically, the Father is the Principle (the "Cause") *without principle* (the Father is not begotten). The distinctive property of the Son is *filiation* (he is begotten). And, as the following text of St. Gregory of Nazianzus explains, the characteristic property of the Holy Spirit is *procession.* "The Father is *father* and without principle (*anarchos*), because he does not come from anyone. The Son is *son* and he is not without principle, because he comes from the Father. . . . The Holy Spirit is truly the *Spirit* coming forth from the Father, not by filiation, because it is not by generation, but by procession (*ekporeutos*)."[7] These characteristic properties enable one to grasp the *hypostases,* that is to say, the distinct persons of the Father, Son, and Holy Spirit who are one God. The "redoubling" or *redoublement* of the language of Trinitarian faith, which connects the level of "substance" and that of "properties" in order to express the mystery of the Trinity, is well illustrated by this extract from St. Gregory of Nazianzus:

When I speak of *God,* you must be illumined at once by one flash of light and by three: three in properties, or hypostases (*hupostaseis*), if any one prefers so to call them, or persons (*prosopa*) . . . but this light is one in respect of the substance (*ousia*), that is, the Godhead.[8]

---

fact that God's essence has no cause. The same applies to the procession of the Holy Spirit.

6. St. Basil of Caesarea, *Against Eunomius* 2.28 (*SC* 305:120).

7. Saint Gregory of Nazianzus, *Oration* 39.12 (*SC* 358:174); emphasis mine.

8. St. Gregory of Nazianzus, *Oration* 39.11 (*SC* 358:170–72).

The Father, Son, and Holy Spirit are "others" in the sense of personal otherness: the Father is "another" (*allos*) than the Son and the Holy Spirit; but they are not a "different thing" (*allo*), because "the three are one and the same thing qua Godhead."[9] These explanations of St. Gregory of Nazianzus are found again in the West in St. Augustine: "The Holy Spirit is another (*alius*) than the Father and the Son, for he is neither the Father nor the Son. I say 'another' (*alius*), not 'another thing' (*aliud*), because, equally with them, he is the simple, unchangeable, co-eternal Good."[10]

Faced with the challenge posed by heresies—particularly that of Eunomius of Cyzicus—this doctrinal elaboration enables one to show that "not being the Father" takes nothing away from the divinity of the Son and Holy Spirit, because the name *Father* expresses not the divine substance but the relation of the Father to the Son whom he begets. "All that the Father has belongs likewise to the Son, except unbegottenness; and all that is the Son's belongs also to the Spirit, except his sonship."[11]

The properties of the divine persons involve an "opposition": the Father is not the Son; the Son is not the Spirit. "When we hear of the *unbegotten light,* we think of the Father; of the *begotten light,* we think of the Son. As regards light and light there is no contrariety between them, but as regards begotten and unbegotten one

9. Saint Gregory of Nazianzus, *Letter* 101.21 (*SC* 208:44–46); it is the inverse, St. Gregory explains, that one finds in the person of Christ: in Christ, there is "one thing and an other" ("different things": divinity and humanity, the invisible and the visible) but Christ "is not one and an other," because he is one and the same hypostasis, one single person (*Letter* 101.20; *SC* 208:44); St. Gregory of Nazianzus, *On God and Christ: The Five Theological Orations and Two Letters to Cledonius* (Crestwood, New York: St. Vladimir's Seminary Press, 2002), 157.

10. St. Augustine, *The City of God* 11.10; English translation from Saint Augustine, *The City of God: Books VIII–XVI*, trans. Gerald G. Walsh and Grace Monahan, The Fathers of the Church: A New Translation 14 (Washington, D.C.: The Catholic University of America Press, 1952), 202 (translation slightly modified); see on this subject the explications of St. Thomas Aquinas, *Summa theologiae* I, q. 31, a. 2.

11. St. Gregory of Nazianzus, *Oration* 34.10 (*SC* 318:216); see also *Oration* 29.16 (*SC* 250:210) in St. Gregory of Nazianzus, *On God and Christ,* 84: "*Father* designates neither the substance nor the activity, but the relationship (*schesis*), the manner of being, which holds good between the Father and the Son."

considers them under the aspect of their opposition (*antithesis*)."[12] The Catholic tradition will speak of a "relative opposition" or of "opposed relations" in order to signify the distinction of divine persons by such relative properties. The distinctive properties of the divine persons have to do with *origin*, that is to say, with generation or procession. It is in this sense that one speaks of "relations of origin" ("opposed relations of origin"). The *Catechism of the Catholic Church* explains, on the subject of the Father, Son, and Holy Spirit: "They are distinct from one another in their relations of origin: 'It is the Father who generates, the Son who is begotten, and the Holy Spirit who proceeds.'"[13] Put otherwise, the distinction of divine persons comes from the fact that one person is the *principle* of another person. The Orthodox East employs the term "cause" ("*aitia*," applied to the Father alone) for designating the relation of *principle* that one person has toward another. So as to manifest the order (*taxis*) that accounts for the distinction of the Holy Spirit, St. Gregory of Nyssa explains:

Our account is the same concerning the Holy Spirit, having a difference only in the order. For just as the Son is joined to the Father, and, while having his being from him, is not posterior to the Father according to his existence, so again the Holy Spirit has to do with the Only-begotten, for only notionally by reason of causality is [the Son] considered before the hypostasis of the Spirit; for temporal extensions have no place in that eternal life. Therefore, *leaving aside the notion of causality, the Holy Trinity has no difference in itself.*[14]

The Catholic Church developed this teaching following a rule formulated at the Council of Florence in A.D. 1442 (the application of this rule to the procession of the Holy Spirit posed an ecumen-

12. St. Basil of Caesarea, *Against Eunomius* 2.28 (SC 305:120); see also 2.26 (SC 305:108).
13. *Catechism of the Catholic Church*, 2nd ed. (Vatican City: Libreria Editrice Vaticana, 1997), no. 254 (with a quote of the Fourth Lateran Council).
14. St. Gregory of Nyssa, *Contra Eunomium* 1.691, in *Gregorii Nysseni Opera*, vol. 1, *Contra Eunomium libri, Pars Prior: Liber I et II*, ed. Werner Jaeger (Leiden: Brill, 1960), 224–25; emphasis mine.

ical difficulty that we will treat further on): "These three persons are one God, not three Gods, because there is one substance of the three, one essence, one nature, one Godhead, one immensity, one eternity, and everything is one where the opposition of a relation does not prevent this."[15] The same council specifies that, by reason of this unity, "the Father is whole in the Son, whole in the Holy Spirit; the Son is whole in the Father, whole in the Holy Spirit; the Holy Spirit is whole in the Father, whole in the Son."[16]

This teaching emphasizes the mutual indwelling of the three divine persons by reason of their consubstantiality. This mutual indwelling is also manifest when we consider the *relations* that characterize the persons. Each relation implies another corresponding relation, so that the notion of one is found in the other. The notion of "Son" is included in that of "Father," since the Father is Father by his relation to the Son. In the same way, the mutual indwelling of the persons comes into focus when we consider the *origin* of the Son and of the Holy Spirit—that is, generation and procession. The Son is not begotten "outside" of the Father; rather he is begotten within the Father and he remains in the Father. "I am in the Father and the Father in me," says Jesus (Jn 14:10 and Jn 14:11). The same goes for the procession of the Holy Spirit. Following St. Gregory of Nazianzus, who had used the Greek verb "*perichorein*" to describe the communication of the divine nature and the human nature in Christ Jesus, St. John Damascene called this mutual interpenetration of divine persons "perichoresis," their mutual "being in." Each divine person is in the others. Still more, it is necessary to recognize that *each person is in those who are in him*. Whatever the aspect under which one contemplates this Trinitarian mystery, the mutual indwelling of the divine persons shows their personal distinction in the most profound unity.

15. Council of Florence (*Decrees of the Ecumenical Councils* 1:570–71, translation slightly modified); emphasis mine; see also the *Catechism of the Catholic Church*, no. 255. This formulation goes back to St. Anselm of Canterbury.

16. Council of Florence (*Decrees of the Ecumenical Councils* 1:571); see also the *Catechism of the Catholic Church*, no. 255.

The "mature" doctrine of the Fathers of the Church (starting from around the year A.D. 350) can be described by the three following characteristics: first, a clear version of the distinction between person and nature, entailing the principle that all that is attributed to the divine nature is found in an equal and simple way in each divine person; second, a formulation of the generation of the Son that clearly signifies that this generation occurs within the incomprehensible divine being; third, a clear expression of the inseparable action of the divine persons.[17] The technical vocabulary, however varied, serves to express these fundamental themes that constitute the foundation of a Trinitarian theological culture. These themes should not be filed away as mere relics of the past. Rather, they form the matrix of Christian reflection on the mystery of the triune God. Three aspects deserve special attention: the simplicity of God, the unity of action of the three persons, and the analogical mode of thought that is required to render an account of faith in God the Trinity.

God the Trinity is *simple*. This affirmation means that God is exempt from all forms of composition that characterize creatures: composition of act and power, of essence and existence, of substance and accident, of whole and parts, of form and matter. God is not a mixture of this and that. He is without any composition. Showing the identity of nature of the Father and the Son, St. Hilary of Poitiers explains: "God is not made up of composite things in a human fashion, so that 'what He has' within Him is one thing and 'what He Himself is' is something else, but everything that He has is life, that is to say, a perfect, complete, and infinite nature."[18] St. Augustine sums this up in a striking formulation: "Our reason for calling the Trinity simple is because *it is what it has*—with the

17. Lewis Ayres, *Nicaea and Its Legacy: An Approach to Fourth-Century Trinitarian Theology* (Oxford: Oxford University Press, 2004), 236–40.

18. St. Hilary of Poitiers, *The Trinity*, 8.43, in Saint Hilary of Poitiers, *The Trinity*, trans. Stephen McKenna, 309–10 (New York: Fathers of the Church, 1954).

exception of the real relations in which the Persons stand to each other."[19] The divine simplicity is a Trinitarian doctrine. It is essential for grasping the identity of substance of the three persons.

Extending this teaching, St. Thomas Aquinas explains that God is "pure Act." In him there is not the mixture of actuality and potentiality that characterizes creatures. The essence of God, that is to say, what God is, is his existence: God is sheer subsisting being (*Ipsum esse subsistens*). Not only is God "what he has," as St. Augustine put it, but also what is God (his essence) is his very existence. Thus, God is "outside every genus": there is no category of being in which we could place God and creatures together. No concept can encompass God and creatures.[20] The incomprehensibility of God is connected to his simplicity. This forces us to use analogy.

The simplicity of God likewise implies that God is immutable: being perfectly actualized (or rather, beyond all actualization of a potentiality) and without mixture (since he is pure Act), God is beyond all change. The incarnation, passion, and resurrection of the Son do not modify the Trinity. In becoming man, the Son "enhanced the human without diminishing the divine."[21] "Even when the Word takes a body from Mary, the Trinity remains a Trinity, with neither increase nor decrease. It is for ever perfect."[22]

Today, with the goal of promoting a conception attentive to the concrete and historical dimension of the revelation of God in Jesus Christ, it is not rare for theologians to employ the notion of "event"

19. St. Augustine, *The City of God* 11.10, in Saint Augustine, *The City of God: Books VIII–XVI*, trans. Gerald G. Walsh and Grace Monahan (Washington, D.C.: The Catholic University of America Press, 1952), 202; emphasis mine.

20. St. Thomas Aquinas, *Summa theologiae* I, q. 3; q. 4, a. 2.

21. Pope St. Leo the Great, *Tome to Flavian*: "humana augens, divina non minuens" (*Decrees of the Ecumenical Councils* 1:78). On the teaching of the Fathers, see Paul L. Gavrilyuk, *The Suffering of the Impassible God: The Dialectics of Patristic Thought* (Oxford: Oxford University Press, 2004, reprinted 2005). For a contemporary discussion, see James F. Keating and Thomas Joseph White, eds., *Divine Impassibility and the Mystery of Human Suffering* (Grand Rapids, Mich.: Eerdmans, 2009).

22. St. Athanasius of Alexandria, *Letter to Epictetus* 8–9 (translation of the *Liturgy of the Hours* for the Office of Readings of January 1; cf. *PG* 26, col. 1064–1065).

for expressing the Trinitarian being of God: "God is event." At times, some authors even seek to replace the category of substance with that of event. Certainly, the notion of event suggests that the being of God is a veritable fullness of life. However, we cannot simply discard the notion of substance, because an "event" requires an acting reality, without which it lacks meaning. Likewise, it is necessary to recall that God is absolutely simple: he is Act, without composition, without movement, and without becoming. Illumined by the affirmation of God as "pure Act," the notion of "event" can be considered as a *metaphor* that suggests the eternal newness of the divine being,[23] but caution is necessary here, since its use can also cause confusion.

Absolute simplicity is the exclusive property of God alone. To say that God is simple is therefore to affirm the *divinity* of God. This property concerns the being of God in himself as well as his action in the world: God does not enter into composition with creatures; he does not mix himself or intermingle himself with his creatures. Above all, this rule is verified in the incarnation of the Son. In the incarnation, which is the highest union of God with a creature, the divine nature remains distinct from the human nature (dogma of Chalcedon). Put otherwise, the affirmation of the divine simplicity, applied to the action of God, shows that God creates and saves *as God*. The simplicity of the triune God belongs to the faith of the Church.[24] The recognition of the simplicity and incomprehensibility of God ranks among the fundamental elements of a Christian culture that respects the mystery of the Trinity.

This leads us to a second principle: the three persons act in one and the same operation. "The Father does all things through the

23. St. Thomas Aquinas observed that the Platonists held that "God moves himself," inasmuch as God knows and loves (acts of the divine life); but in this affirmation it is necessary to exclude movement and change which imply a potentiality incompatible with the simplicity of God (*Summa theologiae* I, q. 9, a. 1, ad 1).

24. Council of Lateran IV, in 1215, Constitution *Firmiter credimus*, ch. 1 (*Decrees of the Ecumenical Councils* 1:230); Council of Vatican I, in 1870, Constitution *Dei Filius*, ch. 1 (*Decrees of the Ecumenical Councils* 2:805).

Word in the Holy Spirit. Thus the unity of the Holy Trinity is pre-
served."[25] The community of action of the Trinity manifests the one
divinity of the three persons. "It is very necessary for us to be guided in our investigation of the divine nature by its operations. . . . If
we consider the operation (*energeia*) of the Father and of the Son
and of the Holy Spirit to be one, differing or varying in no way at
all, it is necessary because of the identity of the operation for the
oneness of the nature (*phusis*) to be inferred."[26] In creation and salvation, the effects produced by the three divine persons show the
unity of their activity and uncover, at the root of their activity, the
unity of their power (*dunamis*).[27] All things issue from the will of
the Father, are actualized by the Son, and brought to perfection by
the Holy Spirit. A number of patristic texts explain or express the
consubstantiality of divine persons by their unity of activity and
of power. The common nature of the Father, Son, and Holy Spirit is often described as a unity of operation and of power: asserting the unity of operation is a way of confessing the one essence of
the three persons. This teaching constitutes a leading component of
Christian Trinitarian monotheism.

Since the Holy Trinity fulfills every operation . . . not by separate action
according to the number of the Persons, but so that there is one motion
and disposition of the good will, which is communicated from the Father
through the Son to the Spirit, so neither can be called Those Who exercise this Divine and superintending power and operation towards ourselves and all creation, conjointly and inseparably, by Their mutual action,
three Gods.[28]

---

25. St. Athanasius of Alexandria, *Letter to Serapion* 1.28, in *The Letters of Saint Athanasius Concerning the Holy Spirit,* trans. C. R. B. Shapland (London: Epworth Press,
1951), 135.

26. St. Basil the Great, *Letter* 189, in St. Basil, *Letters,* vol. 2 (186–368), trans. Sister
Agnes Clare Way (Washington, D.C.: The Catholic University of America Press, 1969), 31.

27. On the centrality of "power," see Michel René Barnes, *The Power of God: 'Dunamis' in Gregory of Nyssa's Trinitarian Theology* (Washington, D.C.: The Catholic University of America Press, 2001).

28. St. Gregory of Nyssa, *That There Are Not Three Gods,* in Johannes Quasten, *Patrology,* vol. 3 (Westminster, Md.: Newman Press, 1960), 286–87.

One can see in this text the "redoublement" of St. Gregory of Nyssa's explanation: the affirmation of the unity of power and operation is specified by the order of the distinct divine persons. The Father does nothing that the Son does not do, and the Son does nothing that the Holy Spirit does not do, but the same power of action is communicated by the Father to the Son and to the Holy Spirit. In the West, St. Augustine professes a similar teaching: "As the Father, the Son, and the Holy Spirit are inseparable, so do they work inseparably."[29] "The work of Father and Son is indivisible, and yet the Son's working is from the Father just as he himself is from the Father."[30] St. Thomas Aquinas teaches the same: the power of action is common to the whole Trinity, according to an order. "The Son holds his being and his action from the Father, and this is why the Father acts through the Son."[31] "The Father acts through the Son, because the Son is the cause of what is accomplished in virtue of one same and indivisible power, a power that the Son possesses in common with the Father but which he receives, nonetheless, from the Father through his generation."[32] This teaching is an integral part of the Catholic doctrine. "As the Trinity has only one and the same nature, so too does it have only one and the same operation."[33] To reject this rule would be to destroy Trinitarian faith.

Lastly, the Catholic expression of the incomprehensible mystery of the Trinity requires a mode of thought guided by *analogy*. This is the third essential rule. Analogy is distinguished from univocity and equivocity. There is univocity when a perfection or a term is attributed to many realities according to the same content. For example, the name "animal" is applied in a univocal manner to a cow or a horse. By reason of his supreme transcendence and his simplicity, God is not in the same genus as his creatures: God is not

---

29. St. Augustine, *On the Trinity* 1.4.7, in St. Augustine, *The Trinity*, trans. Edmund Hill, O.P. (Brooklyn, N.Y.: New City Press, 1991), 70 (translation slightly adapted).

30. St. Augustine, *On the Trinity* 2.1.3 (trans. Edmund Hill, 99).

31. St. Thomas Aquinas, *Commentary on the Sentences*, Bk. 2, dist. 13, q. 1, a. 5, ad 4.

32. St. Thomas Aquinas, *Commentary on the Sentences*, Bk. 2, dist. 13, q. 1, a. 5, corp.

33. *Catechism of the Catholic Church*, no. 258.

included in any genus. It is necessary therefore to exclude univocity. Inversely, there is equivocity when a term is applied to many realities according to a totally diverse meaning. This is the case, for example, with the word "dog" when one uses it to signify the domestic quadruped and the astral constellation. It is likewise necessary to deny that all names used to signify God and creatures are equivocal: this would imply that it is impossible for us to know anything of God (because, if we know God, it is through creatures); were this the case, our human words and the words of the Bible would be completely meaningless when applied to God.

The path of knowledge of God passes therefore through analogy. Here, a term (a name, a perfection) is attributed to several things according to a signification that is both partly similar and partly different. For example, there is an analogy, that is to say a proportion, between food declared "healthy" and a "healthy" person. Food is called healthy because it produces good health in those who eat it. The analogy between God and creatures rests on the action of God that communicates to creatures a participation in his perfection. The noble properties that one finds in creatures are caused by God, in whom these perfections exist in a supereminent and transcendent mode. Thus, God is called "good" and the creature is called "good," but the goodness of God and that of creatures are not situated at the same level. God is the transcendent source of the goodness of creatures. God is his very goodness by essence (the goodness of God is his very being), while creatures are good inasmuch as they participate in the goodness of God, in a radically limited mode.

In order to illustrate the importance of this doctrine beyond confessional differences, consider the position of Karl Barth. A Protestant theologian, Barth did not accept the Catholic doctrine of the "analogy of being" (the analogy that enables us to know God by the natural light of our human reason), but he showed the importance of the analogy of faith that enables one to know God in his revelation.

When we speak of God, we speak in relation to the world created by Him, its beauty and goodness and being. But: "They [namely, creatures] are not beautiful, they are not good, they do not exist, in the same way as Thou, their Creator; in comparison with Thee, they are neither beautiful, nor good, nor do they even exist" (St. Augustine, *Confessions* 11.4.6). . . . Does there exist a simple parity of content and meaning when we apply the same word to the creature on the one hand and to God's revelation and God on the other? . . . Obviously we cannot affirm this. . . . Ought we, then, to speak of a disparity of content and meaning when we apply a description to the creature on the one hand and to God's revelation and God on the other? . . . This kind of disparity necessarily means that in fact we do not know God. For if we know Him, we know Him by the means given us; otherwise we do not know Him at all. . . . The older theology accepted the concept of analogy to describe the fellowship in question. By this term both the false thesis of parity and the equally false thesis of disparity were attacked and destroyed, but the elements of truth in both were revealed. It could therefore be claimed as the correct definition of the matter. . . . If in this fellowship there can be no question of either parity or disparity, there remains only what is generally meant by analogy: similarity, partial correspondence and agreement. . . . The object itself— God's truth in His revelation as the basis of the veracity of our knowledge of God—does not leave us any option but to resort to this concept.[34]

According to the Catholic doctrine, analogy is based not only on the revelation of God, but first on the creation. The created world participates in God, in such a way that the created universe is a first and constant manifestation of God. The Creator God is the productive ("efficient") cause and the "exemplary" cause of the created world. By creation, the world bears in itself some "likenesses" of God. These likenesses or similitudes enable one to be raised "by analogy" to the contemplation of God (Sg 13:5). This is why, according to Catholic faith, the human being can, through the natural light of his reason, know the existence of God as well as the attributes that belong necessarily to God, inasmuch as he is the principle of creatures. In addition, at the superior level of faith in the Trinity (which only revelation enables one to know), the believing mind also discovers in the created world some "similitudes" of God the Trinity. The Catechism of the Catholic Church explains:

> All creatures bear a certain resemblance to God, most especially man, created in the image and likeness of God. The manifold perfections of creatures—their truth, their goodness, their beauty all reflect the infinite perfection of God. Consequently we can name God by taking his creatures' perfections as our starting point, "for from the greatness and beauty of created things comes a corresponding perception of their Creator" (Sg 13:5).[35]

This provides a solid foundation for knowing God himself.[36] The transcendent simplicity of God imposes an important limit, however, because God remains beyond all created representations. "For between Creator and creature there can be noted no similarity (similitudo) so great that a greater dissimilarity (maior dissimilitudo) cannot be seen between them."[37]

The path of our knowledge of God by analogy has three moments. The first is that of affirmation, by virtue of the "efficient" and "exemplary" causality of God (creation and participation). We know God through creatures. Recall the example given above by St. Augustine: God is good. The second moment is that of negation. God is not good in the same manner as creatures. His manner of being good—his very goodness—is radically different from what we observe in creatures. The third moment is that of eminence. The goodness of God surpasses all goodness: God is truly good, in a sovereign and supereminent manner that infinitely goes beyond what we can understand.

The attribution of a perfection to God by analogy implies that

---

35. *Catechism of the Catholic Church*, no. 41.

36. *Catechism of the Catholic Church*, no. 43: "Admittedly, in speaking about God like this, our language is using human modes of expression; nevertheless it really does attain to God himself."

37. Fourth Lateran Council, Constitution *Damnamus* (*Decrees of the Ecumenical Councils* 1:232; this teaching can be found in St. Augustine, for instance, in his *On the Trinity* 15.20.39; 15.23.43.

one distinguishes, on the one hand, the *perfection signified* (for example, goodness), and, on the other, the *manner of signifying* this perfection. Under the first aspect, when it is a matter of properties worthy of God, the names that we use are applied properly to God. The *perfection signified* really exists in God: God is good. Still more, the goodness belongs to God more properly than to creatures: "No one is good but God alone" (Lk 18:19). But under the second aspect, our "mode of signifying" is connected with the manner in which we understand creatures; it is attached to the mode according to which the perfections exist in creatures. Now this mode is radically marked by composition and imperfection. Under this second aspect, our words do not apply properly to God. Thus, far from enclosing God in our concepts, analogy leaves completely unlimited the reality of God, which is beyond our comprehension.[38] In this way, analogy procures a true knowledge, and it profoundly respects the incomprehensibility of God. God can be known "in a mirror" (1 Cor 13:12), but we cannot know him as he is knowable in himself.

Here, we should be very precise. Our words and concepts do not "represent God"; rather, they signify him. No concept can represent God. It is important to distinguish clearly between representation and signification. Naming God by analogy does not pertain to the realm of representation, but to that of signification. Our words (the words of the Bible) do not represent God; they *signify* him; and they give us true knowledge of God, all the while respecting his incomprehensibility.

St. Augustine explained: "*The Word was God* (Jn 1:1). We are talking about God; so why be surprised if you cannot grasp it? I mean, if you can grasp it, it isn't God. Let us rather make a devout confession of ignorance, instead of a brash profession of knowledge. Certainly it is great bliss to have a little touch or taste of God with the mind; but completely to grasp him, to comprehend him, is altogether im-

---

38. St. Thomas Aquinas, *Summa theologiae* I, q. 13, a. 3 and a. 5.

possible."[39] "So what are we to say, brothers, about God? For if you have fully grasped what you want to say, it isn't God. If you have been able to comprehend it, you have comprehended something else instead of God. If you think you have been able to comprehend, your thoughts have deceived you. So he isn't this, if this is what you have comprehended; but if he is this, then you haven't comprehended it."[40] This was recalled by the First Vatican Council:

Now reason, if it is enlightened by faith, does indeed—when it seeks persistently, piously and soberly—achieve by God's gift some understanding, and that most profitable, of the mysteries, whether by analogy from what it knows naturally, or from the connexion of these mysteries with one another and with the final end of humanity; but reason is never rendered capable of penetrating these mysteries in the way in which it penetrates those truths which form its proper object. For the divine mysteries, by their very nature, so far surpass the created understanding that, even when a revelation has been given and accepted by faith, they remain covered by the veil of that same faith and wrapped, as it were, in a certain obscurity, as long as in this mortal life *we are away from the Lord, for we walk by faith, and not by sight* (2 Cor 5:6–7).[41]

Consequently, dogmatic reflection on the generation of the Son and the procession of the Holy Spirit, on the divine persons and their personal properties, excludes all pretention to "comprehend" the Trinity. Human intelligence can neither demonstrate the mystery, nor explain it by sufficient reasons. Rather, human intelligence undertakes a contemplative labor "for the exercise and support of the faithful."[42] This labor always depends upon the revelation of Christ, Son of the Father and Giver of the Holy Spirit. The labor is fueled by the hope of seeing God face to face in the heavenly Church. In

39. St. Augustine, *Sermon* 117.5 (*PL* 38, col. 663), in St. Augustine, *Sermons*, vol. 4, *Sermons 94A–147A*, trans. Edmund Hill, O.P. (Brooklyn: New City Press, 1992), 211.

40. St. Augustine, *Sermon* 52.6.16 (*PL* 38, col. 360), in St. Augustine, *Sermons*, vol. 3, *Sermons 51–94*, trans. Edmund Hill, O.P. (Brooklyn: New City Press, 1991), 57 (with a slight modification).

41. *Decrees of the Ecumenical Councils* 2:808; cf. Denzinger, *Enchiridion symbolorum*, no. 3016.

42. St. Thomas Aquinas, *Summa contra Gentiles*, Bk. I, ch. 9 (no. 54): "ad fidelium quidem exercitium et solatium."

this hope, the theologian seeks to explain the faith by manifesting the Trinitarian mystery to the minds of believers insofar as he is able. He does so with the aid of what is better known to us ("similitudes"). "And such a search is not useless, since it elevates the mind and gives it enough of a glimpse of the truth to steer clear of errors."[43]

In this project, we necessarily have recourse to analogy, because we know God through creatures. Even the names transmitted by the Bible and received in faith (Father, Son, Love) require us to know God through our experience of the world. It is through our experience of the world that these names have a meaning for us and that they serve the revelation of God (without which we could indeed affirm that God is "Father," but this affirmation would leave our mind completely empty!). This holds for all the names that are applied to God in a proper manner, both the names signifying perfections common to the three divine persons (wisdom, goodness, love, power), and the names signifying distinctly each person according to his property (Father, Son, Spirit). We will observe this in considering the name "person."

WHAT IS A PERSON?

We encounter today, in Western culture, various conceptions of the person that put a principal accent on the subjective aspects of the person. Since the seventeenth century, following Locke and Descartes, an important philosophical current offers a "psychological" notion of the person: a person is a subject who thinks and who has self-consciousness. One likewise finds, following Kant in particular, a "moral" notion of the person: to be a person is to be able to dispose freely of oneself and to be autonomous in one's action; the person is then defined by freedom. One also finds other approaches that place the principal accent on the relational and social dimension of the per-

43. St. Thomas Aquinas, *De potentia*, q. 9, a. 5: "nec talis inquisitio est inutilis, cum per eam elevetur animus ad aliquid veritatis capiendum quod sufficiat ad excludendos errores."

son: the person is then defined by his or her responsibility for others, or by his or her insertion into the network of social relationships.

For its part, the Christian dogmatic tradition developed a metaphysical approach to the person, in which psychological, moral, and relational aspects are integrated. As has been observed above, the word and the notion of "person" are first employed in order to respond to unitarian monarchianism, in a Trinitarian context. Tertullian and other Christian authors who developed the use of this term were able to rely on the meaning that the word *persona* possessed in classical Latin culture (with a social, literary, theatrical, juridical background) and on the Greek term *prosopon* (common in the Greek Bible, this word corresponds to the Latin term *persona*, with certain nuances), as well as on exegetical methods that sought to identify the "person who speaks" in certain passages of the Bible ("prosopological" exegesis). To speak of "person," from the beginning of the Trinitarian use of this word, is to signify the being that exists truly in itself, the reality that underlies the manifestation to others, the foundation of what appears in the action. The word "person," as applied to God in this sense, is not found in the Bible, but "what the word *person* signifies is found to be affirmed of God in many places of Scripture":[44] a being who exists through himself, who acts by his wisdom and will, who speaks and listens, who sends messengers, who manifests himself in his wise and good action, who loves, to whom one prays wholeheartedly, who is praised in worship, who is "imitated" by the holy people of God, and with whom believers have an intimate relationship.

The affirmation of "three divine persons" aims precisely to maintain, against unitarian monarchianism, that the tri-personal "disposition" that *appears* in the history of salvation exists in the *very reality* of God. To say that the Son of God is a "person" is to affirm that he has a proper existence or subsistence in himself. A similar purpose inspires the development of the Trinitarian concept of *hypos-*

44. St. Thomas Aquinas, *Summa theologiae* I, q. 29, a. 3, ad 1.

tasis in the East: the hypostasis signifies that which subsists individually through itself. The person or hypostasis is a subsisting reality endowed with a proper mode of existing. It includes a special mode of action and a relational capacity, but it is defined foremost by its existence in itself and through itself.

Christian reflection has progressively elaborated an understanding of the person that applies to the triune God (and therefore to Christ Jesus), as well as to human beings and to angels. This analogical understanding of what is a *person* is well-expressed in the definition given by Boethius at the end of antiquity: "A person is an individual substance of rational nature (*naturae rationabilis individua substantia*)."[45] This metaphysical understanding of the person is not the first thing we notice in our experience of being "persons." It is not spontaneous, but we discern it by reflecting on the immediate given of our experience. At the root of free action and of self-consciousness, we discover a being who holds himself in existence, that is to say, the deep reality that is the radical principle of free action, of openness to others, and of self-consciousness. Let us briefly explain this definition of the person with St. Thomas Aquinas.[46]

According to St. Thomas, the person is defined by the integration of the following three elements: (1) individuality; (2) substance; (3) a nature endowed with faculties of intelligence and will. This position is somewhat difficult, but it deserves attention.

The *individual* signifies that which is "undivided" in itself and that is also distinct from others. To speak of the individual is to signify the singular being in its distinction and undividedness. Far from setting in opposition the individual and the person, Thomas Aquinas places the individual in the definition of the person, in order to signify the "individual *mode of being*" of the real singular.[47]

The individual finds its supreme realization in the *substance*. The substance designates that which is apt to exist through itself,

45. Boethius, *Treatise against Eutyches and Nestorius,* ch. 3 (PL 64, col. 1343).
46. St. Thomas Aquinas, *Summa theologiae* I, q. 29, a. 1.
47. St. Thomas Aquinas, *De potentia,* q. 9, a. 2, ad 5.

in itself, and not in another (substance is distinguished from accident). The "individual substance" signifies the individual whose "special mode of existence" is to subsist through himself and in himself.[48] Defined as individual substance, the person is a reality that possesses its proper being in a complete manner, in himself and through himself, and which exercises on his own the act of existing. The manner of acting characterizing the person (acting through himself) will be proportionate in a special way to his mode of being (being through himself). Thus in the definition inherited from Boethius, the "individual substance" signifies the subsisting singular who exists through himself and in himself, according to an irreducible mode, as a complete whole, a "hypostasis" who exercises the act of existing on his own account.

The third element of the definition of the person is *rational nature*—that is to say, the essence of beings endowed with intelligence. Rationality implies will and freedom. It characterizes the mode of being and of acting proper to those beings who direct themselves freely toward an end that they know by their intelligence. Free will is the characteristic of beings endowed with intelligence: they are not merely "propelled" toward an end to attain, but instead they have the capacity to direct themselves freely, by their will, toward the end that they have apprehended by their mind. This is the ultimate determination that makes a person of an individual substance: it is the faculty, belonging to the nature, of understanding the truth and of freely loving the good. In the human being, this "rational nature" implies a principle defined by an end, certain dynamisms, certain active and passive powers, as well as a communal dimension that belongs to the very nature. Since the rational nature is a principle of being and acting, the rational nature manifests itself by free action. It blossoms and makes itself known by the voluntary command of acts (the will as liberty), which has its root in the intelligence. The mode of intelligent and free action reveals the spiritual nature that characterizes the person. By virtue of this nature, the hu-

48. St. Thomas Aquinas, *De potentia,* q. 9, a. 2, ad 6.

man person possesses the ability to relate to the world, to others, to himself or herself, and to God through intelligence and love.

The metaphysical approach, it should be clear, excludes neither the psychological, moral, and relational features of the person, nor the importance of action. Rather, it enables one to integrate these aspects, and it guarantees their foundation. One can observe this, for example, in the teaching of the Third Council of Constantinople (in A.D. 680–681). The document by which this council addressed its results to the emperor explains that, since Christ assumed a true human nature, he exercises a true human activity. The document continues: "Nothing other constitutes the perfection of the human substance than the essential will by which the power of free choice (*autexousiotes*) is inscribed in us."[49] Established on a solid metaphysics of the person-hypostasis, the Church's doctrine regarding Christ Jesus was led to place the *will* and *freedom of action* at the heart of the Christian understanding of the human being. This is precisely what the theme of the image of God expresses, as Thomas Aquinas explains: the human being has been created to the "image" of God, which means that the human being "is endowed with intelligence and free will, and has the power to act by itself."[50] In this way, Christian theology elaborated a conception of the person marked by proper subsistence, individuality, unity, and totality, as well as by an intelligent and free nature.

PERSON AND NATURE, DIVINE PERSON AND HUMAN PERSON

The maturation of Trinitarian doctrine in the second half of the fourth century brought numerous decisive elements regarding the

49. Greek text with Latin translation in *Sacrorum Conciliorum nova et amplissima collectio*, ed. J. D. Mansi, vol. 11 (Paris: H. Welter, 1901), 663–64; French translation in Francis Xavier Murphy and Polycarp Sherwood, *Constantinople II et Constantinople III* (Paris: Editions de l'Orante, 1974), 321.

50. St. Thomas Aquinas, *Summa theologiae* II, prologue; this prologue specifies the aspect under which moral theology studies the human being.

notion of person. We will recall two in particular, which have not lost any of their importance. The first element is the clear distinction between, on the one hand, nature (*phusis*) associated with essence (*ousia*) and with power (*dunamis*), and person or hypostasis on the other. The second element is the recognition of the personal property that distinctly characterizes each divine hypostasis. Persons or hypostases of the same essence and of the same power are distinguished by individual characteristics that are exclusive "properties." In the divine Trinity, as we have already noted, these properties are of the order of relation (*schesis*)—that is to say, of the order of a "mode of being" that consists in relation to each other: paternity, filiation, procession.

In order to reflect on these two elements, one can start with the language of faith. The Church confesses three divine persons, but it affirms only one nature in the Trinity. And Christ, who is one of the Trinity, is one person existing in two natures (dogma of Chalcedon).[51] This implies clearly that "*person* has a different meaning from *nature*."[52] This affirmation will permit us to understand better the analogical dimension of the notion of person, and it also provides light for catching a glimpse of the mystery of God the Trinity.

Let us first consider creatures. The *nature* is the interior principle of the action of a being and of its development. By extension, the word *nature* signifies the specific essence of a being, what the thing is, that by which the thing is what it is: a rose, a horse, a man.[53] For its part, a *person* is a singular being existing distinctly from others. When we speak of a "human person," the word *person* does not signify only the human nature, but the singular, concrete, and distinct individual who exists. Thus, the person includes the nature and signifies "something more" than the nature. First, the nature as

51. On the intrinsic connection between a Trinitarian understanding of the divine Mystery and a unified conception of the person of Christ, see Brian E. Daley, "The Persons in God and the Person of Christ in Patristic Theology: An Argument for Parallel Development," in *The Mystery of the Holy Trinity in the Fathers of the Church*, edited by D. Vincent Twomey and Lewis Ayres, 9–36 (Dublin: Four Courts Press, 2007).

52. St. Thomas Aquinas, *Summa theologiae* III, q. 2, a. 2.

53. St. Thomas Aquinas, *Summa theologiae* III, q. 2, a. 1; these meanings are drawn from Aristotle.

principle or as essence does not include the concrete act of existing. The essence of creatures is not identical to their existence. The
person adds to the nature *the very act of existing*. Second, the person
adds to the nature the features that give it *its singularity, its individuality*. In us, human persons, this individuation comes from matter.
In the human person, *this* flesh is substantially united to *this* soul.
To sum up: The "human person" adds two things to the "human nature": *the proper act of existing,* which the nature does not include in
itself; and what *individualizes* this human nature, what gives it its irreducible singularity.

We can now attempt to direct our reflection toward God the
Trinity. The divine person is an "individual substance of rational nature," but in a manner profoundly different from human persons.
There is, however, an analogy. In God, this spiritual nature (an "intellectual nature") is the transcendent divine nature identical to the
very existence of God, and indeed identical in the three persons, as
the doctrine of the divine simplicity reminded us. It is necessary
even to affirm that the three persons *are* their identical divine nature. Between the divine persons and the divine nature, there is no
real difference, but only a conceptual distinction. The sole real distinction that is found in God is the distinction between the persons
themselves (and not between the persons and the divine nature).
Trinitarian faith holds firmly to the unity of God. But what accounts
for the otherness among the divine persons, or what mutually distinguishes them? The response, insofar as our mind can give one,
resides in the doctrine of relations or relative properties explained
above. We repeat: insofar as our mind is capable of understanding—that is, in a limited way. The divine persons are distinguished
by virtue of their relative properties: paternity, filiation, procession.
Although the divine nature is indivisibly one in itself and in operation, the hypostases or persons are really distinct according to their
relative properties. The *Catechism of the Catholic Church* summarizes this teaching:

The divine persons are relative to one another. Because it does not divide the divine unity, the real distinction of the persons from one another resides solely in the relationships which relate them to one another: "In the relational names of the persons the Father is related to the Son, the Son to the Father, and the Holy Spirit to both. While they are called three persons in view of their relations, we believe in one nature or substance" (Council of Toledo XI, in A.D. 675).[54]

In a discovery that constitutes the summit of theological reflection on the "divine person," St. Thomas Aquinas showed that the divine person is a "relation that subsists."[55] A real relation possesses two aspects. On the one hand, the real relation exists: it is not only thought by our mind, but rather it possesses a standing in the reality of things. On the other hand, the relation consists in a pure relation to another (this is the very definition of a relation). On these grounds, we raise our mind to the relations that, in God, distinctly characterize the persons: paternity (the relation of the Father to his Son), filiation (the relation of the Son to the Father who begets him), and procession (the relation of the Holy Spirit to the Father and the Son from whom he proceeds). As regards their standing in being, these relations are identical to the very being of God; they are identified with the essence of God, which is his pure existence: these relations subsist. The divine person is not the result of a composition of the divine being with another thing. God is simple. As regards relation to another—and a relation is defined precisely through reference to another—these relations distinguish the divine persons. This is because, as we have seen, they concern properties that are not interchangeable, since they are mutually "opposed": the Father is not Son, the Son is not Father, but the Father is Father of the Son and the Son is Son of the Father. The notion of "opposition," which we have encountered in St. Basil of Caesarea, should be taken in a formal sense and not, of course, in a moral sense. Wher-

54. *Catechism of the Catholic Church*, no. 255.
55. St. Thomas Aquinas, *Summa theologiae* I, q. 29, a. 4.

ever there is a distinction, there is some "opposition." The relations
not only distinguish the persons, but also they constitute these persons. To affirm that the relation constitutes the person (to say, for
example, that filiation constitutes the Son) is to recognize that this
relation is not added to the person and is not involved only in manifesting the person, but rather that the person consists in this very relation insofar as the relation possesses the divine being.

The divine person is a *subsisting relation*. The divine relation includes in itself the unity of the divine being and the personal distinction. This teaching (St. Thomas Aquinas) enables one to grasp,
however slightly, what "person" in God means, without destroying
the mystery. Such a theological contemplation does not pretend to
comprehend God, but it gives an account of faith in three persons
who are one God.

There is thus, first, a common notion of *person* that is applied by
analogy to the divine Three, to angels, and to human beings. This
common notion, which is analogical, is expressed by the definition
of Boethius. And there is, second, a special notion of *person* that
is applied distinctly either to human beings, or to God the Trinity. This special notion considers the manner according to which the
person is "one" in itself and is distinguished from others; in other
words, it emphasizes what accounts for the distinct individuality of
one person. For its part, the human person is composed of a soul
and a body. The substantial unity of *this* body and *this* soul constitutes one human person. According to the special notion that characterizes it, the human person is a substantial existent of an intelligent and free nature, individualized by and subsisting in matter. As
regards the divine person, which is not composed but which is perfectly simple, it is a relation that subsists in the perfection of the divine nature. The Father is paternity insofar as this relation of paternity subsists in the divine being. The Son is filiation insofar as this
filiation has the mode of existing of the divine nature. The Holy
Spirit is his relation to the Father and the Son from whom he receives himself. Produced by the need to answer heresies and sus-

tained by the quest for the understanding of the faith, Trinitarian theology leads the believing mind to this contemplation: the Father, who is God, is relative to the Son and to the Holy Spirit; the Son, who is equally God, is relative to the Father and to the Holy Spirit; and the Holy Spirit, who is the same God, is relative to the Father and to the Son.

The constitution of a person by a relation remains the exclusive prerogative of the divine Trinity, because only in God does a relation "subsist." In a human being, a relation does not constitute the person. Rather, a relation is a determination of the person (an "accident" added to substance). This is not to imply that relations have no ontological weight: one is really determined by one's relation to God, by one's relation to one's parents, and by all of the other relations that a human being has (fulfillment of the "image of God"). But these are determinations *of* the person.

MODERN DIFFICULTIES REGARDING THE
AFFIRMATION OF "THREE PERSONS"

Christian monotheism holds that, in God the Trinity, the three persons are one understanding and one will, one freedom, exercising one operation as one identical essence: one single God. Consequently, if one defines the person just by reason, or freedom, or the capacity for autonomous action, how can we recognize "three persons" in God? This would imply three intelligences, three freedoms, three centers of spiritual life, in brief, three gods (tritheism). This is far from a false or superficial difficulty. It has been vividly perceived by Christian theologians, sometimes dramatically, ever since the seventeenth century when, following Locke and Descartes, the person began to be understood in terms of self-consciousness or of acts of thought.[56]

The problem is found also in Christology: how can we profess

56. See Philip Dixon, *"Nice and Hot Disputes": The Doctrine of the Trinity in the Seventeenth Century* (London: T. and T. Clark, 2003).

that Christ Jesus is "one single person" while recognizing in him a true and complete human mind (with intelligence and freedom) that remains really distinct from his intelligent and free divinity? To define the person by the life of the mind would lead one to posit two persons in Christ. For these reasons, in the twentieth century, certain theologians distanced themselves from the word "persons" in speaking of the Trinity. Karl Barth preferred to speak of three "modes of being" (*Seinsweisen*) in God the Trinity. For his part, Karl Rahner proposed to specify the "personality" of the Three by the notion of "distinct modes of subsistence" (*distinkte Subsistenzweisen*).[57] Besides, they adopted a conception of the human person based on the life of the mind and subjectivity. These theologians' proposals have not succeeded in resolving the difficulty.

The "classical" tradition, which we have presented drawing on Thomas Aquinas and his interpretation of Boethius's definition, still offers today, we think, the best resource for pursuing Christian reflection on the human being and on the triune God. It places the metaphysical foundation of the person in the foreground. This foundation is at the root of the dignity of the person. The person is "what is most worthy" and "what is most perfect,"[58] not only by reason of his faculties of understanding and free will, but also *and first* by reason of his mode of existing through himself. The approach to the person in terms of *substance* and of *nature* grounds and promotes the psychological, ethical, relational, and social traits of the person. This approach constitutes the indispensable foundation for understanding *analogically* the divine person and the human person. It enables one to express the faith in the Father, Son, and Holy Spirit, three persons who are one single God.

57. Karl Barth, *Church Dogmatics*, vol. 1, *The Doctrine of the Word of God*, part 1, *The Word of God as the Criterion of Dogmatics: The Revelation of God*, 2nd ed. (Edinburgh: T. and T. Clark, 1975), § 9: 355–68; Karl Rahner, *The Trinity*, trans. Joseph Donceel (New York: Crossroad, 1997), 103–15.

58. St. Thomas Aquinas, *De potentia*, q. 9, a. 3; *Summa theologiae* I, q. 29, a. 3.

5

Doctrinal Synthesis on the Father, Son, and Holy Spirit

This chapter examines the Father, Son, and Holy Spirit in their distinctive properties. The divine persons are not blended: each person possesses his own personal traits. These distinct personal features constitute the "property" of each divine person: paternity and innascibility (Father), filiation (Son), and procession (Holy Spirit). The properties regard the eternal existence of the divine persons, and they allow us likewise to grasp the mode of action of these persons in creation and in salvation. We will direct our attention principally to the property of each divine person in his eternal existence, while indicating briefly the creative and salvific action that these properties illumine. The following chapter will try to show more fully the light that this dogmatic reflection brings for understanding the action of the divine persons in the world. The discussion of the Holy Spirit will be a bit longer than those on the Father and the Son, because the doctrine of the Holy Spirit unites the teaching on the Father and the Son. In reality, each time that we direct our attention to a divine person, we consider simultaneously the two others, because the three persons are relative to each other and they are present in each other, both in their innermost being and in their action for us.

THE FATHER

When we reflect on the person of the Father, our mind must undertake an important work of purification. Faced with currents that did not accept the teaching of the Council of Nicea, Christian teachers of the fourth century showed that a Catholic faith in the Father excludes corporeal generation, change and temporal succession, and sexual difference. The person of the Father should be approached, in accordance with revelation, in a manner befitting his spiritual nature. As we purify from our conception of the Father everything incompatible with his perfection, what precisely must we retain? Three principal traits should be acknowledged. First, the Father is Father of the Son whom he begets: this is his "relative personal property" of paternity. Second, the Father does not have an origin. He is unbegotten, without principle. This is his property of innascibility (the word "innascible" means not begotten). Third, with the Son whom he begets, the Father is also the principle of the Holy Spirit; however, since it is a matter of an aspect that the Father communicates to the Son ("The Holy Spirit proceeds from the Father as the first principle and, by the eternal gift of this to the Son, from the communion of both the Father and the Son"),[1] the Catholic theological tradition sees here a common characteristic that makes known to us the Father and the Son: this is the "notion" of spiration (in this context, the word "notion" designates a characteristic that makes known to us a divine person, and the word "spiration" relates to the act of "breathing forth the Holy Spirit").[2] The Father is the "principle without principle." According to traditional Catholic doctrine, we grasp distinctly the person of the Father—insofar as the weak-

1. St. Augustine, *De Trinitate* 15.26.47, quoted in the *Catechism of the Catholic Church,* 2nd ed. (Vatican City: Libreria Editrice Vaticana, 1997), no. 264.

2. The Father, as "the principle without principle," is the "first principle" or the "first origin" of the Holy Spirit: this belongs to the Father alone (*Catechism of the Catholic Church,* no. 248). And "as Father of the only Son, he is, with the Son, the single principle from which the Holy Spirit proceeds" (ibid.). In this context, "first principle" means the same as "principle not from a principle." Put otherwise, in the formula "first principle," the adjective *first* refers to a mere order, namely, the order of divine persons.

ness of our mind allows—by his paternity, his innascibility, and the spiration of the Holy Spirit: "Three properties belong to the Father: one by which he is distinguished from the Son alone, and this is paternity; another by which he is distinguished from two, namely the Son and the Holy Spirit, and this is innascibility . . . ; the third is that by which the Father himself, together with the Son, is distinguished from the Holy Spirit, and it is called common spiration."[3]

The Paternity of the Father

In following the explanations of St. Thomas Aquinas, we have noted that the divine persons are characterized by a relation (a relative personal property), and that in reality they are this relation that subsists. Now, the personal relation by which the Father is Father is his paternity. To reflect on this paternity is therefore to focus our attention on the Father himself: "This name Father signifies not only a property, but also the person itself. . . . Because this name Father signifies the relation which is distinctive and constitutive of the hypostasis."[4] In addition, to place paternity at the beginning of the study of the person of the Father is to recognize that the name Father is the most proper name for designating his person, in accordance with the teaching of the New Testament. "A name proper to any person signifies that by which the person is distinct from all others. . . . Now that which distinguishes the person of the Father from all others is fatherhood. Thus the name Father, signifying his fatherhood, is the name proper to the person of the Father."[5] These considerations recall the stakes of the Council of Nicea. To name the first person Father is not to have recourse to a metaphor, and it is not a manner of speaking of the activity of the Unbegotten, but rather it is to name the Father of Jesus by his proper name, in accordance with what Jesus revealed. In her confession of faith, as in her liturgy and her catechesis, the Church follows the language of Jesus himself: Father.

3. St. Thomas Aquinas, *Compendium theologiae* I, ch. 57.
4. St. Thomas Aquinas, *Summa theologiae* I, q. 40, a. 2.
5. St. Thomas Aquinas, *Summa theologiae* I, q. 33, a. 2.

Paternity, which is made known to us by the personal relation of Jesus with his Father, includes all the relations that God the Father has with his Son. These relations, as we have observed above in chapter 2, are characterized by the fact that Jesus came forth from the Father as regards his very being. They possess a dimension of knowledge and love, of common action and mutual indwelling. All these aspects are summed up in the affirmation: *the Father is the principle of the Son.* This manner of signifying the paternity of the Father can seem a little dry. This is why it is important to note that, by this affirmation, one expresses the depth of the personal relation of the Father to his Son, in all its richness, with the dimensions of life that we have evoked. The Father is the Source of the Son. Paternity signifies the relation of principle that the Father has with his Son, that is to say the paternal gift of the fullness of divine being to the Son. The Greek Fathers, followed by Orthodox theologians, speak of the "Cause" (*aitia*) or the "Principle" (*arche*) in designating the Father. Latin theologians prefer to use the term "Principle" (*principium*) because, following an important current of the Western cultural tradition, the word "cause" connotes a dependence and an inferiority of the effect in relation to its cause, while the word "principle" is clearer. "Principle" simply signifies a relation of origin. However, given the usage of the Greek Fathers, the Catholic Church welcomes both words: *cause* or *principle.*[6] Paternity does not imply the priority of the Father or a hierarchy in the Trinity, but only the relation according to which he is the principle of the Son.

The divine paternity with respect to Jesus includes some traits that, *among human beings,* belong to mothers in the begetting and care of a child: conception, giving birth. The Son is "conceived" and "given birth to" by his Father; he dwells "in the bosom of the Father" (Jn 1:18). These *maternal traits* are integrated into the divine name *Father,* while safeguarding against anthropomorphisms, be-

6. Council of Florence, in 1439 (*Decrees of the Ecumenical Councils* 1:527); see also Heinrich Denzinger, *Enchiridion symbolorum, definitionum et declarationum de rebus fidei et morum,* 37th ed., ed. Peter Hünermann (Freiburg im Breisgau: Herder, 1991), no. 1301.

cause God is not Father of the Son in the manner of human beings (neither in the way of human fathers, nor in the way of human
mothers).[7] The paternity of God is not a virility. *God is Father, but
he is not male.* It is necessary to recall here the rule of divine names:
what these names signify is only properly attributed to God to the
degree that this accords with his divine spiritual nature, in conformity with revelation. The name *Father* is a proper name insofar as
it means *Source* and *Principle* of the Son in the same divine nature,
giver of the divine fullness to the Son through eternal generation.
The property of the Father as "unbegotten" emphasizes likewise the
necessity of going beyond human representations, that is to say, of
conceiving the Father according to the purifications required by the
rules of an analogy that respects God's transcendence.

The Analogical Meanings of the Name "Father"

The name Father signifies a relation of paternity. Now, it is necessary to recognize many relations by virtue of which God is named
Father: he is (1) the Father of his only Son; (2) our Father in the
Son; (3) Father of all human beings; (4) Father of the world. In the
four cases, the word "Father" does not have exactly the same meaning. Rather, there is an analogy. The name "Father" is applied by
analogy to God in order to signify, first, his relation to the eternal
Son, second, his relation to the just who live by grace, third, his relation of provident Creator to all human beings and fourth, his relation to all creatures.

In the first and most proper sense, the name *Father* signifies the
person of the Father in his eternal relation to the only Son. "Fatherhood and sonship in their fullest meaning are to be found in God
the Father and God the Son, since their nature and glory are one."[8]
"To be Father" is to give life to another of the same nature. The supreme realization of paternity is found in the gift of the fullness of

---

7. We speak of the maternal traits of the Father, but we do not name him "Mother
of Jesus." This would diverge from the New Testament and introduce a grave confusion.

8. St. Thomas Aquinas, *Summa theologiae* I, q. 33, a. 3.

the divine nature to the Son, in the unity of the divinity. Paternity exists in its most perfect mode in the eternal relation of the Father to his only Son. To say *Father,* in the full sense of Trinitarian faith, is not to designate first of all the relation of God to his creatures, but rather to signify before all else the eternal relation of the Father to his only Son. The paternity of the Father to his consubstantial Son is absolutely first.

The Holy Spirit is not absent from the relation of paternity and filiation that "constitute" the Father and the Son. The Holy Spirit is present in the very act of the eternal generation of the Son, not that the Holy Spirit is the principle of this generation (this would break the order of the persons in the Trinity, introducing confusion), but because the Father, in begetting his Son, gives to his Son the power to "breathe forth" or to "spirate" the Holy Spirit. The Father *as Father* gives to the Son the power to spirate with him the Holy Spirit, and the Son *as Son* receives from the Father the power (the active power) of spirating with him the Holy Spirit. The power of spirating the Holy Spirit is *included* in the generation of the Son: by his generation, the Son receives from the Father to be with him the principle of the Holy Spirit. Put otherwise, the procession of the Holy Spirit is inscribed in the mutual relation of the Father and the Son. This means that the procession of the Holy Spirit is connected *in itself* to the generation of the Son by the Father.

The paternal relation of God toward human beings is not pushed aside, but it stands in second place, derived from the first and dependent on it. Paternity in God regards first a relation of divine person to divine person, and then the relation of God the Father to the angels and the humans who receive a *participation* in the divine life. This means that the Father is not our Father in the same way that he is Father of his only Son. He is Father of the Son by nature, while he is our Father by grace: he enables humans to participate in the sonship of his only Son; he makes them "children of God." This adoptive sonship is accomplished by the Holy Spirit, who inscribes in believers a "likeness" of the Son. By conforming them to the Son, the Holy Spirit enables them to be children of God *in the Son,* and to lead a filial life toward God the Father, following the example of Christ.

Here it is necessary to be precise. Adoptive sonship, that is to say, "being children" adopted by God, can be considered under two aspects. If we consider "being children" under its "ontological" aspect, that is to say as a created effect in its relation to its cause, it is necessary to recognize that, by grace, humans are children of the whole Trinity, since created effects have for their cause the whole Trinity. In this sense, one can say that the Trinity is our Father. But if we consider "being children" under its "intentional" aspect, that is to say, according to the dynamism of the gifts of grace that enable humans to be united to God in faith and charity by conformation to the Son and to the Holy Spirit, sonship refers us to the person of the Father in his personal distinction.

Consider the prayer of the *Our Father.* We can envision the words "Our Father" from three points of view. (1) Under the aspect that we called "ontological," one can understand that the whole Trinity is our Father. The great theologians of medieval scholasticism sometimes explained the expression "Our Father" under this aspect. The daily bread, the forgiveness of sins, the deliverance from temptations, and the liberation from evil are given to us by the whole Trinity. The whole Trinity is the cause of our sonship and of the gifts that God gives us. So, if one considers our sonship (our relation to "Our Father") under the aspect of its cause, it refers us to the whole Trinity. (2) Still ontologically, but with a consideration of the divine persons' *order,* "Our Father" refers to the distinct person of the Father insofar as he is the principle of the Son and of the Holy Spirit. What we ask for in the "Our Father" is procured by the Father *through* the Son and *in* the Holy Spirit, by virtue of one operation common to the three persons (an operation which the Son and the Holy Spirit receive from the Father). Thus, the "Our Father" is addressed to the distinct person of the Father, insofar as the Father is the principle of the Son and of the Holy Spirit with whom

he is God and through whom he procures for us the goods of life.[9]
(3) Taken under the "intentional" aspect, that is to say, under the aspect of faith and charity that unite us to God, we pray to the distinct person of the Father insofar as we have a personal relationship with the Father through the Son and in the Holy Spirit. Here the personal dimension becomes especially clear, since this aspect stresses the communion of the Church with the Father through the Son, in the Holy Spirit. Indeed, Christian prayer is addressed distinctly and properly to the person of the Father:

When we pray to "our" Father, we personally address the Father of our Lord Jesus Christ. By doing so we do not divide the Godhead, since the Father is its "source and origin," but rather confess that the Son is eternally begotten by him and the Holy Spirit proceeds from him. We are not confusing the persons, for we confess that our communion is with the Father and his Son, Jesus Christ, in their one Holy Spirit. The Holy Trinity is consubstantial and indivisible. When we pray to the Father, we adore and glorify him together with the Son and the Holy Spirit.[10]

When Christians pray to God the Father by addressing themselves distinctly to the person of the Father, they signify first his relation to the only Son, Jesus. It is in the Son and through the Son that believers address themselves to God as Father, meaning by this the Father of the Son. To name God Father in the personal, distinct sense of Trinitarian faith is always to name him as Father of his only Son, because it is in his eternal relation to the Son that the Father is personally and distinctly Father. When this Trinitarian relation of paternity is extended to us by the dynamism of the gifts of grace

9. St. Thomas Aquinas observed that we pray to God insofar as God is fully happy and gives us a share in his beatitude. And since this belongs to God by virtue of his divine essence, we pray to God by reason of his essential attributes. As St. Thomas says: "What belongs to the [divine] essence is in the other persons from the Father; and therefore the other persons are somehow brought back to the Father. . . . And on account of this, the Father is called 'the principle of the whole deity.' And thus leading us back to the Father, as to the principle without a principle, Christ taught us to direct our prayer to the Father through the Son" (St. Thomas, *Commentary on the Sentences*, Bk. IV, dist. 15, q. 4, a. 5, quaestiuncula 3).

10. *Catechism of the Catholic Church*, no. 2789.

that unite us to the Father through the Son in the Spirit, the relation of the Father to his eternal Son remains in the foreground. Prayer is addressed distinctly to the person of the Father, meaning by this his relation to the Son and, through the Son and in the Spirit, the relation by which his children are united to him.

Let us briefly summarize these explanations. On the one hand, the Father appears in his personal distinction when we have in view *the order of persons* who are the cause of the gift of sonship: the Father makes us his children through his Son and in the Holy Spirit. There is no access to the person of the Father outside the relation that he has eternally with his Son and that, in the Spirit, he causes to overflow into the just who live by his grace. On the other hand, Christian prayer is addressed distinctly to the person of the Father under the "intentional" aspect of faith and charity. Through the Son and the Holy Spirit, the children of God are united to the Father whom they contemplate in faith and whom they love in charity. This aspect not only views the Trinity as the cause or origin of the gifts that we receive, but it signifies that, through the Son and in the Holy Spirit, believers are in communion with the Father.

Third, the name *Father* can designate the relation that God has with all human beings whom he creates in his image, through the Son and the Holy Spirit, that is to say, the relation that God has with all humans by virtue of creation. Even when humans reject grace, God remains their Father, but in a sense somehow different from the preceding one (analogy). Even when the image of God is obscured by sin, the sonship by creation remains, because the paternal gift of life still remains and, indeed, our human nature still points beyond itself to its fulfillment in God.

At the most universal level, the paternity of God extends to purely material creatures. In this case, by the name *Father*, we mean the *Creator of the world* who governs and cares for all beings in his *Providence*. In all cases, when we reflect on the name *Father*, it is necessary to seek to discern the relation signified by this name and its effects (the life of grace, human natural life, the existence of things).

The name *Father* is analogous: it designates different relations of which the first (from which all the others derive by participation) is the eternal relation of the Father to his only Son. The paternity of the Father to his Son is the source of all the gifts that descend from the "Father of Lights" (James 1:17); it is at the origin of the whole human family, of every gift of life: "I bow my knees before the Father, from whom every family on heaven and on earth is named" (Eph 3:14). The same goes for other human acts of spiritual paternity and maternity, for caring for life, for helping others progress in the true and good: in all these, we can discover a participation in the paternity of God the Father. Every true gift, every fruitful action comes back to the paternity of the Father who is the transcendent and mysterious archetype.

The Unbegotten Father, Principle without Principle

The Father, who begets his Son and who is the principle of the Holy Spirit, is not begotten and does not proceed. He is "not begotten," "unbegotten," "without principle," or "innascible." This is the second property that characterizes the Father. We find the reflection or expression in the economy of salvation: the Son is sent by the Father, the Holy Spirit is sent by the Father and the Son, but the Father is not sent. Having no origin, the Father has no principle that could send him. This property of innascibility retains a negative content (the Father is "not begotten") that enables one better to glimpse the mystery of the Father. The Father is known to us, in faith, as not coming forth from another person. Innascibility also combats the temptation to think of the Father like a human parent. Human parents transmit what they have received, but God the Father alone gives to the Son and to the Holy Spirit what he has from no other person.

Thus, paternity and spiration show the fecundity or the "fontality" ("plenitude of the Source") of the Father: he is the Source, the principle of the Son and of the Holy Spirit. Moreover, if one takes account of innascibility, one sees better what constitutes the unique "personality" of the Father: he is the "principle *without prin-*

ciple," the Source who has no origin. Thus, for instance, St. Thomas Aquinas refers to the Father with expressions such as "the fontal principle of the whole divinity" and "the source and principle of the whole deity."[11] The Latin Catholic tradition uses at times the word "Author" (*Auctor*) for signifying that the Father is the Source, the principle of the Son and of the Holy Spirit, but that he himself comes forth from no principle.[12] In summary:

> On the one hand, the Father is known to us by his paternity and by spiration, that is to say, through his relation to the persons who proceed from him. On the other hand, in so far as he is "principle *not from a principle*," the Father is known to us under the aspect in which he himself does not come from another person; and this belongs to the property of innascibility, which is signified by this word *Unbegotten*.[13]

There is, however, a difference in how the Catholic (Latin) and Orthodox (Greek) traditions speak about the Father. It concerns the "monarchy of the Father." For the Orthodox doctrine, the "monarchy" signifies that the Father is the sole Source, the sole "Cause" or the sole "principle" in the Trinity, in a way that denies that the Son could be, with the Father, the principle of the Holy Spirit.[14] According to Catholic doctrine, the characteristic of the Father as "principle without principle" (and consequently "first origin" of the Holy Spirit) does not exclude that the Son is, with the Father and by virtue of his generation by the Father, the principle of the Holy Spirit. But the two traditions, Orthodox and Catholic, fundamentally meet in the recognition of the Father as unbegotten Source, princi-

---

11. St. Thomas Aquinas, *Commentary on the Sentences,* Bk. I, dist. 34, q. 2, a. 1: "Fontale principium totius divinitatis"; *Commentary on Dionysius' Divine Names,* ch. 2, Lesson 4 (no. 181): "Fons et principium totius deitatis."

12. In his discussion of intratrinitarian relations, St. Thomas Aquinas reserves the word "Author" (*auctor*) to the person of the Father. The name "Author" also applies to the Father in the economy: the Father is the "Author of the Incarnation" (St. Thomas Aquinas, *Commentary on the Gospel of St. John* 7:29, no. 1065).

13. St. Thomas Aquinas, *Summa theologiae* I, q. 33, a. 4.

14. See Boris Bobrinskoy, *The Mystery of the Trinity: Trinitarian Experience and Vision in the Biblical and Patristic Tradition* (Crestwood, N.Y.: St. Vladimir's Seminary Press, 1999), 265–66.

ple without principle, principle of the Son and principle of the Holy Spirit. The two traditions likewise recognize that the Father is the source of the unity of the Trinity. To confess the Father as "principle without principle" is to recognize that the Trinity derives its unity from the Father, because it is the Father who communicates the one divine nature to the Son and (with the Son, according to Catholic teaching) to the Holy Spirit. From the Catholic perspective, St. Thomas Aquinas explains: "When we consider the properties of the persons, we find the notion of first principle, as it were, in the Father. And it is in virtue of the unity of a principle without principle that the same nature is communicated to all, within each nature. This is why all are one by reason of the Father."[15]

These explanations clarify how the Father acts in the economy of creation and grace. The Father's mode of action is that of the "principle without principle" or of the Source of the Trinity: the Father acts through the Son and in the Spirit who come forth from him. For example, consider creation. The Father creates the world and fashions human beings through his Son and his Spirit, who are like his "two Hands," according to the beautiful expression of St. Irenaeus. Put otherwise, it is through the eternal generation of the Son and the procession of the Holy Spirit that the Father exercises his paternal activity of creation in time. He is, in this sense, the Source of creation, because he is the Source of the Son and of the Spirit through whom he creates the world.

After creation, let us consider the final fulfillment ("eschatology"), according to the plan that God has revealed: to enable humans to participate in his own happiness in his kingdom. In the same way that the Father creates humans through the Son in the Spirit, it is through this same Son and in this same Spirit that the Father leads to himself redeemed human beings. On the one hand, the Father is the "principle without principle" from whom all things have come forth. On the other hand, the Father is the "ultimate term" to

15. St. Thomas Aquinas, *Commentary on the Sentences*, Bk. I, dist. 31, q. 3, a. 2; see also *Summa theologiae* I, q. 39, a. 8: "The other persons derive their unity from the Father."

which the divinizing action of the Son and of the Holy Spirit leads humans. All three divine persons are one same and single end of the universe. And, within this one end, the Father is somehow the "ultimate term," just as he is the "principle without principle." The Father thus appears as "the ultimate principle to whom we are led back," in the words of St. Augustine.[16] It is in this final fulfillment, when "God will be all in all" (1 Cor 15:28), that the mystery of the Father will be fully manifested to the saints. In summary: Principle without principle in the intimate life of the Trinity, the Father is also the principle of the divine economy, and he is also the "ultimate term" of that economy. Humans receive participation in the divine nature in the Holy Spirit, who imprints in them the image of the Son, in order to enable them to enter into the communion of the Father. Thus, thanks to the Spirit, through the mediation of the Son, all things are led back to the Father.[17] In this sense, the Father is "the alpha and the omega of the Trinitarian life."[18] He reveals himself as the Source of the Son and the Holy Spirit, as the personal source of the economy, and also as the ultimate personal end to whom the Son and Holy Spirit lead the saints. Through the Son and in the Spirit, all comes from the Father; through the Son and in the Spirit, angels and human beings (and, in humans, the whole universe together) are renewed and elevated so as to rejoin the Source, the Father, in whom resides the final fulfillment of the promises.

THE SON, WORD AND IMAGE OF THE FATHER

The revelation of Christ Jesus in the economy of salvation is the sole path of access to the divine mystery of his filiation. The Fathers of

---

16. St. Augustine, On True Religion 55.113 (CCSL 32:260): "Principium ad quod recurrimus."

17. See, for instance, St. Cyril of Alexandria, On John 11.10 (PG 74, col. 541); cf. Norman Russell, The Doctrine of Deification in the Greek Patristic Tradition (Oxford: Oxford University Press, 2004); Daniel A. Keating, The Appropriation of Divine Life in Cyril of Alexandria (Oxford: Oxford University Press, 2004).

18. Following the title of the work of Emmanuel Durand, Le Père, Alpha et Oméga de la vie trinitaire: De la paternité eschatologique au Père en son mystère (Paris: Cerf, 2008).

the Church insisted on the incomprehensible and ineffable character of the eternal filiation of the Son. "How has the Son been begotten? . . . God's begetting ought to have the tribute of our reverent silence. The important point is for you to learn that he has been begotten. As to the way it happens, we shall not concede that even angels, much less you, know that. Shall I tell you the way? It is a way known only to the begetting Father and the begotten Son. Anything beyond this fact is hidden by a cloud and escapes your dull vision."[19] With a comparable sense of mystery, St. Thomas Aquinas continues:

It is not permitted to scrutinize the mysteries on high with the intention of comprehending them. This appears in what St. Ambrose writes: "One can know *that* the Son is born, but one must not question *how* he is born." Because to question the mode of his birth is to seek to know what his birth is. Now, on the subject of divine realities, we can know *that* they are but not *what* they are.[20]

The doctrinal study of the Son, like theological research on the Father and on the Holy Spirit, should therefore be undertaken as we put it in chapter 4: it is a contemplative study "for the exercise and comfort of the faithful." In explaining Scripture and in showing that faith in the Son is intimately connected to all the other mysteries of faith, this study uses created "likenesses" or "similitudes." By means of what is better known to us, it seeks to manifest the faith more fully to the minds of believers. "And such a search is not useless, since it elevates the mind and gives it enough of a glimpse of the truth to steer clear of errors."[21]

---

19. St. Gregory Nazianzen, *Oration* 29.8 in St. Gregory of Nazianzus, *On God and Christ: The Five Theological Orations and Two Letters to Cledonius,* translated by Frederick Williams and Lionel Wickham (Crestwood, New York: St. Vladimir's Seminary Press, 2002), 76.

20. St. Thomas Aquinas, *On Boethius' De Trinitate,* q. 2, a. 1, ad 4; emphasis mine. The word "birth" designates here the eternal generation of the Son.

21. St. Thomas Aquinas, *Summa contra Gentiles,* Bk. I, ch. 9 (# 54), and *De potentia,* q. 9, a. 5.

The Eternal Filiation of the Son

The tradition of the Church finds in the name of Son the expression of the intimate and eternal being of Christ Jesus. He is the eternal and consubstantial Son of the Father, preexistent to creation and to his sending by the Father, manifested to humans in the mysteries of his flesh, and he dwells eternally as Son with his Father. The incarnation, the earthly life, and the Pasch of Jesus are the expression, in the humanity that he assumed, of the eternal communion of the Son with his Father. This communion, which is manifested particularly in the reciprocal knowledge and love of the Son and of his Father, and in their mutual indwelling, regards the very being of the Son. Jesus' human life is the revelation of his eternal divine sonship. The deepening of the notion of relation by St. Thomas Aquinas, especially the doctrine of "subsisting relation,"[22] fosters the recognition that the Son is his filial relation itself ("sonship"), which subsists in the divine being. The Son is completely ordered to the Father who begets him: "his relation (namely, sonship) is his characteristic personhood."[23]

The name *Son* thus enables us to apprehend and to signify, in faith, the fullness of the divinity of the second person. The Son receives the nature and the goods of the Father, all the goods of God. "All that the Father has is mine," says Jesus (Jn 16:15). With the term "filiation," the dogmatic tradition has underscored that the entire divine nature is communicated to the Son, who has it in a distinct mode, namely, as received from the Father. The Son has *the divine fullness received by generation.* When one speaks of the communication of the divine "nature," this includes all the plenitude of God: wisdom, love, power. The Son is Son in the eternal act by which he receives from the Father, in the filial mode of generation, all the di-

---

22. See above in chapter 4: "Person and Nature, Divine Person and Human Person."

23. St. Thomas Aquinas, *Commentary on the Sentences,* Bk. I, dist. 19, q. 3, a. 2, ad 1: "sua enim relatio est sua personalitas."

vine being, wisdom, and love of the Father. The property of the Son consists in this relation to the Father. By his generation, he eternally receives his being *God as Begotten.* This "filial mode of being," which is a mode of being relative to the Father, belongs only to the Son in the Trinity. Filiation thus designates the distinct relation that characterizes the divine personal existence of the Son.

The Son is begotten by the Father in a way that is not the human manner of being born. His begetting is also radically distinguished from the act of creation. The Son is not produced by the will of the Father, as are creatures, but rather he is begotten from the substance of the Father, by nature. The same affirmation should be applied to the Holy Spirit: the Holy Spirit proceeds naturally from the substance of the Father. The Catholic and Orthodox doctrine avoids all that would imply an inferiority of the Son or of the Holy Spirit in relation to the Father. The Son is consubstantial with the Father; he has the same substance as the Father, the same divine nature and the same power, the same operation. "All mine are thine, and all thine are mine" (Jn 17:10). The Father and the Son are one in all things except what concerns their personal properties: the Son is all that the Father is, except that he is not Father and not without principle. In the Father, in the Son, and in the Holy Spirit, the divine nature therefore is identical and the same. One speaks at times of "numerical unity" in order to designate such transcendent unity (the divine essence is "numerically one" in all three divine persons), far beyond all forms of unity that can be found among human persons. The Father and the Son do not only have a similar nature, like human persons in whom the same specific nature is multiplied, but rather the Father and the Son exist in a nature that is absolutely one and identical.

The filiation of the Son is the foundation of all human sonship and of filial adoption by the Father: "God has sent the Spirit of his Son into our hearts, crying, 'Abba! Father!'" (Gal 4:6; cf. Rom 8:15; Eph 3:14–15). Salvation consists in the reception of adoptive sonship by which humans become children of God. This sonship by grace is a participation in the natural sonship of the Son, that is to say a participation in his personal relation to the Father, an assimilation to his mode of existence that is completely referred to the Father. "The Word of God, born once in the flesh (such is his kindness and his goodness), is always willing to be born spiritually in those who desire him. In them he is born as an infant as he fashions himself in them by means of their virtues. He reveals himself to the extent that he knows someone is capable of receiving him."[24]

Sonship by grace conforms believers to the Son; it "makes them similar" to the Son; it enables them to be associated with the very sonship of the Son in relation to his Father. This conformation to the Son, by the Holy Spirit, renews human beings who thereby become "new creatures." "If any one is in Christ, he is a new creation" (2 Cor 5:17). The Son is the "ontological" model of the new *being* of believers. This new being blossoms in the imitation of the holy life of Christ, lived wholly for his Father. The Christian vocation is thus filial by essence. Through the mysteries of his life in our flesh, the Son associates himself with humans in order to make them children of God; he keeps them from sin and enables them to participate by grace in his filial relation to the Father. In the same way, belonging to the Church, which is an incorporation in Christ by the grace of the Holy Spirit, is essentially filial.[25]

The participation of human beings in the sonship of Christ Jesus is an analogical reality that is accomplished according to diverse modes or degrees. (1) It finds its highest realization in the blessed, who see God face to face and who are fully united with him in eternal life (sonship of glory). (2) In the human earthly condition, it finds its fulfillment in the saints, vivified by faith and charity (sonship of grace). These just persons are associated with Christ inasmuch as Christ is united with his Father and inasmuch as Christ

24. St. Maximus the Confessor, *Centuries* 1.8, translation of the *Liturgy of the Hours* for the Office of Readings of 4 January (or, of Wednesday, from January 2 to Epiphany); cf. *PG* 90, col. 1181.

25. See notably Eph 1:23; Eph 5:30; Col 1:18; cf. Eph 3:6; 1 Cor 6:15; 1 Cor 12:27.

was tested by suffering: "Although he was a Son, he learned obedience through what he suffered" (Heb 5:8). (3) A more general mode of sonship belongs, lastly, to all humans by reason of their human condition, that is to say, inasmuch as each human being is created in the image of God and, on this basis, is capable of receiving the grace of knowing and loving God (sonship by creation, which remains even in humans who separate themselves from God, since their human nature remains).

In an even broader manner, sonship regards the whole creation. God "has spoken to us by a Son, whom he appointed the heir of all things, through whom also he created the world" (Heb 1:2). The eternal generation of the Son is the source, the model, the uncreated and transcendent exemplar of creation. One can understand this in the following way. Creation is the action by which God freely communicates, *ex nihilo,* a participation in being to creatures. As regards the eternal generation of the Son, it is the act by which the Father begets the Son from his own substance. Under this aspect, the total communication of the divine nature of the Father to the Son appears in some way as the uncreated "model" of creation. It is necessary to specify that the Son is the *uncreated* and *transcendent* model. Moreover, creation was not necessary; the world was produced by a free decision of God. God created the world by his will, whereas he begets the Son by nature. Put otherwise, the generation of the Son, in which the Father communicates to his Son the fullness of divinity, sheds light on the gift of being that God makes to creatures by creation. *Human life and the existence of the created world find their full intelligibility only in the "filial mystery" of the uncreated Son who is begotten by the Father.*

The Word of the Father

The Son is the Word, the Logos (Jn 1:1; Jn 1:14; cf. 1 Jn 1:1; Rev 19:13). This name Word designates, first, the person of the Son in his divine being and in his eternal relation to the Father. Second, it expresses the work that the Son freely accomplishes for us. On the biblical foundation of the Word, of Wisdom and the Law, the name

Word highlights the preexistence of the Son and his divine intimacy with the Father, as well as his action of creation, revelation, and salvation. The Word reveals and manifests the Father: by nature, the word is a manifestation. Moreover, the Father creates, causes creatures to come to be, and sustains them in existence through his powerful Word (Jn 1:3). The Word is, so to say, the uncreated model of what the Father accomplishes (one can speak here of "exemplar causality"), and he possesses the effective power, the dynamic action of God himself (in order to describe this aspect, one can speak of "efficient causality"). By coming to dwell with his own, the Word saves and procures the divine life: "To all who received him, who believed in his name, he gave power to become children of God" (Jn 1:12).

In naming the Son *"Word,"* one signifies a twofold aspect in the Son himself. First, the Word comes forth from the one who speaks him or pronounces him. A word is spoken by someone. The tradition flowing from St. Augustine meditated on the divine Word by considering, by analogy, the "interior word" that a human being forms or conceives by his mind and that remains in his mind. This "likeness" allows one to show believers that the Word is characterized by a relation of origin to the One who speaks him from all eternity: the Father. Second, the Word is the perfect and full expression of the Father. We can see this by considering the following: by the human interior word, which the vocal word signifies exteriorly, our human mind *expresses what it conceives.* By analogy, the Father, by knowing himself in a personal and fruitful act, pronounces a Word who expresses all that he is. The Word is the full expression of the whole divine being of the Father. Despite the limits of the "likeness" (analogy) that our interior human word offers, it allows one to show the perfect equality of the Word with his Father: the Son is the very expression of the Father. The name *Word* also removes the temptation to conceive of the filiation of the Son on the model of the begetting of a human being. Indeed, this name is especially apt to show that the generation of the Son is accomplished in a purely spiritual way, and is neither material nor sexual.

The name *Word* covers all major aspects that characterize the Son in God: his origin from the Father (the Word is *conceived by the Father,* that is, *born from the Father*), his immanence in the Father (the Word remains *within the Father*), and his perfect identity of nature with the Father (the Word is the *perfect expression of the Father*). This is why St. Thomas Aquinas uses the name *Word* in order to show what the name *Son* signifies in God.[26] It is also what theology tries to express when it affirms that the Son is *begotten* "by mode of intellect." This does not mean that there would be in the generation of the Son more intelligence than in the procession of the Holy Spirit (indeed, the fullness of all the divine attributes is given to the Holy Spirit as well as to the Son), but rather it signifies that the Son is begotten as Word of the Father by a fecund act of "speaking": the Father "speaks" or "pronounces" from all eternity his own Word that is distinct from him, while remaining in him.

The property signified by the name *Word* sheds light on the free activity that the Son exercises in creation, in revelation, and in salvation. The personal expression of the Father, the Word is the one through whom the Father creates and saves, through whom the Father manifests himself and gives a share in the divine life. The Christian doctrine of the Word underscores the *personal* dimension of the manifestation of God. In creating, God offers a first manifestation of himself: the Father creates through his Word who is his own expression. This allows one to understand better that the created world offers a path capable of inspiring man to raise his mind toward the Creator and toward his wisdom. More profoundly still, the doctrine of the Word illumines revelation and its fulfillment in Christ who is the Word incarnate in person. By speaking to human beings, by sending to them his own Word, God does not only reveal "some thing" but rather it is *himself* that he reveals. And, through the "Word made flesh" who is "full of grace and truth" (Jn 1:14), grace is given to humans (Jn 1:17). The sanctifying knowledge of God, the

26. See St. Thomas Aquinas, *Commentary on the Gospel of St. John* 1:1 (no. 29); *Summa theologiae* I, q. 34, a. 2.

gift of wisdom that unites humans to God, is a participation in the
Son who is the Word and the Truth (cf. Jn 14:6; Jn 17:17).

Finally, the contemplation of the divine Word enables one to
apprehend the unity of the divine work of creation, revelation, and
salvation. The wisdom and love of God are supremely manifested in
the incarnation of the Word. On the one hand, "the renewal of creation has been wrought by the self-same Word who made it in the
beginning. . . . The Father effected the salvation of the world in the
same Word by whom he made it in the beginning."[27] On the other
hand, "the Word of God has a special affinity with human nature,
because he is the concept of the eternal Wisdom, from which all human wisdom comes. . . . And so it was fitting that the Word of God
personally united himself to a human nature (in the incarnation)."[28]

The Image of the Invisible God

Christ is "the image (eikon) of the invisible God, the first-born of
all creation" (Col 1:15); he is "the likeness of God" (2 Cor 4:4). The
name Image signifies Christ as preexistent to creation, working in
creation and in the Church. In his quality of Image, the Son is the
author and the model of creation and re-creation.

In a way similar to the name *Word,* this name *Image* signifies first
the relation of the Son to his Father: the Son comes forth from the
Father, and he is the perfect expression of the Father. Christians use
the name *Image* for signifying that the Son is fully like and equal to
the Father. The theological tradition associates the name *Image* with
the names *Son* and *Word.* The personal name *Image* places a special
accent on the full resemblance of the Son in relation to the Father. It
also expresses the communion of the Son with his Father in the same
nature (this aspect is especially signified by the name *Son*), and it
designates equally the Son as the expression of the wisdom of the Father (this aspect is specially signified by the name *Word*). In the gold-

27. St. Athanasius of Alexandria, *On the Incarnation of the Word* 1.1 (or 1.4 in SC
199:262); English translation from http://www.ccel.org, with a slight modification.

28. St. Thomas Aquinas, *Summa theologiae* III, q. 3, a. 8.

en age of patristic Trinitarian theology, the theme of the Son-Image summarizes the doctrine of the consubstantiality of the Father and the Son as well as the affirmation of their personal distinction.

On this basis, the name *Image* enables one to express the completely free work of creation, revelation, and salvation accomplished by the Son. Being the perfect Image of the Father, the Son is also, for this reason, the "exemplar" or the model according to which creatures were made, the model in which the Father conceived his plan of creation and grace. Under this aspect, the theme of the Image is close to that of the Word. Conceived by the Father, the Son is the expression of the Father; he represents the very being of the Father. And the Father expresses creatures in his Word who is his Image. The Son-Image is thus the uncreated Model of creatures that the Father makes through him. This Model is endowed with the same divine power as the Father.[29] The work of revelation and of salvation is equally signified by the theme of the Image. The Son reveals the Father because he is the Image of the invisible God, the Icon of the Father. The Son seated at the right hand of the Father, after having accomplished the purification of sins, is the very Son through whom God created the world: he "reflects the glory of God and bears the very stamp of his nature" (Heb 1:3).

In particular, faith in the *Son-Image* enables one to apprehend better the creation and re-creation of human beings *in the image of God.* On the one hand, the Son is not mixed with human creatures: the Son is the divine and perfect Image of the Father, while human beings are made "in the image" of God. On the other hand, to call the Son *Image* is to recognize an affinity between humans and the Son who models them. Human beings are created "in the image of God" by a participation in the Son-Image. In his Incarnation and his Pasch, the Son-Image reestablishes and reshapes in humans the image that sin deformed, and he elevates humans to divine communion. Salvation is a new creation, a "re-formation" by conformation

29. On these positions, see for example St. Thomas Aquinas, *Summa contra Gentiles,* Bk. IV, ch. 11 (no. 3474).

to the Son: "For those whom he foreknew he also predestined to be conformed to the image of his Son, in order that he might be the first-born among many brethren" (Rom 8:29). By the gift of the Holy Spirit, the Father reproduces the image of his Son in all those who receive a participation in his sonship. This conformation to the Son is accomplished by an interior and progressive transformation (cf. 2 Cor 3:18) that will find its complete fulfillment in eternal life.

The theme of the "Son-Image" and that of the human being "in the image of God" are drawn together in patristic teaching, which presents the incarnation of the Word as the work of restoration of the human being to the image of the Son, and as the gift of knowledge of God: "The Word of God came in his own person, that, as he was the Image of the Father, he might be able to recreate man after the image."[30] We can recall this beautiful explanation of St. Thomas Aquinas with regard to the incarnation of the Son: "In as far as he is the Image, the Son has a kinship with that which he must restore, that is to say, with man who is created to the image of God (cf. Gen 1:27). This is why it is fitting that the Image assumes the image, that is to say, that the uncreated Image assumes the created image."[31] Signifying the personal being of the Son in his eternal relation to the Father, the name *Image* is thus expressive of the whole creative and re-creative work of the Son.

The study of the names *Son, Word,* and *Image* manifests the divine being of the Son and his mode of existence, which is completely relative to the Father. This same study enables one to describe the act of the Son in light of what he is: Son, Word, and Image of the Father. It is in considering the Son in his personal divine being that one discovers the foundations of his work for the world and for us. The creative, revelatory, and salvific action of the Son is grounded in his divinity, in his personal relation to the Father, and in his eternal relation to the Holy Spirit.

30. St. Athanasius of Alexandria, *On the Incarnation of the Word* 3.13.7 (SC 199:312); English translation from http://www.ccel.org (with a slight modification).
31. St. Thomas Aquinas, *Commentary on the Sentences,* Bk. III, dist. 1, q. 2, a. 2.

THE HOLY SPIRIT, LOVE AND GIFT OF THE
FATHER AND THE SON

Faith in the Holy Spirit, rooted in the teaching of revelation, is connected to the gift of grace and of salvation. The knowledge of the Holy Spirit that the Church expresses in the liturgy and in the creed is first. It precedes all theological reflection. The active presence of the Holy Spirit is fundamental to the Christian life. It is in the Holy Spirit that, through the Son, humans have access to the Father. The Holy Spirit reveals to us the Father and the Son, and in doing so, he also reveals himself. He "comes to us as the Spirit of the Father and of the Son, revealing the Father in the Son and the Son in the Father, and thus as himself God through whom God reveals himself."[32] The personality of the Holy Spirit remains mysterious. Moreover, for the Father and the Son we have names that, in our human experience, designate persons ("father," "son"); we can approach their meaning by means of analogies that evoke fundamental personal relations (paternity, begetting, birth, sonship). The same does not hold for the Holy Spirit: in created things, the name "spirit" or "breath" does not signify a person. In order to try to clarify faith in the Holy Spirit, we should therefore specially direct our attention to the action of the Holy Spirit, to his community of action and presence with the Father and the Son, as well as to the relations that the Holy Spirit has with the Father and the Son.[33]

The Procession of the Holy Spirit

In the history of doctrines, the dogmatic teaching on the property of the Holy Spirit came in the wake of the teaching on the Son. Catholic doctrine on the Holy Spirit benefitted from previous precisions regarding the generation of the Son. The essential approach of the Fathers of the fourth century was to clarify two fundamental aspects:

32. Thomas F. Torrance, *The Trinitarian Faith: The Evangelical Theology of the Ancient Catholic Church* (Edinburgh: T. and T. Clark, 1995), 203.
33. See above in chapter 2: "The Gift of the Holy Spirit."

the divinity of the Holy Spirit and his personal existence as a hypostasis in the Trinity. The second element raises a difficult but necessary
question: what is the personal "property" that distinguishes the Holy
Spirit from the Father and from the Son? From the historical perspective, this question comes from the necessity of defending faith in the
Holy Spirit in the face of heterodox currents that did not acknowledge the true divinity of the Holy Spirit and his existence as a person
equal to the Father and to the Son. How can the Holy Spirit be God,
since he is not the Father and is not begotten? From the contemplative side, this question comes from the quest for a deeper understanding of the faith and of the ecclesial experience of salvation.

One of the first responses was furnished by St. Basil of Caesarea.
St. Basil suggests that the property of the Spirit who is "breathed"
(and not begotten) can be disclosed in holiness or in the power
of sanctification;[34] that is to say, in radiant sanctity. In the wake of
St. Basil, St. Gregory of Nazianzus will affirm vigorously that the
property of the Holy Spirit is procession (*ekporeusis*). The Greek
word "*ekporeusis*," which we render in English by "procession," corresponds to the verb employed in John 15:26 ("The Spirit of truth, who
proceeds [*ekporeuetai*] from the Father"). However, since in the vocabulary of the Latin Catholic Church the word "procession" is applied both to the generation of the Son and to the origin of the Holy
Spirit (both the Son and the Holy Spirit "proceed" from the Father), it could be preferable, in order to avoid confusion, to keep the
Greek term *ekporeusis* for signifying the proper and distinct origin

34. St. Basil the Great, *Letter* 214: "Thus, the meaning of substance (*ousia*) is common (*koinon*), as in 'goodness' or 'divinity' or anything else that may be conceived, but
the hypostasis is perceived in the peculiar property (*idioma*) of paternity or sonship
or sanctifying power"; in St. Basil, *Letters* 2 (186–368), trans. Sister Agnes Clare Way
(Washington, D.C.: The Catholic University of America Press, 1969), 102. St. Basil holds
firmly the unity of power and action of the three divine hypostases: "Equally the Father
and the Son and the Holy Spirit sanctify and vivify and enlighten and console and do all
things. And let no one especially assign the sanctifying power to the action of the Spirit,
after he has heard the Savior in the Gospel saying to His Father concerning the disciples, *Father, sanctify them in thy name*" (*Letter* 189, 31–32). All operations are equally per-
formed by the Father and by the Son and by the Holy Spirit.

of the Holy Spirit. Nevertheless, we will keep the word "procession," with the added precision that the term is used in the special sense in which it exclusively designates the origin of the Holy Spirit.[35]

Thus, St. Gregory of Nazianzus explains: "The Holy Spirit is truly the Spirit coming forth from the Father, not by filiation, because it is not by generation, but by procession (*ekporeutos*)."[36] This procession accounts for the personal existence of the Holy Spirit. "*The Holy Spirit who proceeds from the Father.* Insofar as he proceeds from the Father, he is no creature; inasmuch as he is not begotten, he is no Son; and to the extent that procession is the mean between ingeneracy and generacy, he is God."[37] The affirmation of the origin of the Holy Spirit by procession underscores also the ineffable and mysterious character of the provenance of the Holy Spirit: "What, then, is 'proceeding' (*ekporeusis*)? You explain the ingeneracy of the Father and I will give you a biological account of the Son's begetting and the Spirit's proceeding—and let us go mad the pair of us for prying into God's secrets."[38]

Like the Greek tradition, the Latin tradition insists upon the incomprehensible character of the origin of the Holy Spirit. In fully preserving the sense of mystery, St. Augustine sought to show believers something of how one can perceive, in faith, the distinct procession of the Holy Spirit. In his *De Trinitate*, St. Augustine recalls that we must not confuse the procession of the Holy Spirit with the generation of the Son: *the Holy Spirit is not begotten.*[39] How can this

35. It is thus that the Catholic theologians of the Latin Middle Ages understood it. They distinguished, first, a common usage of the word "*processio*" for designating the origin of the Son and that of the Spirit, and, second, a special usage that is applied exclusively to the origin of the Holy Spirit; see for example, St. Thomas Aquinas, *Summa theologiae* I, q. 28, a. 4; q. 32, a. 3; q. 37, a. 1.

36. St. Gregory of Nazianzus, *Oration* 39.12 (*SC* 358:174).

37. St. Gregory of Nazianzus, *Oration* 31.8 (*SC* 250: 290) in St. Gregory of Nazianzus, *On God and Christ: The Five Theological Orations and Two Letters to Cledonius,* translated by Frederick Williams and Lionel Wickham (Crestwood, New York: St. Vladimir's Seminary Press, 2002), 122.

38. Ibid.

39. St. Augustine, *On the Trinity* 1.5.8; 2.3.5; 5.14.15. The question is reprised with greater amplitude in Book 15 (15.25.45; 15.26.47; 15.27.48; 15.27.50).

be manifested to the believing mind? When one affirms that the Holy Spirit "proceeds" in a way that is really distinguished from the generation of the Son, one expresses the true faith, but this remains profoundly obscure. How can we show the distinction between the "procession" of the Holy Spirit and the generation of the Son, which is likewise immaterial and divine? This question, explains St. Augustine, is "extremely difficult."[40]

In order to try to respond—in a manner that he himself judged greatly insufficient (since the mystery is so great!)—St. Augustine considered the "likeness" offered by love and the will in our human mind. Our mind "conceives" a word.[41] This permits one to show believers something of the "generation" of the Word, the Son, who is "conceived by the Father," "born from the Father." Now love, which is related to the will, is not begotten.[42] The characteristic of the will and of love is not to be produced like an "offspring" from a "parent," but rather is *to unite* the begetter and the begotten.[43] The Holy Spirit is not begotten, but proceeds in the manner of love. The likeness of love—however limited this likeness may be—thus enables one to show that the procession of the Holy Spirit is not confused with the generation of the Son. Without such a likeness, one could indeed affirm that the procession of the Holy Spirit is really distinguished from the generation of the Son, but one would hardly have manifested to our understanding the meaning of this affirmation. St. Augustine specifies: to manifest "somewhat," to enable to glimpse "imperfectly," to show "as much as the weakness of our mind permits," because the generation of the divine Word and the procession of the Holy Spirit infinitely go beyond what we can understand (the likeness found in

40. St. Augustine, *On the Trinity* 15.27.48: "difficillimum."

41. According to St. Augustine, the "conception of the word," when we love temporal and material things, is different from the "birth of the word." "But the *conceived* word and the *born* word are the same thing when the will rests in the act itself of knowing, which happens in the love of spiritual things"; *On the Trinity* 9.9.14; trans. Edmund Hill, O.P. (Brooklyn: New City Press, 1991), 278.

42. St. Augustine, *On the Trinity* 9.12.17–18.

43. St. Augustine, *On the Trinity* 14.6.8; 14.7.10; 14.10.13; 15.27.50; see also 11.7.12; 11.8.15–11.9.16; 11.11.18.

the human mind cannot offer a comprehensive explanation of Trinitarian persons). This teaching is animated by the quest for happiness. In seeking understanding of faith, the believing mind discovers a foretaste of the joy that he or she hopes to receive in the vision of the Trinity in the heavenly Church.

This doctrinal deepening with respect to the Holy Spirit merits some attention. It is necessary at least to note the four following aspects. First, it is faith alone, founded on the revelation transmitted by the apostles, that teaches the personal existence of the Holy Spirit and the action that he exercises with the Father and the Son. In this domain, human reason can demonstrate nothing. Second, the recourse to the likeness of the word and of love in the human mind (the doctrine of the image of God) seeks to make manifest the teaching of holy Scripture, starting from what God himself has done. The God who inspires holy Scripture is also the God who created the world and human beings, in such a way that attentive observation of the world can help us to understand better the meaning of Scripture, to know better God the Trinity and to love him more.[44] Third, if the mystery of God the Trinity can be "manifested" by the image of God in the human mind (likeness of the word and of love), this is because God himself casts his own light on his image. Put otherwise, it is by catching the light that comes from God's action that the human mind becomes to some extent luminous by reflection. Fourth, the doctrine that makes manifest the Trinitarian faith by means of the likeness of the word and of love is not a stranger to the economy of salvation, as at times some have wrongly charged. This approach to understanding the faith is directly connected to the teaching of revelation concerning the salvific action of the Holy Spirit: "God's love has been poured into our hearts

---

44. St. Augustine, *On the Trinity* II, Prologue: "I will not be idle in seeking out the substance of God, either through his scriptures or his creatures (*siue per scripturam eius siue per creaturam*). For both these are offered us for our observation and scrutiny in order that in them he may be sought, he may be loved, who inspired the one and created the other"; Saint Augustine, *The Trinity*, trans. Edmund Hill, O.P. (Brooklyn, New York: New City Press, 1991), 97; see also *On the Trinity* 15.20.39 (trans. Edmund Hill, 426).

through the Holy Spirit who has been given to us" (Rom 5:5). The Holy Spirit manifests himself in the communion of love that is poured out when he dwells in the heart of believers. Through what he does, the Holy Spirit reveals who he is: the radiance of the divine communion, the Love of the Father and the Son, the Charity that is God's greatest gift.

Since there is nothing greater than charity among God's gifts, and since there is no greater gift of God's than the Holy Spirit, what must we conclude but that he is this charity, which is called both God and from God? And if the charity by which the Father loves the Son and the Son loves the Father ineffably shows forth the communion of them both, what is more suitable than that he who is the common Spirit of them both should be distinctively called *charity*? This, surely, is the sounder way for us to believe and understand the matter: that the Holy Spirit is not alone charity in that Trinity, but that there is a good reason for properly calling him *charity*.[45]

During the centuries, Catholic theology has worked to deepen the heritage of St. Augustine by associating him with the approach of other Fathers of the Church, Greek and Latin. In what follows, we illustrate this deepening of the Augustinian heritage (the Holy Spirit is the Love and the Gift of the Father and the Son) in St. Thomas Aquinas. However, before entering into this teaching, it is necessary to consider the doctrine of Catholic faith concerning the origin of the Holy Spirit: he proceeds from the Father and the Son.

The Holy Spirit Proceeds from the Father and the Son

The Catholic Church professes that "the Holy Spirit proceeds from the Father as the first principle and, by the eternal gift of this to the Son, from the communion of both the Father and the Son."[46] The Latin tradition of the creed confesses that the Spirit "proceeds from the Father and the Son." This teaching poses a doctrinal difficulty in

---

45. St. Augustine, *On the Trinity* 15.19.37 (trans. Edmund Hill, 424, slightly modified).
46. *Catechism of the Catholic Church*, no. 264; the English formula "first principle" is a translation of the Latin adverb "principaliter."

the dialogue with the Orthodox Churches. At times, due to the ecumenical debate, this teaching also raises a feeling of reserve among the Catholic faithful themselves. This is why, without judging in advance the deepening that the expression of Catholic dogma can still receive, it is important to understand the traditional teaching of the Catholic Church. It is necessary first of all to distinguish carefully two things: (1) the addition of the Latin phrase Filioque ("and the Son") in the Creed of Constantinople by the Catholic Church; (2) the doctrine of faith, which constitutes the more profound and more important aspect.

Concerning the first point, it seems that it was first in Spain and in Gaul, at the turning point between antiquity and the Middle Ages, that the procession of the Holy Spirit "from the Father *and the Son*" was introduced into some confessions of faith. The occasion was quite probably the necessity of affirming the faith in the divinity of the Son and the Holy Spirit in the face of heterodox Western currents that did not recognize the full divinity of the Son. To affirm that the Holy Spirit proceeds from the Father *and the Son* was to profess the consubstantial unity of the Father and the Son, and therefore to affirm the true divinity of the Son, as well as the true divinity of the Holy Spirit. The Third Council of Toledo, in A.D. 589, illustrates this teaching: "We should confess and preach that the Holy Spirit proceeds from the Father and the Son, and that with the Father and the Son he is one single substance."[47] The symbol of faith *Quicumque,* which comes probably from southern Gaul toward the end of the fifth century, offers another example: "The Father has neither been made by anyone, nor is he created or begotten (*a nullo*); the Son is from the Father alone (*a Patre solo est*), not made nor created but begotten; the Holy Spirit is from the Father and the Son (*a Patre et Filio*), not made nor created nor begotten, but proceeding."[48]

The use of the phrase "and the Son" enters little by little into the

---

47. Denzinger, *Enchiridion symbolorum,* no. 470.
48. Ibid., no. 75.

Western liturgy, between the eighth and the eleventh centuries.[49] The theologians of Charlemagne's court contributed to promoting it. It is at the beginning of the eleventh century, under Pope Benedict VIII, that the *Filioque* was introduced into the Creed of the Mass at Rome. Orthodox Christians often resent this addition of the *Filioque* by the Catholic Church as an act that morally wounded ecumenical unity. In 1439, the Council of Florence explains: "We define . . . that the explanation of those words 'from the Son' (*Filioque*) was licitly and reasonably added to the creed for the sake of declaring the truth and because of urgent necessity at the time."[50]

The *doctrine* of the procession of the Holy Spirit from the Father and the Son is more important than the *Filioque* addition in the Latin text of the creed (it is not added in the Greek text of the Niceno-Constantinopolitan symbol, even in its liturgical use by Catholics). This doctrine is well rooted in an ancient tradition. It is found, in various forms (the interpretation of texts is at times debated), in many Fathers of the Church, notably St. Hilary of Poitiers and St. Ambrose of Milan. Pope St. Leo the Great professed it. For many centuries, the Orthodox Churches did not find in the Catholic doctrine a reason for rupture with the Catholic Church, as for instance St. Maximus the Confessor witnesses in the seventh century— although St. Maximus held clearly that the Father is the sole "Cause" of the Son and of the Holy Spirit. This fact calls us to relativize somewhat the role of the *Filioque* in the rupture between the Orthodox Churches and the Catholic Church. Nonetheless, from the ninth century onward, the question of the procession of the Holy Spirit occupies an important place in the dispute between the Catholic Church and the Orthodox Churches. The difficulty remains in ecumenical dialogue today. We emphasize, however, that the difference

49. See Yves Congar, *I Believe in the Holy Spirit*, vol. 3, *The River of the Water of Life Flows in the East and in the West*, trans. David Smith (New York: Seabury Press, 1983), 53–54; see also the *Catechism of the Catholic Church*, no. 247.

50. *Decrees of the Ecumenical Councils* 1: 527; cf. Denzinger, *Enchiridion symbolorum*, no. 1302.

in *expressions* of faith in the Holy Spirit does not prevent unity of *faith* in the Holy Spirit. When doctrinal expressions do not become "rigid," they do not affect "the identity of faith in the reality of the same mystery confessed."[51] The Catholic Church and the Orthodox Churches share the same faith in the Holy Spirit, although they express this faith from different perspectives, and with a different vocabulary. We will come back to this later. On the Catholic side, St. Thomas observed: "If we take careful note of the statements of the Greeks we shall find that they differ from us more in words than in meaning."[52]

One can observe *two principal foundations* of the Catholic doctrine. These foundations concern the revelation and witness of holy Scripture. The first foundation consists in the correspondence between, on the one hand, the action of God the Trinity in the economy, and, on the other hand, the eternal being of God the Trinity. We have noted above, in chapter 2 (in our survey of the teaching of St. John and of the Acts of the Apostles), that the Holy Spirit is *sent* and *given* to the Church *by the Father and by the Son*. Similarly, Scripture teaches that the Spirit of the Father is also the Spirit of the Son: he is the "Spirit of Jesus" (Acts 16:7), the "Spirit of Christ" (Rom 8:9), the "Spirit of his Son" (Gal 4:6), the Spirit who "receives what is the Son's" (cf. Jn 16:14–15). Now the mission of the Holy Spirit manifests his personal being: the sending of the Holy Spirit makes known his eternal procession. Put otherwise, the economy, in which the Holy Spirit is poured out by the Father and the Son, is the *expression* of what the Holy Spirit is from all eternity. Just as the Holy Spirit proceeds from the Father and the Son in eternity, he comes forth from the Father and the Son in the economy. The economy of divine persons in time is conformed to the eternal order of origin of these persons. To be precise: Catholic doctrine does not conceive the eternal procession of the Holy Spirit by a "projec-

---

51. *Catechism of the Catholic Church*, no. 248.
52. St. Thomas Aquinas, *De potentia*, q. 10, a. 5: "*a nobis magis differunt in verbis quam in sensu.*"

tion" of the economy into the inner life of the Trinity, but rather it holds that the mission reflects the origin. Just as the Son who is begotten by the Father is sent by the Father, so also the Holy Spirit who proceeds from the Father and the Son is sent by the Father and the Son. This first foundation is clearly set forth by the *Catechism of the Catholic Church:* "The eternal origin of the Holy Spirit is revealed in his mission in time."[53]

The second foundation is directly connected to the first: it has to do with the divine unity of the Father, Son, and Holy Spirit. In professing that the Holy Spirit proceeds from the Father and the Son, the Catholic Church expresses the *consubstantiality* of the Father, Son, and Holy Spirit, in the distinction of persons. We have noted above that the phrase "and the Son" highlights the full divinity of the Son: it emphasizes the consubstantial communion of the Son with the Father, and it also underscores the true divinity of the Holy Spirit, because he proceeds from the Father and the Son. The Catholic tradition shows a direct affinity between the affirmation of the substantial unity of the three persons ("one single substance") and the recognition of the procession of the Holy Spirit from the Father and the Son.

These two foundations are rooted in the Word of God. The Word of God, interpreted by the Church, is directly homogeneous to the faith, and it is this Word that grounds the conviction of the Catholic Church. On the basis of these two foundations, Trinitarian faith is expressed in terms of *substance* and of *relations.* The distinction of divine persons concerns their relations (as we saw in chapter 4). The following passage from the *Catechism of the Catholic Church* sums up the traditional teaching.

The divine persons are relative to one another. Because it does not divide the divine unity, the real distinction of the persons from one another resides solely in the relationships which relate them to one another: "In the

---

53. *Catechism of the Catholic Church,* no. 244; the *Catechism* continues: "The Spirit is sent to the apostles and to the Church both by the Father in the name of the Son, and by the Son in person, once he had returned to the Father (cf. Jn 14:26; 15;26; 16:14)."

relational names of the persons the Father is related to the Son, the Son to the Father, and the Holy Spirit to both. While they are called three persons in view of their relations, we believe in one nature or substance" (Council of Toledo XI, in A.D. 675). Indeed "everything (in them) is one where there is no opposition of relationship" (Council of Florence, in A.D. 1442).[54]

The last phrase merits particular attention: in God the Trinity, all is one where there is no opposition of relations. This phrase was promoted by St. Anselm of Canterbury at the turn of the eleventh and twelfth centuries, but we have seen in the preceding chapter that it possesses a solid patristic grounding. Put otherwise, the Trinitarian plurality is characterized by an order, and it is this order that one expresses in affirming that the Son is begotten by the Father, and that the Holy Spirit proceeds from the Father and the Son.

The two foundations that we have presented have an immediate relationship with the ecclesial experience of salvation and of divinization: the Spirit conforms his beneficiaries to the Son; he procures for them adoptive sonship to the image of the Son; he sanctifies them by associating them with the mystery of the passion and resurrection of the incarnate Son, through whom humans have access to the Father. In his action as in his being, the Holy Spirit is relative to the Father and to the Son.

In order to understand well the traditional teaching of the Catholic Church, it is necessary to bring forward three additional, yet important, precisions. First, the Father and the Son are *one single principle* of the Holy Spirit. Catholic doctrine denies that there are two different principles of the Holy Spirit (this would divide the Holy Spirit). There is not a "double procession" of the Holy Spirit, but there is *a single procession,* by a *single act* of the Father and the Son. The Father and the Son, as St. Augustine already explained, are "one principle relatively to the Holy Spirit."[55] This also belongs to

---

54. *Catechism of the Catholic Church,* no. 255.

55. St. Augustine, *On the Trinity* 5.14.15: "Pater et Filius . . . relatiue ad Spiritum Sanctum unum principium"; Sanctus Aurelius Augustinus, *De Trinitate libri XV,* ed. W. J. Mountain, vol. 1, *Libri I–XII* (Turnhout: Brepols, 1968), 223.

the solemn teaching of the Catholic Church: "We profess faithfully and devotedly that the Holy Spirit proceeds eternally from the Father and the Son, not as from two principles, but as from one principle; not by two spirations, but by one single spiration."[56] It is in their unity that the Father and the Son spirate the Holy Spirit. This unity is not only the essential oneness of the Father and the Son but, more precisely, it concerns their personal union ("notional," in the sense of a trait common to the Father and the Son) as *spirative principle.* The principle of the Holy Spirit, for Catholic doctrine, is the Father and the Son in their communion.

The second precision is no less important: it is from the Father that the Son has the power to spirate the Holy Spirit. This also belongs to the doctrine of Catholic faith. "And since the Father gave to his only-begotten Son in begetting him everything the Father has, except to be the Father, so the Son has eternally from the Father, by whom he was eternally begotten, this also, namely that the Holy Spirit proceeds from the Son."[57] This precision is important for correctly understanding the Catholic teaching. In begetting his Son, the Father gives him to be, with the Father, the principle of the Holy Spirit. This affirmation emphasizes that the Father is the *Source* of the whole divinity, the "principle without principle," because it is from the Father that the Son is begotten, it is from the Father that the Holy Spirit proceeds, and it is from the Father that the Son is (with the Father) the principle of the Holy Spirit. In this sense, St. Augustine explained that the Holy Spirit proceeds "principally (*principaliter*) from the Father," because the Father begot the Son "as that the Common Gift would proceed from the Son too, and

56. Second Council of Lyons, in 1274, *Decrees of the Ecumenical Councils* 1:314; see also Denzinger, *Enchiridion symbolorum,* no. 850. The affirmation was reprised at the Council of Florence, in 1439: "The Holy Spirit proceeds from both (the Father and the Son) eternally as from one principle and by one single spiration"; *Decrees of the Ecumenical Councils* 1:526; see also Denzinger, *Enchiridion symbolorum,* no. 1300.

57. Council of Florence, *Decrees of the Ecumenical Councils,* 1: 527; see also Denzinger, *Enchiridion symbolorum,* no. 1301. This teaching is reprised in the *Catechism of the Catholic Church,* no. 246.

the Holy Spirit would be the Spirit of them both."[58] And St. Thomas Aquinas explained that the Father alone is the "Author" (*auctor*), since "Author" means the principle without principle.[59] "The Holy Spirit is said to be *principally* from the Father because the *authority of spiration* is in the Father (*in Patre est auctoritas spirationis*), from whom the Son has spirative power."[60] The Son *himself* spirates and sends the Holy Spirit, although he does this not from himself, but *from the Father,* since everything the Son does, he has from the Father. The Catholic doctrine therefore affirms clearly that the Father is the Source of the Deity, the "principle without principle" of the Trinity (this is what the adverb "principally" emphasizes),[61] but this does not deny that the Son receives from the Father his being the principle of the Holy Spirit along with the Father. This "principal" place of the Father is also expressed by the phrase "the Holy Spirit proceeds from the Father *through the Son.*" This phrase is already attested in Tertullian, at the beginning of the third century: "The Spirit proceeds from no other than from the Father through the Son (*a Patre per Filium*)."[62]

In affirming that the Holy Spirit proceeds from the Father "*and the Son,*" one emphasizes the unity of the Father and the Son as one "spirative principle" of the Holy Spirit. In holding that the Holy Spirit proceeds from the Father "*through the Son,*" one emphasizes the personal distinction of the Father and the Son, that is to say, the fact that the Father is the principle of the Son and the only "principle without principle" in the Trinity: the Holy Spirit takes his ori-

58. St. Augustine, *On the Trinity* 15.17.29 (trans. Edmund Hill, 419, slightly adapted); "The Holy Spirit also proceeds from the Son. But this too was given the Son by the Father, not given to him when he already existed and did not yet have it; but whatever the Father gave to his only-begotten Word he gave by begetting him" (ibid.).

59. St. Thomas Aquinas, *Commentary on the Sentences,* Bk. I, dist. 29, q. 1, a. 1.

60. St. Thomas Aquinas, *Commentary on the Sentences,* Bk. I, dist. 12, q. 1, a. 2, ad 3.

61. "The Father alone is the principle without principle (*arche anarchos*) of the two other persons of the Trinity, the sole source (*pege*) of the Son and of the Holy Spirit"; Pontifical Council for Promoting Christian Unity, *Clarification* on "The Greek and Latin Traditions Regarding the Procession of the Holy Spirit," in *L'Osservatore Romano,* September 20, 1995, weekly edition in English.

62. Tertullian, *Against Praxeas* 4.1 (CCSL 2:1162).

gin from the Father in a principal manner. It is necessary to hold together these two formulations in order to have a full expression of the Catholic teaching. This also implies that the generation of the Son and the procession of the Holy Spirit are intrinsically connected. The Holy Spirit is present in the very act of the generation of the Son, not that he begets the Son, but because he proceeds from the Son insofar as the Son is begotten by the Father. In begetting his Son, the Father gives him the power to spirate with him the Holy Spirit: this belongs to the generation of the Son as such. The procession of the Holy Spirit is therefore connected, in itself, to the generation of the Son. The teaching on the generation of the Son requires that one consider, simultaneously, the procession of the Holy Spirit.[63]

It is necessary to make one last fundamental precision. The generation of the Son and the procession of the Holy Spirit are absolutely "simultaneous," in the simultaneity that is the very eternity of God and that excludes all succession. One does not happen before the other. There is not *first* a relation between the Father and Son, and *then* their relation to the Holy Spirit. Thomas Aquinas explains: "In the divine reality, the begetting of the Son has *no priority at all* over the procession (of the Holy Spirit)."[64] "As the begetting of the Son is co-eternal with the begetter, in such a way that the Father does not exist before begetting the Son, so the procession of the Holy Spirit is co-eternal with its principle (the Father and the Son). Hence, the Son was not begotten before the Spirit proceeded, but the begetting of the Son and the procession of the Holy Spirit are co-eternal."[65] Catholic doctrine affirms a pure relation of origin of the Holy Spirit to the Son, without any dependence or posteriority,

63. This aspect has already been emphasized above in the exposition of the paternity of the Father.

64. St. Thomas Aquinas, *Commentary on the Sentences*, Bk. I, dist. 12, q. 1, a. 1 (emphasis mine); if there is a "priority," this is only in our "mode of knowing," "by reason of likenesses that one finds in creatures and which are deficient for representing generation and procession such as they are in God."

65. St. Thomas Aquinas, *Summa theologiae* I, q. 36, a. 3, ad 3.

that is to say, a pure *order of origin*. The procession of the Holy Spirit is not subordinate to paternity or filiation: the Father is no less related to the Holy Spirit than he is to the Son. One can express it thus: *in begetting his Son, the Father spirates with him the Holy Spirit*. This point is capital. Catholic doctrine does not entail any minimization of the Holy Spirit, either on the doctrinal level or, correlatively, on the level of ecclesial and spiritual experience.[66]

Between the Latin and the Eastern traditions, there is a *difference of perspective* on the same mystery. "At the outset the Eastern tradition expresses the Father's character as first origin of the Spirit. . . . The Western tradition expresses first the consubstantial communion between Father and Son, by saying that the Spirit proceeds from the Father and the Son."[67] For its part, the Eastern tradition expresses the relationship of the Holy Spirit to the Son with the formula "through the Son" (the Holy Spirit takes his origin from the Father through the Son). And the Latin tradition recognizes that the Father alone is the "principle without principle," the "first origin" of the Holy Spirit (the Father is the ultimate "Source" of the Holy Spirit).[68]

There is also a *difference of vocabulary*. In the Eastern tradition, the Greek word "*ekporeusis*" characterizes the Spirit's relationship of origin from the Father alone as "principle without principle." But in the Western Catholic tradition, the Latin word "*processio*" is used to signify the origin of the Holy Spirit from the Father and the Son. These two words are not used with exactly the same meaning.[69]

---

66. See the nuanced observations of Yves Congar, *I Believe in the Holy Spirit*, vol. 3, *The River of the Water of Life Flows in the East and in the West*, trans. David Smith (New York: Seabury Press, 1983), 208–12; see also Congar, *La Parole et le Souffle* (Paris: Cerf, 1983), 179–87.

67. *Catechism of the Catholic Church*, no. 248.

68. Ibid.

69. Perhaps we could add that the *use* of the word "principle" also offers such a difference. What the Orthodox tradition means by "principle" (when it says that the Father alone is the principle of the Holy Spirit) corresponds to what the Latin tradition refers to in speaking of the "principle without principle" (or the "first origin," following the *Catechism of the Catholic Church*, no. 248).

One can consider that the principal divergence between the Catholic Church and the Orthodox Churches consists in the way of conceiving (and of expressing) the manner in which the Father is the Source of the Trinity. For the Orthodox, the "monarchy" of the Father excludes the position that the Holy Spirit also proceeds from the Son. For the Catholic Church, the recognition of the Father as "the source and origin of the whole divinity"[70] does not exclude the position that the Holy Spirit proceeds from the Father *and the Son,* but rather it *includes* this position by affirming an order of origin between the Son and the Holy Spirit. "The eternal order of the divine persons in their consubstantial communion implies that the Father, as 'the principle without principle,' is the first origin of the Spirit, but also that as Father of the only Son, he is, with the Son, the single principle from which the Holy Spirit proceeds."[71] This is what St. Augustine meant by affirming that the Holy Spirit proceeds "principally" from the Father: the Father is the sole "principle without principle" in the Trinity. From the Catholic side, ecumenical study especially requires showing in a more developed way that the procession of the Holy Spirit "from the Father and the Son" does not contradict the recognition of the Father as the "principle without principle" or the "Source" of the whole divinity.[72]

The Love and Gift of the Father and the Son

The personal property of the Holy Spirit is procession. By "procession," according to the teaching that we are setting forth here, we understand the relation of origin that the Holy Spirit has with the Father and the Son, the Father being the principle without principle. The Holy Spirit exists in a proper mode that is relative to the Father and to the Son, from whom he receives himself. This does not imply any "passivity" in the Holy Spirit, any more than generation

70. *Catechism of the Catholic Church,* no. 245.
71. *Catechism of the Catholic Church,* no. 248.
72. See the *Clarification* issued in 1995 by the Pontifical Council for Promoting Christian Unity, "The Greek and Latin Traditions Regarding the Procession of the Holy Spirit," in *L'Osservatore Romano,* September 20, 1995, weekly edition in English.

implies "passivity" in the Son who is begotten. To proceed is an act.

When we consider the generation of the Son and the procession of the Holy Spirit, it is necessary to avoid any idea of passivity. Our thinking must pass through an important work of purification when we apply it to the mystery of the holy Trinity. It is by one operation that the Father begets and that the Son is born from all eternity, but this one operation is in the Father and in the Son under *distinct relations:* paternity and filiation.[73] Therefore the Father's act of begetting the Son implies no passivity in the Son: "Action, insofar as it implies origin of motion, involves passion; but that is not the way we affirm action of the divine persons."[74] Similarly, it is by one operation that the Father and the Son "breathe" ("spirate") the Holy Spirit and that the Holy Spirit proceeds; but this operation is in the Father and the Son, and in the Holy Spirit, under *distinct relations.* In the Father and the Son, this action possesses the relative mode of "spiration," while in the Holy Spirit, this action possesses the relative mode of "procession." This "procession" is the relative property that distinguishes and constitutes the person of the Holy Spirit. Our vocabulary is limited. This is why, for lack of another term, we employ the word "procession" for designating the eternal *coming forth* of the Holy Spirit, and we employ this same word for designating his personal *relation* (his relative *property*). Lastly, the deepening of the notion of relation by St. Thomas Aquinas (particularly the doctrine of "subsisting relation") enables one to recognize that the person of the Holy Spirit is identified with his relation of procession. "The procession is the person of the Holy Spirit proceeding."[75]

73. St. Thomas Aquinas, *Commentary on the Sentences,* Bk. I, dist. 20, q. 1, a. 1, ad 1: "Generation signifies relation by way of an operation. . . . And although 'to beget' does not belong to the Son, this does not mean that there would be some operation belonging to the Father and not to the Son. Rather, it is by one and the same operation that the Father begets and the Son is born, but this operation is in the Father and in the Son according to two distinct relations."

74. St. Thomas Aquinas, *Summa theologiae* I, q. 41, a. 1, ad 3: "The only 'passive' that we posit among the divine persons is grammatical, according to our mode of signifying; i.e., we speak of the Father begetting and of the Son *being begotten.*"

75. St. Thomas Aquinas, *Summa theologiae* I, q. 30, a. 2, ad 1.

The procession of the Holy Spirit is the procession of *Love* in person. When saying this, we must take care not to confuse the person of the Holy Spirit with the essential act of loving that is common to the three divine persons. The Father, Son, and Holy Spirit are Love by essence, in the same degree to which they are God. St. Augustine was well aware of this difficulty. On the one hand, the "substance" of God is Love, and this substance is one and the same in the Father, Son, and Holy Spirit. On the other hand, "the Holy Spirit is properly called Charity."[76] Put otherwise, when one designates the Holy Spirit as Charity or Love in person in the Trinity, one seeks to signify the "property" of the Holy Spirit without confusing it with the Love that is an attribute common to the three persons. Thus, in order to make manifest that the Holy Spirit is *Love in person*, it would be necessary to show that this "Love" proceeds and that it is characterized by a relation of origin, that is to say that it possesses a relative mode of being conformed to its procession. And it would be necessary to establish that this accounts for the action of the Holy Spirit attested by holy Scripture.

Concerning the first point, we have no other way than to look for a "likeness" drawn from our experience, that is to say, a reality arising from what is proportionate to our understanding, in order to show by analogy, under the guidance of faith, how we can perceive that the Holy Spirit is Love in person. Without such a "likeness," one could affirm that the Holy Spirit proceeds as Love, but one could hardly make manifest to our understanding what this means. Concerning the Son, numerous Christian teachers (and not only St. Augustine) have found such a "likeness" in the word formed by our mind—that is, in the word that our mind conceives and expresses when it knows. Concerning the Holy Spirit, St. Thomas Aquinas proposes to consider the likeness offered by the impres-

76. St. Augustine, *On the Trinity* 15.17.28–29: "What is meant is that while in that supremely simple nature substance is not one thing and charity another, but substance is charity and charity is substance, whether in the Father or in the Son or in the Holy Spirit, yet all the same the Holy Spirit is distinctively named charity" (trans. Edmund Hill, 419).

sion or "imprint" of the beloved in the will of the one who loves. This teaching deserves attention.

When St. Thomas Aquinas teaches that the Holy Spirit proceeds as Love (the procession of the Spirit is the procession of Love), the "likeness" that he holds up to clarify somewhat this affirmation is not our act of loving as such. Rather, Aquinas observes that, when the human will loves, "an imprint, so to speak, of the reality loved" is produced in the affection of the lover, an imprint that "moves and pushes the will of the lover towards the beloved."[77] When we love someone, our beloved is "engraved" in our heart, like a weight of love that pulls us and draws us to our beloved. Thus, at the point of departure of the act of love, an "imprint" of the good that we love is engraved in our will. This imprint is a principle of impulsion toward the good loved; it pushes our will toward this good. The "affectionate impression of the beloved" in the will of the one who loves is the dynamic principle of the inclination of love. The "likeness" by means of which St. Thomas proposes to perceive somewhat the property of the Holy Spirit, by analogy, is this "impression" or "imprint of the beloved" in the will of the one who loves, an imprint that proceeds from the will in act and that remains in the will. And it is this affection or imprint of love that, by an accommodation of language (because we lack a more precise word), we designate *here* by the word "love": the love—the imprint of the beloved—that proceeds.

It is therefore by considering this "imprint of the beloved in the affection of the lover" that, by analogy and by a kind of accommodation of language, St. Thomas Aquinas shows that the Holy Spirit is *Love* in person. The affectionate impression, which is the principle of the impulsion toward the beloved, enables us to make manifest a fecund act of spiration in God who loves himself. In our human will, this "imprint" of love possesses a relation of origin to the will from which it proceeds and in which it remains; and this rela-

77. St. Thomas Aquinas, *Summa theologiae* I, q. 36, a. 1; q. 37, a. 1; see also *Summa theologiae* I-II, q. 28, a. 2, corp. and ad 1.

tion is different from the relation of the word conceived by our understanding. In God the Trinity, Love is a reality infinitely superior to our human love, but one can recognize there, in a transcendent mode, the uncreated Model that our "impression of the beloved" reflects. Thus, with the aid of this "likeness," St. Thomas shows to believers that *Love proceeds,* and that the relation that characterizes this "Love that proceeds" *is distinguished from the relation that characterizes the Word.*[78]

It is therefore necessary to note with care that, in our language about God the Trinity, the word "Love" designates first the very being of God the Trinity,[79] that is to say, the whole Trinity. And, *according to the accommodation of language* that we have tried to explain with "the imprint of the beloved that emanates in the will of the one who loves," the name "Love" designates properly the very person of the Holy Spirit. "In his intimate life, God 'is love' (cf. 1 Jn 4:8 and 1 Jn 4:16), the essential love shared by the three divine Persons; personal love is the Holy Spirit as the Spirit of the Father and the Son."[80]

In order to understand this theological elaboration well, it is necessary to avoid all rationalistic approaches to the mystery of God. Rather, approaching this mystery theologically is a spiritual exercise. This exercise begins with faith and is accomplished in faith. It involves an attentive study of the human mind, because the human mind is made in the image of God and it reflects the light that comes to it from God. Under the guidance of faith, and insofar as our human intelligence is capable, the believer who seeks an "understanding of faith" thus renders an account of the property of the Holy Spirit. In an imperfect but enlightening manner, this exercise of believing intelligence shows the personal distinction of the Holy Spirit by relation to the Father and to the Son, while respecting the incomprehensibility of the mystery.

78. St. Thomas Aquinas, *Summa theologiae* I, q. 37, a. 1.

79. *Catechism of the Catholic Church,* no. 221.

80. John Paul II, *Lord and Giver of Life: Encyclical Letter Dominum et Vivificantem,* no. 10 (Washington, D.C.: Office of Publishing and Promotion Services, United States Catholic Conference of Bishops, 1986), 17–18.

On this basis, St. Thomas develops his teaching by considering the Augustinian theme of the Holy Spirit as *mutual Love* of the Father and the Son. This theme of mutual Love does not mean that the Holy Spirit is the cause by reason of which the Father loves the Son and vice versa. The Holy Spirit is not a principle with respect to the Father and the Son (this would break the order in the Trinity). To affirm that the Holy Spirit is the *mutual Love* of the Father and the Son, or to say that he is the *Bond of love* of the Father and the Son, means that the Holy Spirit is *the Love who proceeds from the Father and the Son*. The Father and the Son love each other in a common act of which the Holy Spirit is, so to say, the personal "fruit." The Father loves the Son and the Son loves the Father, in the single act that the Son receives from the Father.

These reflections are directly connected to the economy of creation and grace. Just as the Father creates and re-creates through his Word, he creates and saves by his Love. The Father fashions us and renews us through his Word and by his Love. St. Thomas Aquinas summarizes this in a rigorous and beautiful sentence: "The Father and the Son love each other and love us by the Holy Spirit or Love proceeding."[81] The Father and the Son love us by the *same Love* by which they love each other eternally. They love us in the radiance of their mutual Love.

These explanations offer a very suggestive way to understand the action of the Holy Spirit. Consider first the creation. The Father creates the world and human beings through the Son, in his Spirit who is Love. Now, Love is characterized by a force of impulsion that puts creatures in movement and that establishes them in a harmonious order. "God saw that it was good," as we read in the first chapter of Genesis. "When thou sendest forth thy Spirit, they are created; and thou renewest the face of the ground" (Ps 104:30). This permits us to grasp better the particular mode of action of the Holy Spirit in creation and in the exercise of divine providence: he is the Love

81. St. Thomas Aquinas, *Summa theologiae* I, q. 37, a. 2.

who perfects creatures in their being and in their action, the Love who gives life and who leads creatures to their fulfillment.

Theological meditation on the Holy Spirit as Love likewise offers a profound light for understanding his work of salvation. The Holy Spirit "has spoken through the prophets," we confess in the creed. God reveals his wisdom "through the Spirit" (1 Cor 2:10). Of course, it is by reason of friendship that one confides one's secrets to one's friends: it is through his Love that God reveals to us his mystery. The charisms that serve the mission of the Church and the gifts that sanctify the Church, particularly charity, the most excellent gift, are distributed by the Holy Spirit (1 Cor 12–13). "God's love has been poured into our hearts through the Holy Spirit who has been given to us" (Rom 5:5). By coming to dwell in hearts, the Holy Spirit procures charity. The Holy Spirit enables one to share in what he is: Charity itself. Those who have been enlightened by baptism, as the epistle to the Hebrews says, "have become partakers of the Holy Spirit" (Heb 6:4). The reception of charity and of the sanctifying gifts can be understood as a *conformation* to the person of the Holy Spirit, a participation in the Holy Spirit. The new life is procured by the Holy Spirit: "Come from the four winds, O breath, and breathe upon these slain, that they may live" (Ezek 37:9). "It is the spirit that gives life," says Jesus (Jn 6:63). By the vital impulsion that he communicates inasmuch as he is Love (and love involves a motive power of inclination toward the beloved), the Holy Spirit enables one to participate in the very life of God. This vital action of the Holy Spirit is emphasized by St. Paul in his teaching on adoptive sonship and the freedom of the children of God: "For all who are led by the Spirit of God are sons of God" (Rom 8:14). Faith living through love unites believers to Christ by the action of the Holy Spirit. The Spirit enables one to confess Christ the Lord in living faith (1 Cor 12:3); he makes one belong to Christ (Rom 8:9); he procures life for the disciples of Christ (Rom 8:11). The Holy Spirit is like "the soul" or "the heart of the Church."[82]

82. St. Thomas Aquinas, *Homilies on the Apostles' Creed,* art. 9 (no. 971): "The Catholic Church is one body and has different members. And the soul which vivifies this

In sum, the Holy Spirit confers the divine friendship and procures the very presence of God. "If a man loves me, he will keep my word, and my Father will love him, and we will come to him and make our home with him" (Jn 14:23). We can discern here the action par excellence of the Holy Spirit. The Holy Spirit enables one to love Jesus, and he thus procures the presence of Christ and of his Father. He causes humans to enter into the mystery of the Trinity who is communion, enabling humans to live for God and in God: "He who abides in love abides in God, and God abides in him" (1 Jn 4:16). The Spirit of Love makes God present to humans and he makes humans present to God.

Being Love, the Spirit is also "Gift" in person. On the one hand, all the spiritual gifts come from the Holy Spirit (cf. 1 Cor 12:4), in particular charity, which is the greatest gift (cf. 1 Cor 13:13) and which St. Paul describes as the first "fruit" of the Spirit with joy, peace, patience, kindness, goodness, faithfulness, gentleness, and self-control (Gal 5:22). Sins are forgiven by the gift of the Holy Spirit (cf. Acts 2:38), because pardon comes from charity: "Love covers a multitude of sins" (1 Pet 4:8). On the other hand, the Holy Spirit procures not only certain particular gifts, but he *himself is given* (Rom 5:5). The Spirit is, in person, the "Gift of God Most High," as the Church chants in the hymn *Veni Creator Spiritus*. The Holy Spirit is the Gift of the Father and of the Son in the same manner that he is the Love of the Father and of the Son. The first Gift of God is Love himself.

When one designates the Holy Spirit as *Gift,* one signifies that, because he is the Love of the Father and the Son, the Holy Spirit is eternally inclined to be given to angels and to humans in grace. He is the Gift poured out by the Father and the Son, because he is the Love proceeding from the Father and the Son. This is why the Father and the Son are themselves given *in the Holy Spirit.* By virtue of his personal property, which is to be the Love of the Father and

body is the Holy Spirit." For the image of the heart, see *Summa theologiae* III, q. 8, a. 1, ad 3.

Son, the Holy Spirit possesses, as it were, a special aptitude to be given in grace, because the first Gift that God pours out is his own Love. To receive the Holy Spirit in person only pertains to creatures made in the image of God, capable of knowing and loving God: angels and humans. Thus, the Holy Spirit is from all eternity *Gift,* and in the economy he is *given* to angels and to humans who welcome him and receive divinization from him.

In his encyclical *Divinum illud munus,* Pope Leo XIII summarized Catholic teaching on the Holy Spirit in the following manner. "We have said that the Holy Ghost gives Himself: 'the charity of God is poured out into our hearts by the Holy Ghost who is given to us' (Rom 5:5). For He not only brings to us His divine gifts, but is the Author of them and is Himself the supreme Gift, who, proceeding from the mutual love of the Father and the Son, is justly believed to be and is called 'Gift of God most High' (*altissimi donum Dei*)."[83]

Sanctifying grace, which elevates human nature so as to make it participate in the divine life, as well as the theological virtues, which elevate human actions so as to enable humans to be united to God in knowledge and love, are poured out by the Holy Spirit, and the Holy Spirit is given with them. When the Holy Spirit is given, charity is given. When charity is given, the Holy Spirit is also given. In any case, absolute priority belongs to the Holy Spirit who is the *uncreated Gift.* The created sanctifying gifts *are caused* by the uncreated Gift, and they *dispose* one to receive this uncreated Gift in person.

A special place belongs to the "seven gifts" of the Holy Spirit: wisdom, understanding, counsel, fortitude, knowledge, piety, and fear of the Lord. These gifts perfect the life of sanctity and enable humans to obey promptly the movements of the Holy Spirit and to follow "the instinct of the Holy Spirit."[84] Between the Holy Spirit and the human being, these gifts establish a coordination similar to

83. Pope Leo XIII, Encyclical *Divinum illud munus,* no. 9; English translation taken from http://www.vatican.va.

84. St. Thomas Aquinas, *Summa theologiae* I-II, q. 68.

the communion of wills in a friendship, a communion so direct that it becomes, so to say, connatural. The model par excellence of this communion is contemplated in Christ Jesus who led his earthly existence under the guidance of the Holy Spirit. "Those who are perfected by the seven gifts of the Holy Spirit, and united in faith in the Trinity, come to the Father."[85]

By focusing our attention on the procession of the Holy Spirit, on his personal property as Love and Gift of the Father and the Son, we have distinguished, on the one hand, the eternal existence of the Holy Spirit within the Trinity, and, on the other, the action of the Holy Spirit and his presence in the world. But we have also observed that the economy of the Holy Spirit reflects his very being. The eternal existence of the Holy Spirit is revealed to us by the mission of the Son and by the mission of the Holy Spirit himself. And it is by contemplating the Holy Spirit in his personal divine being that we discover the depth of his action in the world and in the Church. The Holy Spirit unites humans to the Son and he leads them to the Father, because he is the Spirit of the Father and the Son. The Holy Spirit procures life and he pours out charity because he is Love in person. The Holy Spirit is poured out in hearts because he is Gift. *The Father and the Son love each other and love us by one and the same Love, the Holy Spirit who proceeds and who introduces the Church into the Trinitarian communion.*

85. St. Thomas Aquinas, *Commentary on the Gospel of St. John* 21:11 (no. 2605).

6

Returning to the Creative and Saving Action of the Trinity

The preceding chapters have presented the doctrine of the Church on the divine persons and their properties, by explaining it with the help of St. Thomas Aquinas and other teachers. This study has undertaken to purify our understanding in order to elevate our gaze, in faith, to the mystery of God the Trinity. It is now necessary for us to return to the action of the Trinity in his work of creation, revelation, and salvation. The teaching concerning the properties of the divine persons offers a precious light for understanding more profoundly the action of these persons.

THEOLOGY AND ECONOMY

In this book, we have constantly moved from the "economy" to "theology." Recall that, by economy, we mean the action by which the Trinity reveals and communicates himself, particularly the incarnation of the Son and the sending of the Holy Spirit; by theology, we mean the life of the Trinity in itself in its eternal being. Trinitarian doctrine consists in two paths or complementary movements. The first path is that of our discovery of the mystery. It starts from the "economy" and leads to the "theology": it is in receiving the revelation of the gift of God in the economy that believers are led to contemplate God himself. In order to unite the "economy" with the "theology," we have had recourse to analogy. Starting from the effects of the action of God in the world, and under the guidance of faith, analogy helps our mind to raise itself to a true and correct knowledge of the divine persons, by respecting the transcendence of the mystery of God. The second path goes from the "theology" to the "economy": our knowledge of the Trinity in his intimate being clarifies our understanding of the action of the Trinity in the world.

The Fathers of the Church distinguish between theology (*theologia*) and economy (*oikonomia*). "Theology" refers to the mystery of God's inmost life within the Blessed Trinity and "economy" to all the works by which God reveals himself and communicates his life. Through the *oikonomia* the *theologia* is revealed to us; but conversely, the *theologia* illuminates the whole *oikonomia*. God's works reveal who he is in himself; the mystery of his inmost being enlightens our understanding of all his works. So it is, analogously, among human persons. A person discloses himself in his actions, and the better we know a person, the better we understand his actions.[1]

The place that belongs to the "economy" and to the "theology" is well put in the following text from St. Thomas Aquinas concerning Christ Jesus:

According to the order of nature, in Christian doctrine the beginning and the principle of our wisdom is Christ inasmuch as he is the Wisdom and Word of God, i.e., in his divinity. But as to ourselves, the beginning is Christ himself inasmuch as he is the Word who has become flesh, i.e., in his incarnation.[2]

In these explanations, the "order of nature" corresponds to the "theology" and to the order of doctrinal exposition: it regards the Word in his divine being with the Father. For its part, the expression "as to ourselves" corresponds to the "economy" that regards the Word

1. *Catechism of the Catholic Church*, 2nd ed. (Vatican City: Libreria Editrice Vaticana, 1997), no. 236.
2. St. Thomas Aquinas, *Commentary on the Gospel of St. John* 1:1 (no. 34).

in the mysteries of his flesh. As regards the reality itself ("the order of nature"), the eternal divinity of the Word is first. However, as regards the path of our understanding ("as to ourselves"), the incarnation is first. It is necessary first of all to receive the nourishment of the "Word made flesh" in order to grow and to become able to receive the teaching regarding "the Word that is in the beginning with God."[3]

We now focus our attention on the path that goes from "theology" to the "economy." When, in faith, we have been able to discern the eternal properties of the persons, this permits us to perceive better their action in the world. Why is this so? Because it is in the eternal mystery of God the Trinity that one finds the origin, transcendent and free, of his action in the world. God acts according to what he is in himself. The believer's knowledge of the Trinity in his intimate life enables a better discernment of the features proper to the action of each person in the economy. It is not only a matter of "describing" the Trinity's works, but of showing their meaning to believers—that is to say, of offering a doctrine of the action of the divine persons. We have already sketched this aspect in the two preceding chapters. Without repeating all the explanations that we have already given, this last chapter proposes to return to the creative and saving action of the divine persons in order to shed light on the Trinitarian nature of creation and grace.

THE "PROPER MODE OF ACTION" OF DIVINE PERSONS AND "APPROPRIATION"

In order to do justice to the teaching that we have surveyed, we should distinguish and reunite three complementary aspects in our knowledge of the action of the Trinity: (1) the common action of the three divine persons in virtue of their one power and their one nature; (2) the proper mode of acting of each person; (3) the appropriation of certain actions, and of certain effects, to one person in particular.

3. St. Thomas Aquinas, *Summa theologiae* II-II, q. 189, a. 1, ad 4.

Let us briefly recall the first aspect. The three persons act together, not by the juxtaposition or the superimposition of three different actions, but in one same action, because the three persons act by the same power and in virtue of their one divine nature. This affirmation, as we indicated above in chapter 4, constitutes a fundamental element of patristic theology and of the teaching of the Church. "The whole divine economy is the common work of the three divine persons. For as the Trinity has only one and the same nature so too does it have only one and the same operation."[4] To reject this profound truth would be to divide the Trinity.

The second aspect is no less important: "However, each divine person performs the common work according to his unique personal property."[5] In the common action of the Trinity, each person acts according to the distinctive trait that characterizes him. The Father acts as the Source of the Son and of the Holy Spirit, and he always acts thus: *the Father acts through the Son and in the Holy Spirit.* This mode of acting is proper to the Father. He is the only one who, in the Trinity, creates and saves through his Son and in his Holy Spirit. The Son acts in a filial way—that is to say, inasmuch as he is turned toward the Father who begets him, and inasmuch as he is eternally in relation with the Holy Spirit who proceeds. The Son always acts according to this twofold relation. *The Son is, in a proper and distinct way, the Word through whom the Father acts, with the Holy Spirit.* The Holy Spirit acts in the mode of his relation to the Father and to the Son from whom he proceeds. According to the tradition that we presented above, we can say that *the proper mode of the Holy Spirit is to act as the Love and Gift of the Father and the Son.*

In order to understand this mode of action, it is necessary to return to the teaching concerning the "properties" of the persons. What is proper to each person, in the intimate life of the Trinity whose nature is one and simple, is to exist according to a "distinct mode of being." This mode of being is relative because it concerns

4. *Catechism of the Catholic Church*, no. 258.
5. Ibid.

the relation of each divine person with the others. In the one divinity, the Father exists in the mode of the Source without origin who is the principle of the Son, with whom he "breathes" the Holy Spirit. The Son exists personally in the mode of his filial relation to the Father, which implies his relation to the Holy Spirit. The Holy Spirit exists in the mode of his relation of procession from the Father and the Son, as the Love and Gift of the Father and Son from all eternity. In sum: in the one divine substance, each person is characterized by a distinct mode of existence, and this mode corresponds to the relative property of each person.

Just as each divine person is characterized by a *distinct mode of existence*, each person possesses likewise a *distinct mode of action*. This mode of action is strictly conformed to the mode of existence of the divine person. As one is, so one acts. It is therefore necessary to recognize that the proper mode of action concerns *the eternal relations of divine person to divine person*. When he acts in the world, the Son does not cease to receive himself from the Father by generation: the Son is turned toward the Father who begets him. The proper mode of existence of divine persons does not disappear when these persons act in the world; rather, this proper mode remains present as a constitutive feature of each person's action.

The Father works through his Son and in the Spirit to whom he eternally communicates the divine fullness. The Father did not create the world by a necessity imposed on him, nor does he act in the world in an arbitrary manner; he acts through his Son who is his Word full of wisdom. And the Father did not create the world in order to increase his happiness, but purely through the superabundance of his generosity: he creates and gives life through his Holy Spirit who is Love in person. The Son acts insofar as he is the personal expression of the wisdom of the Father—that is to say, insofar as he is God the Word from whom bursts forth Love. And the Holy Spirit acts insofar as he is the Communion and the Love of the Father and the Son: his personal mode of action is to work insofar as he is the Love and the Gift proceeding from the Father and the Son.

One can summarize this teaching with the following affirmation: "The Father does all things through the Word in the Holy Spirit."[6] There is therefore a single power and one action of the whole Trinity, within which each person acts according to what distinctly characterizes him—that is to say, in the relative mode that is proper to him.[7] Each person acts *in virtue of the common nature* and *according to the mode of his personal property.*

The third doctrinal element regarding the action of the Trinity consists in the Trinitarian "appropriations." Before presenting these "appropriations," we recall some preliminary precisions. The divine nature in virtue of which the three persons act is identical; the power and the action are equally common; the effects will therefore be common to the three persons. "The gifts which the Spirit divides to each are bestowed from the Father through the Word. For all things that are of the Father are of the Son also; therefore those things which are given from the Son in the Spirit are gifts of the Father."[8] One cannot affirm that a divine work (for example creation, grace, or a miracle) is the work of one person alone. In the same way, no divine action is accomplished by one person "more" than by the other two.

Why is it thus? On the one hand, because the three persons act by the same divine nature (they *are* this same divine nature); on the other hand, because each person's distinct mode of action, as we have observed, concerns the eternal relations of divine person to divine person and not an exclusive relation that the action of one person has with creatures. When St. John writes that everything

6. St. Athanasius of Alexandria, *Letter to Serapion* 1.28, in *The Letters of Saint Athanasius Concerning the Holy Spirit,* trans. C. R. B. Shapland (London: Epworth Press, 1951), 135.

7. See Gilles Emery, *The Trinitarian Theology of Saint Thomas Aquinas,* trans. Francesca A. Murphy (Oxford: Oxford University Press, 2007), 347–55; Emery, *Trinity, Church, and the Human Person: Thomistic Essays* (Naples, Fla.: Sapientia Press, 2007), 126–43.

8. St. Athanasius of Alexandria, *Letter to Serapion* 1.30, in *The Letters of Saint Athanasius Concerning the Holy Spirit,* translated by C. R. B. Shapland, 141–42 (London: Epworth Press, 1951).

was made through the Word (Jn 1:3: "all things were made through him"), this does not mean that, by creation, creatures have a primary relationship with the Word, a second one with the Father, and finally a third relation with the Holy Spirit. Rather, it signifies that the Father accomplishes all things through the Word whom he has begotten, in such a way that the universal action of the Word is marked by his relation with God his Father. Within the one action of the Trinity, the *distinct* manner according to which the Son acts in the world does not concern his relation to creatures (because the three persons are together the one principle of creatures), but rather his relation to the Father and to the Holy Spirit. This is why one cannot say that a divine action is proper to one person, nor that an effect of God in the world is exclusively produced by one person. It is necessary rather to speak of a "proper *mode* of action" of each person, understanding that this proper mode regards the relations between the divine persons themselves: it is a relational mode of action.

On these foundations, the Catholic theological tradition developed the doctrine of "Trinitarian appropriations." This theological teaching was only theorized in the twelfth and thirteenth centuries, but the reality that it describes is fundamental. The New Testament offers numerous "appropriations": it frequently attributes an action or an effect to a divine person in a special way, without excluding the two others. Let us first give a definition. One calls *appropriation* (from the Latin *ad* and *proprium:* "to draw toward the proper," "to put nearer to the proper") the procedure of the language of the faith by which a reality common to the three persons (a trait that concerns the essence of God the Trinity, or a divine action, or an effect of the action of the Trinity in the world) is attributed in a special way to a divine person. The foundation of the appropriation is the real affinity of an "essential" attribute (common to the three persons) with the distinctive property of a person. The goal of appropriation is to make better manifest the divine persons, in their distinctive properties, to the mind of believers. The means of appropriation reside in the essential attributes (realities common to the whole Trinity) through which one indirectly makes manifest the persons. Put otherwise, "to appropriate" an essential attribute or a divine action to one person is to look upon this attribute or this action *in the person to whom one specially associates it.*

Let us take the example of divine power. Power is common to the Father, Son, and Holy Spirit. Each person is all-powerful. There is only one divine omnipotence, which is equal in the Three. The divine persons are not distinguished by a power more or less great, or more or less efficacious. However, power is attributed in a special way to the person of the Father. It is thus that we confess in the *credo:* "I believe in God the Father almighty." Without excluding the Son or the Holy Spirit, power is specially attributed to the Father by reason of the affinity or kinship that this attribute of power possesses with the distinctive property of the Father. The Father is the Source in the Trinity. He is the Principle without principle. Now, there is clearly an affinity between power and the property of the Father as *Principle without principle,* because power also signifies a "principle": power is the principle of action and of the effects that come forth from this action. In virtue of this real proximity or affinity between the notion of power and that of *Principle without principle,* we therefore attribute power to the Father, without denying that each person is equally powerful. Thus—and this is the goal of appropriation—to attribute power to the Father is to render the property of the Father more manifest to our understanding. This better *makes manifest* the Father to our mind as principle without principle of the Trinity, and thus sheds light on the person of the Father. In this way, the theological doctrine of appropriation accounts for numerous affirmations of holy Scripture.

We should take care, however: the appropriated attributes should not be confused with the distinctive properties of the persons. Appropriation *presupposes* the doctrine of personal properties, and it can never be substituted for these properties. Take, for example, goodness, which is appropriated to the Holy Spirit. Goodness is an attribute common to the whole Trinity. By definition, goodness is the motive and object of love. Now, the Holy Spirit is, in person, the Love of the Father and the Son. By reason of this affinity, one appropriates goodness to him. The meaning of this appropriation is the following: When the person of the Holy Spirit is known to us in faith according to his distinctive property (this property is procession), to appropriate goodness to the Holy Spirit helps us to discern better his person by means of a reality that is more accessible to our understanding (because the divine goodness, through its effects in the world, is more easily accessible to us than the Holy Spirit's hypostatic property of procession).

Consider another example: the filial adoption by which God the Father makes of humans his own children, through his Son and his Spirit. To adopt is an *action*. This action entails an *effect* that is adoptive sonship. Ontologically, that is to say, insofar as it is a created effect, filiation has the whole Trinity as its cause. St. Thomas Aquinas explained: "Adoption, though common to the whole Trinity, is appropriated to the Father as its *Author;* to the Son, as its *Model;* to the Holy Spirit as *imprinting in us the likeness of this Model.*"[9] The three persons accomplish together, in a single action, the adoption of the children of God. And in this same action, each person acts according to the distinct mode of his personal property. This is why the act of adoption is appropriated to each person according to an aspect that presents a special affinity with the proper mode according to which that person acts.

Filial adoption is appropriated to the Father as its *Author.* The Father is the Source of the Son and of the Holy Spirit through whom he adopts us as his children. The Father makes us children of God. Under another aspect, filial adoption is appropriated to the Son, because the Son is the *Model* of all filiation. The property of the Son is to be begotten of the Father. He is thus the Model of filiation by which humans are begotten to a new life as children of God. It is therefore with reason that adoption is attributed to the action

---

9. St. Thomas Aquinas, *Summa theologiae* III, q. 23, a. 2, ad 3.

of the Son: the Son makes us children of God. Finally, adoption is appropriated to the Holy Spirit under the aspect in which, being the Gift of the Father and the Son, the Holy Spirit connects humans to the Son and enables them to participate in the sonship of the Son. We shall say therefore quite rightly that it is the Holy Spirit who makes us children of God.

To make us children of God: a common action that is appropriated. The Father makes us his children insofar as he is the *Source of the Son and of the Holy Spirit* through whom he accomplishes filial adoption. The Son procures adoptive sonship insofar as he is the *Begotten of the Father.* And the Holy Spirit makes humans children of God insofar as he is the *Spirit of the Father and the Son.* Here we find the proper features that ground appropriation. These proper traits are taken from the personal properties—that is to say, from the relations *of divine person to divine person.* There is only one action (to adopt) exercised by the three divine persons, with one effect that has the three persons as its principle (adoptive sonship refers us "ontologically" to the whole Trinity), and appropriation enables us to perceive better the profound Trinitarian dimension of filial adoption.

Let us briefly summarize these elements. The three divine persons act in the world by a single action. The effects of the divine action are also common to the whole Trinity. In the one action of the Trinity, each person operates by virtue of the nature common to the Three, and each person acts according to the distinct mode of his property. The affinity of an action, or of an aspect of an action, or of an effect, with the property of a divine person lets us appropriate this action or this effect to a divine person, in such a way that the proper traits of persons are better manifested to us.

THE CREATIVE TRINITY AND THE
TRINITARIAN ECONOMY

Because the whole divine action is Trinitarian, the first work that it is necessary to consider is the creation. God the Father creates by his Word and by his Spirit. St. Irenaeus magnificently explained this in presenting the creation of the human being.

It was not angels, therefore, who made us, nor who formed us, neither had angels power to make an image of God, nor any one else, except the Word of the Lord, nor any Power remotely distant from the Father of all things. For God did not stand in need of these beings, in order to the accomplishing of what he had himself determined with himself beforehand should be done, as if he did not possess his own hands! For with him were always present the Word and Wisdom, the Son and the Spirit by whom and in whom, freely, he made all things, to whom also he speaks, saying, *Let us make man after our image and likeness* (Genesis 1:26), he taking from himself the substance of the creatures, and the pattern of things made, and the type of all the adornments in the world.[10]

The Son and the Holy Spirit are the two "Hands" by which the Father fashions the human being and leads him to his perfection. The existence of the human in the image of God is grounded in the action of the Father through his "two Hands." In this text, St. Irenaeus rejects the gnostic idea according to which the corporeal world came forth from a reality inferior to God. Christian faith denies gnostic emanations. The human being comes from the action that the Father exercises through his Son and through his Spirit. This theme of the "two Hands" shows that the creation and the salvation of human beings are the work of God insofar as he is Trinity. The divine action is one, and its modality is essentially Trinitarian. The same God the Trinity who leads humans to the fulfillment of their vocation is the God who created them. And God creates like he saves, that is to say, in a Trinitarian manner: the Father creates and saves through his Son and his Spirit. We should not limit this Trinitarian mode to grace and salvation, but rather it is necessary to

10. Saint Irenaeus of Lyons, *Against Heresies* 4.20.1 (cf. *SC*, vol. 100, *Contre les hérésies: Livre IV*, ed. Adelin Rousseau, subvol. 2, *Edition critique, texte et traduction* [Paris, Cerf, 1965], 624–26); English translation from http://www.newadvent.org; see also *Against Heresies* 4, Preface 4 (cf. *SC*, vol. 100, subvol. 2:390): "For man is a mixed organization of soul and flesh, who was formed after the likeness of God, and moulded by His hands, that is, by the Son and Holy Spirit, to whom also He said, *Let us make man*"; cf. also 4.7.4:462–64).

recognize the Trinitarian nature of the whole divine economy, and first of the creation by which the universe is produced and by which we exist. Trinitarian salvation has its foundation in the Trinitarian creation.

This passage of St. Irenaeus shows what we have called the "proper mode of action" of the Father: the Father acts through his Son and through his Holy Spirit. St. Irenaeus elsewhere explains: "As God is verbal [*logikos*], therefore He made created things by the Word; and God is Spirit, so that He adorned all things by the Spirit."[11] One can discern here a sort of "appropriation" of diverse aspects of the divine work: the substance of created things, the pattern of created things, and the adornment of things that are ordered. To the Word is attributed the fact of giving form and existence to things. As regards the Holy Spirit, it pertains to him to dispose things in a harmonious order and to achieve in some way the divine work. "The Word 'establishes', that is, works bodily and confers existence, while the Spirit arranges and forms the various 'powers.'"[12] St. Irenaeus shows the distinction of divine persons in their action.

St. Thomas Aquinas expressed the Trinitarian dimension of creation in a brief formula: "The processions of the divine Persons are the cause of creation."[13] God the Father creates through his Son. The eternal generation of the Son by the Father is, as it were, the reason and the model of the production of creatures that receive from God, in creation, a participation of being and life. This creative action is accomplished in the Holy Spirit who is the Love of the Father and the Son. The eternal procession of the Holy Spirit appears as the reason of the works that God produces by his free will. It is by one and the same Love that the Father and Son love each other and love us. Certainly, the generation of the Son and the procession of the Holy Spirit are eternal and "necessary," whereas creation occurs

11. St. Irenaeus of Lyons, *On the Apostolic Preaching* 5, trans. John Behr (Crestwood, N.Y.: St. Vladimir's Seminary Press, 1997), 43 (cf. *SC* 406:90); see Michel René Barnes, "Irenaeus's Trinitarian Theology," *Nova et Vetera* 7 (2009): 67–106.

12. St. Irenaeus of Lyons, ibid.

13. St. Thomas Aquinas, *Summa theologiae* I, q. 45, a. 6, ad 1.

in time and depends on the good divine will; but creation is directly connected to the Trinitarian life.

Making an additional step, St. Thomas Aquinas explained that the universe has for its cause the Trinitarian *relations* themselves.[14] The relations of divine persons (paternity, filiation, procession), insofar as they are identified with these persons themselves, are the origin of the distinction and of the multiplicity of creatures. The plurality of creatures, in the extraordinary diversity of an ordered universe, finds its source in the personal relations of God the Trinity.

Lastly, in the same way that the processions of the divine persons are the cause of the created world, a transcendent and free cause, they are also the source of the union of angels and humans with God. By the "temporal procession" ("mission") of the Son and of the Holy Spirit, angels and humans are united with God, which is their end and their happiness. In humans, it is the whole universe that, in some way, "returns" to God. We will return to this work of divinization later, when we discuss the "missions" of the Son and of the Holy Spirit.

For now, it is necessary to hold to *the unity of the Trinitarian economy in creation and grace.* Like the gift of grace, creation is a work that the Father accomplishes through his Son and his Spirit. Creation is the foundation of salvation: grace presupposes nature. Grace heals nature, strengthens it, and brings it to its fulfillment. The Trinitarian dimension of creation enables one to apprehend the gift of natural life in all its depth. The created universe is the work of the Word full of wisdom (the Father creates through the Son) and of Love (the Father creates by his Spirit). This is why one finds in the world some "likenesses" for speaking of God the Trinity. In creating the world through his Word and his Spirit, God gave to us a "first book" in which he manifests himself in a permanent way and by which he prepares the reception of his revelation.

One calls "vestiges of the Trinity" the traces that the creative

14. St. Thomas Aquinas, *Commentary on the Sentences*, Bk. I, dist. 26, q. 2, a. 2, ad 2.

Trinity has left in all creatures. These vestiges, which only faith enables one to discern, inspire a contemplative regard for the created world. One calls "image" the special imprint that the Trinity inscribed in angels and humans, insofar as angels and humans are capable of knowing and loving God—that is to say, insofar as they are capable of being elevated to communion with God the Trinity by grace, so as to participate in the beatitude of God the Trinity in the communion of saints. At times one distinguishes "image" and "likeness," designating by "image" a quality that the human being received through creation and that he cannot lose, while the "likeness" signifies the development of the image by grace—that is to say, the progressive assimilation to Christ by the gift of the Holy Spirit.[15]

We have emphasized that the divine act is Trinitarian and that the created world offers reflections of it. It is necessary also to add that the divine economy proceeds according to a Trinitarian arrangement or "disposition." We can illustrate this aspect with St. Irenaeus of Lyons, who offered a profound view of the "Trinitarian unfolding" of the divine economy.

For man, by his own power, will not see God. But when God pleases he is seen by men, by whom he wills, and when he wills, and as he wills. For God is powerful in all things, having been seen in the past prophetically through the Spirit, and then seen, too, adoptively through the Son; and he shall also be seen paternally in the kingdom of heaven, the Spirit truly preparing man for the Son of God, and the Son leading him to the Father, while the Father confers upon him incorruption and eternal life, which come to every one from the fact of seeing God. . . . And for this reason, he, who is beyond comprehension, and boundless and invisible, rendered himself visible, and comprehensible, and within the capacity of those who believe, that he might vivify those who receive and behold him through faith. . . . It is not possible to live apart from life, and the means of life is found in participating in God; but to participate in God is to know God, and to enjoy his goodness.[16]

15. See, for instance, Irenaeus of Lyons, *Against Heresies* 5.16.2 (*SC* 153:216).

16. Saint Irenaeus of Lyon, *Against Heresies* 4.20.5 (cf. *SC,* vol. 100, subvol. 2:638–42); English translation from http://www.newadvent.org.

The Trinitarian economy reveals to us who God is. Above all, St. Irenaeus emphasizes that God gives himself to be seen. To see God is to know him by a transformative knowledge that enables one to participate in his life. The goal of the "economies" is the fullness of life for the glory of God. Now the fullness of life consists in knowledge of God: "And this is eternal life, that they know thee the only true God, and Jesus Christ whom thou hast sent" (Jn 17:3). This vision of God does not take place "from the outside," but rather it is in himself that God is seen. The path of salvation is thus structured in a Trinitarian manner around the vision of God, in three moments. The first step is, so to say, confided to the Holy Spirit who prepares human beings for the Son. At the heart of the second step is the incarnate Son, in view of filial adoption (conformation to the Son, union with God by faith). And the Son leads the Church to the fulfillment of the path, which is eternal life flowing from the vision of the Father. In this presentation of the Trinitarian economy, the work of one divine person is referred to another person: the Holy Spirit leads to the Son, and the Son leads to the Father. By associating each step or moment of the economy with one divine person, St. Irenaeus makes manifest the order of persons and their unity. Put otherwise, St. Irenaeus makes manifest the Trinity by presenting the divine economy, and he uncovers this economy by making manifest the Trinity. The doctrine of the Trinity and the history of salvation are intimately connected; they mutually illuminate each other.

Here, then, is the Trinitarian disposition of salvation: "Just as the effect of the mission of the Son was to lead us to the Father, so the effect of the mission of the Holy Spirit is to lead the faithful to the Son."[17] Above, in chapter 3, we already observed this order of divine persons in their action, in reference to baptism.

For those who bear the Spirit of God are led to the Word, that is to the Son, while the Son presents them to the Father, and the Father furnishes them with incorruptibility. Thus, without the Spirit it is not possible

---

17. St. Thomas Aquinas, *Commentary on the Gospel of St. John* 14:26 (no. 1958).

to see the Word of God, and without the Son one is not able to approach the Father; for the knowledge of the Father is the Son, and knowledge of the Son of God is through the Holy Spirit, while the Spirit, according to the good-pleasure of the Father, the Son administers, to whom the Father wills and as He wills.[18]

Baptism summarizes the Trinitarian arrangement of the economy. By the Holy Spirit, humans are led to knowledge of the Son and, through the Son, they have access to the Father. In the passage just cited, one can also observe the twofold relation of the Son and of the Holy Spirit: on the one hand, the Holy Spirit enables one to see the Son; on the other hand, the Son gives the Holy Spirit. This order is connected to the missions of the divine persons (the sending of the Son and of the Holy Spirit). The Father appears as the source and the personal "end" of the economy, because it is he who sends the Son and the Holy Spirit, and it is to him that the Son and the Holy Spirit lead the Church.

The Trinitarian disposition of the economy can be signified in other, complementary ways. One traditional way reproduces the order of persons according to the communication of the divine life within the Trinity itself (the sequence Father-Son-Spirit): creation is attributed to the Father, re-creation to the Son, and the gift of glorious life to the Holy Spirit. This approach can be explained, at least partly, by the process of "appropriation" (creation is attributed to the Father, for example). Without confusing the works common to the whole Trinity with the properties that distinctly characterize the persons, appropriation makes manifest the distinct persons in the arrangement of the economy. In the same sense, Charles Cardinal Journet explained: "The Father is, so to speak, 'located' in the creation, the Son in the Incarnation, and the Spirit in the Church."[19] The history of the world becomes the "place" of the manifestation,

18. St. Irenaeus of Lyons, *On the Apostolic Preaching* 7, trans. John Behr (Crestwood, N.Y.: St. Vladimir's Seminary Press, 1997), 44 (cf. SC 406:92).

19. Charles Journet, *Entretiens sur le Saint-Esprit* (Saint-Maur: Parole et Silence, 1997), 66.

of the presence of the divine persons. This presence of the three divine persons in time constitutes the history of the world. The continuity and distinction of the different stages of history become evident when we consider the presence, under different modes, of the three divine persons in the world: "The Father as Creator—by appropriation—, the Son as Savior, the Holy Spirit as coming to make overflow into the world, by his pressure (so to speak), the grace that is in Jesus and thereby to constitute, wherever it will be received, the Church, his mystical Body."[20]

The *Catechism of the Catholic Church* suggests a related approach when it connects Trinitarian faith to "the gifts that God gives man: as the Author of all that is good, as Redeemer, and as Sanctifier."[21] The three persons work inseparably by one and the same action, in which each person acts in accordance with his relative property.

The economy does not constitute the Trinity (it is not the economy that makes God exist as Triune); rather, the economy makes manifest the eternal Trinity who reveals himself in the incarnation of the Son and in the gift of the Holy Spirit. And when, in faith, we contemplate the distinct persons according to their eternal properties, this helps us to discern better the action of these persons. The economy of creation and grace is marked by the relations of divine persons who work inseparably. Meditation on the Trinitarian economy nourishes and intensifies the desire for union with God the Trinity: "The ultimate end of the whole divine economy is the entry of God's creatures into the perfect unity of the Blessed Trinity (cf. Jn 17:21–23)."[22]

THE "IMMANENT TRINITY" AND THE "ECONOMIC TRINITY"

Today, theological reflection on the Trinity is often undertaken in terms of the "immanent Trinity" and the "economic Trinity." In the

---

20. Journet, *Entretiens sur la Trinité* (Saint-Maur: Parole et Silence, 1999), 97.
21. *Catechism of the Catholic Church*, no. 14.
22. *Catechism of the Catholic Church*, no. 260.

1960s, the Catholic theologian Karl Rahner developed the following principle, which he presented as the "fundamental axiom" of
Trinitarian doctrine: "The Trinity of the economy of salvation *is*
the immanent Trinity and vice versa."[23] "*The 'economic' Trinity is the
'immanent' Trinity and the 'immanent' Trinity is the 'economic' Trinity.*"[24] By "economic Trinity" Rahner means the Trinity who reveals
himself and communicates himself in his action for us, particularly in the incarnation of the Son and the gift of the Holy Spirit. For
its part, the expression "immanent Trinity" signifies the Trinity in
its intimate life. The first phrase of the fundamental axiom ("the
Trinity of the economy of salvation is the immanent Trinity") emphasizes that the economy is truly the manifestation and communication of God the Trinity himself. The second phrase ("and vice
versa") indicates that the Trinity communicates himself in a complete and definitive way in Christ Jesus and in the pouring out of
the Holy Spirit.

Karl Rahner sought particularly to show that the Trinity is the
mystery of salvation par excellence. In his own "self-communication,"
God gives himself as he is. Salvation consists in the gift that God the
Trinity makes of himself. This gift is accomplished in Christ and the
Holy Spirit. Rahner also wished to avoid separating theological teaching on the Trinity and teaching concerning the other realities of faith
(particularly teaching on the work of Christ). He emphasized that the
divine persons act in a differentiated manner and that, in grace, each
divine person communicates himself to us according to his personal
property: "Both mysteries, that of our grace and that of God in himself, are the same fathomless mystery."[25]

The economy is our sole path of access to the mystery of the
Trinity. And in this economy, God reveals himself and communicates himself in accordance with what he is in himself. This is a

23. Karl Rahner, *Theological Investigations,* vol. 4, trans. Kevin Smyth (Baltimore:
Helicon Press, 1966), 87; italics in original.

24. Rahner, *The Trinity,* trans. Joseph Donceel (New York: Herder and Herder,
1970), 22; italics in original.

25. Rahner, *Theological Investigations* 4:98.

truth for which neither Arianism nor Sabellianism succeeded in accounting. In the mysteries of salvation, it is really God the Trinity who manifests himself and who gives himself. The economy is not a "screen" between God and humans, but gives true access to God the Trinity. The mystery of the Trinity is revealed and communicated to us *in the economy* and not "behind" it.

Understanding this "fundamental axiom" requires certain precisions. First, it is necessary not to conflate the eternity of God and the time of the economy. The history of salvation manifests the Trinity, but it is not the economy of salvation that gives to the Father, Son, and Holy Spirit their distinct personality. The economy does not constitute the Trinity. The Father does not become Father by his relation with us in Christ, but rather he is Father from all eternity. Second, the eternal being of God is "necessary," whereas the economy is absolutely free, gratuitous, and not necessary. Nothing obligated God the Trinity to reveal himself or to give himself in grace: it is a purely gratuitous work. Third, we should not conflate the reality of the Trinity in himself, in his transcendent mystery, with the human knowledge and experience that we can have of the Trinity. It is indeed the Trinity in his own mystery who reveals himself and communicates himself in the economy, but humans receive this knowledge and this experience in a limited manner, proportionate to their condition as creatures (in this sense, there is no pure and simple identity between the "immanent Trinity" and the "economic Trinity"). The economy does not exhaust the mystery of the Trinity. This leads us to a fourth precision. The participation of humans in the Trinitarian life will only find its fulfillment beyond history, in the blessed vision of the Trinity. By reason of this expectation, a certain "distance" remains. In sum: God reveals himself and communicates himself as Trinity, because he is in himself Trinity and he acts as he is; however, the reception of the revelation of God and of the gift that God makes of himself in the economy does not exhaust the mystery of the Trinity in itself.

In fact, we should ask whether it is truly wise to exposit Trinitarian faith around the identity and the distinction between the "immanent Trinity" and the "economic Trinity." The reflection connected to this theological elaboration indisputably possesses a real value. And the axiom formulated by Rahner has made a notable contribution to the renewal of Trinitarian theology. However, when the doctrine of the Trinity is posed in these terms, it leads at times to presenting Trinitarian faith in a dialectical and even wooden manner. The theological tradition shows that there are other ways of accounting for the truth of the Trinitarian revelation and of manifesting the gift that the Trinity makes of itself in the economy. One enlightening way consists, undoubtedly, in the doctrine of the "missions" of the divine persons, with which we will complete our exposition.

THE MISSIONS OF THE SON AND
OF THE HOLY SPIRIT

The Trinitarian gift of divine life is accomplished by the mission of the Son and of the Holy Spirit—that is to say, by their salvific sending. In order to render an account of the biblical teaching, a vast current flowing from St. Augustine set forth the saving act of the Trinity by considering the "visible missions" and the "invisible missions" of the Son and of the Holy Spirit. We will begin by explaining briefly the meaning of these expressions.

The "visible mission" of the Son designates his sending in the flesh—that is to say, the incarnation that is unfolded in the mysteries of the life of the Son in his humanity. The visible mission of the Son is unique: there is only one incarnation. But the New Testament bears witness to several "visible missions" of the Holy Spirit.[26] By the expression "visible missions of the Holy Spirit," one des-

26. Receiving the fruits of the tradition that precedes him, St. Thomas Aquinas counts four "visible missions" of the Holy Spirit: two visible missions are made with regard to Christ Jesus (baptism and transfiguration), and two others to the apostles (the breathing forth of the Holy Spirit according to John 20 and Pentecost according to Acts 2); see *Summa theologiae* I, q. 43, a. 7, ad 6.

ignates the sending of the Holy Spirit in abundance with sensible signs. These signs show the fullness of salvation in Christ (particularly at the baptism of Christ) and the gift of the Holy Spirit to the apostles in order to establish the Church in faith and charity (Pentecost). The "visible missions" relate to historical events foundational for salvation, from Christmas to Pentecost.

One calls an "invisible mission" the sending of the Son and of the Holy Spirit into human hearts: "If a man loves me, he will keep my word, and my Father will love him, and we will come to him and make our home with him" (Jn 14:23); "God has sent the Spirit of his Son into our hearts, crying, 'Abba! Father!'" (Gal 4:6). These missions are called "invisible" because, although their fruits are manifested exteriorly in the practice of a holy life, they are accomplished interiorly in the soul of the just. We focus our attention first on the "visible" missions in order then to show their relation with the "invisible" missions, taking our inspiration from the teaching of St. Thomas Aquinas.[27]

The "Visible Mission" of the Son and of the Holy Spirit

The incarnation of the Son and the Pentecost of the Holy Spirit, which we call "visible missions," are ordered to the "invisible" missions that we will discuss further on. The Son of God was made man so that, in faith, we could receive from him grace and truth. The Holy Spirit was manifested by signs in order to show the abundance of grace by which he interiorly sanctifies the Church.

The "visible missions" (the incarnation of the Son and his life in the flesh, as well as the sending of the Holy Spirit under signs attested by witnesses) are at the same time revelatory and salvific. On the one hand, these "visible missions" *reveal the divine persons* and make manifest their gift in grace. God leads us to the invisible through the visible. Such is the mode of knowing that is connatural to us: it is by starting from sensible experience that we are led to realities that are

---

27. For references and more details, see Emery, *The Trinitarian Theology of Saint Thomas Aquinas*, 360–412.

beyond the senses. God uses corporeal realities in order to signify to us his own mystery. On the other hand, the "visible missions" of the Son and of the Holy Spirit *procure sanctification;* they bring salvation. These two aspects, namely the revelation and the gift of the divine persons, are intimately connected. Let us look at them first in the mission of the Son, in order then to observe them in the mission of the Holy Spirit.

"When the time had fully come, God sent forth his Son, born of woman" (Gal 4:4). The Son assumes, in the unity of his own divine person, the humanity conceived in the womb of the Virgin Mary. From the first instant of its conception, this humanity is the humanity of the Son of God. The sending of the Son at the time of his incarnation unfolds in all the mysteries of his existence in the flesh. This sending *manifests* the Son begotten by the Father from all eternity. The life of the Son in human flesh, his words and his acts, reveal his eternal generation by the Father. This sending also *procures* salvation for us. The Son becomes man in order to save humans with the active concurrence of the humanity that he assumes. By the mysteries of his life in the flesh, by his passion and his resurrection, the incarnate Son pours forth the sanctifying Holy Spirit.

We contemplate Christ in the light of the faith of Chalcedon (Christ is true God and true man, one person in two natures united without confusion or separation). In his divinity, insofar as he is true God, the incarnate Son is the principal cause of salvation. In his humanity, insofar as he is true man, the Son is likewise the cause of salvation: his humanity is the "instrument" of the divinity, as was explained by St. Athanasius of Alexandria, St. Cyril of Alexandria, St. John Damascene, and other Christian teachers. The humanity of the incarnate Son possesses this salvific power because it is united to his divine nature in the unity of his own person, and because it is perfected in a unique way by the Holy Spirit. The union of the human nature with the divine nature in the person of the Son (the "hypostatic" union) constitutes this humanity as an instrument of the divinity; the fullness of grace that this humanity possesses (the anointing of Christ by the Holy Spirit) perfects it so that it might adequately accomplish its action of salvation. If we have distinguished the divinity and humanity of the Son, it is in order to show the union and synergy in his one person. The human action of Christ, as instrument of his divinity, collaborates freely with his divine action in order to procure for us the sending of the Holy Spirit and access to the Father. One could include here the whole teaching of the creed regarding Christ.

The "visible missions" of the Holy Spirit are the manifestation, through visible signs, of his abundant gift in human hearts. One notes above all one such visible mission of the Holy Spirit upon the incarnate Son himself, Jesus. At the baptism of Jesus, "the Holy Spirit descended upon him in bodily form, as a dove" (Lk 3:22), and the Father declares him to be his "beloved Son" (Mk 1:11; Mt 3:17).[28] This descent of the Holy Spirit, at the beginning of the ministry of Jesus, shows that Jesus is the Christ, the Son of the Father, the Savior. At the moment in which Jesus inaugurates his public work, the sending of the Holy Spirit under a sign, "as a dove," manifests the plenitude of the Holy Spirit (the "invisible mission" of the Holy Spirit) with which the humanity of Jesus was filled without measure from its conception. A venerable tradition has likewise recognized a similar "visible mission" of the Holy Spirit at the transfiguration of Jesus, by discerning the Holy Spirit in the "bright cloud" from within which the Father declares: "This is my beloved Son, with whom I am well pleased; listen to him" (Mt 17:5). In Aquinas's interpretation, both Christ's baptism and his transfiguration are a manifestation of the Trinity, a Trinitarian "theophany." Christ's baptism is

28. The Gospels present certain differences. According to St. John, it is not Jesus (cf. Mk 1:10), but John the Baptist who sees "the Spirit descend as a dove from heaven" (Jn 1:32). According to St. Matthew (Mt 3:17), the voice coming from the cloud is addressed to the crowd and not to Jesus (cf. Mk 1:11); and in the Fourth Gospel, it is the Baptist who bears witness to Christ (Jn 1:34). Without neglecting these nuances, the notion of the "visible mission of the Holy Spirit" at the baptism of Jesus concentrates on the *sign* that *manifests* the presence of the Holy Spirit in Jesus and the salvific power of Jesus.

"the mystery (or sacrament) of the first regeneration," that is, of the regeneration that takes place though grace, by faith (our filiation in grace). And Christ's transfiguration is "the sacrament (or mystery) of the second regeneration," that is, of the regeneration that will take place through the glorious vision of God in heaven (our filiation in glory).[29] The "visible missions" of the Spirit upon Christ Jesus manifest the interior plenitude of grace with which he was filled from his conception and that he *makes flow out onto others* by his teaching and by his saving action.

In the same way, the Holy Spirit is sent to the apostles. On the evening of the resurrection, according to the witness of the Fourth Gospel, Jesus "breathed on them, and said to them, 'Receive the Holy Spirit. If you forgive the sins of any, they are forgiven'" (Jn 20:22–23). At Pentecost, according to the Acts of the Apostles, the Spirit descends on the gathered apostles; in a noise similar to a "rush of a mighty wind," they received "tongues as of fire": all of them were then "filled with the Holy Spirit" (Acts 2:1–4). The apostles begin to speak in other languages; St. Peter preaches faith in Christ crucified and risen, calling his hearers to conversion and baptism: the Church then increases by many members (Acts 2:5–41). The "signs" accompanying the abundant gift of the Holy Spirit (the breath, the wind, the tongues of fire) are indeed of a completely different order than the humanity assumed by the Son in his incarnation. It is necessary to take the notion of "visible mission" in a differentiated manner, with flexibility. These signs attest to the interior gift of the Holy Spirit, not only for the sake of the apostles, but also for other humans to whom the apostles are sent. They indicate the interior gift of the Holy Spirit to the apostles, given superabundantly, for establishing the Church in faith and charity—that is to say, for communicating the grace of Christ through the ministry of preaching and of the sacraments.

The sending of the Holy Spirit on Pentecost is the last "visible

29. St. Thomas Aquinas, *Summa theologiae* III, q. 45, a. 4, ad 2.

mission." Pentecost sums up and contains all the visible missions of the Spirit. It is also the culminating point of the revelation of the Trinity. It enables us to sum up the traits that constitute the "visible missions." First, we discover here the Holy Spirit in person, sent and given by the Father and the Son. His sending reflects his eternal procession. The mission of the divine person is, so to say, an outflowing in time of his eternal procession. Second, we discern here the new presence of the Holy Spirit by grace with which he fills the apostles and that inspires their ministry of founding the Church. These first two aspects constitute the "invisible mission" of the Holy Spirit to the apostles—this is to say, the interior gift of the Spirit. We will come back to this later. To these two aspects, the "visible mission" adds a third element: manifestation through a sensible sign. This sign (the breath, the tongues of fire) manifests exteriorly the interior abundance of the grace of the Spirit by which the apostles are filled for establishing the Church. Furthermore, by showing the interior sending of the Holy Spirit, this sign manifests likewise his eternal procession. St. Augustine explained this latter aspect in a direct and profound way (which should be understood in light of the whole teaching of the New Testament): "It is not without point that the same Spirit is called the Spirit of the Father and of the Son. And I cannot see what else he intended to signify when he breathed and said *Receive the Holy Spirit* (Jn 20:22). The physical breath that came from his body and was physically felt . . . was a convenient symbolic demonstration that the Holy Spirit proceeds not only from the Father, but also from the Son."[30]

This teaching makes manifest a profound correspondence between, on the one hand, the eternal property of the Son and the Holy Spirit, and, on the other hand, their "visible mission." The Son is begotten from all eternity by the Father. As Son, he receives from the Father his being the principle of the Holy Spirit, along with the Father: with the Father, the Son spirates the Holy Spirit. It there-

---

30. St. Augustine, *On the Trinity* 4.20.29 (trans. Edmund Hill, 174, slightly modified).

fore pertains to the Son, in his very quality as Son, to be sent by the Father as *Author of sanctification*—that is to say, as *Giver of the Holy Spirit*. This is a dimension of the "fittingness" of the Son's incarnation that we discover here. Put otherwise, we can here discern the wisdom of the plan of God that is accomplished in the incarnation of the Son. Sent by the Father, the Son assumes a human nature endowed with intelligence and with will, in order to procure our sanctification through that humanity. In his humanity filled with charity, the Son offers the sacrifice that reconciles humans with God. And, with the active concurrence of his holy humanity that is the "instrument" of his divinity, the incarnate Son spreads the Holy Spirit.

According to the teaching of Charles Cardinal Journet, the grace of Christ possesses many "modalities" that deepen our understanding of the mystery of the Son and of the Church. In Christ Jesus himself, the grace of the Holy Spirit is *connatural, full,* and *filial* (because it is the Son in person who is incarnate): these are the three premier and fundamental characteristics that grace possesses in Christ Jesus himself. The *filial* dimension is also a fundamental modality of grace that Christ communicates to his disciples. Cardinal Journet then notes three secondary modalities of Christic grace— that is to say, of the grace that humans receive from Christ: it is *sanctifying without eliminating trials, conformative* of our lives to the likeness of the temporal life of Christ, and *co-redeeming* of the world with Christ. Journet adds a seventh modality: grace is *nuptial*. The Church, being transformed in Christ, reflects the nuptial love of Christ.

The Holy Spirit himself proceeds from all eternity from the Father and the Son. He is the mutual Love and Gift of the Father and the Son. It thus pertains to him to be sent as the *Gift of sanctification*. The Holy Spirit is not only the Giver, but the *Gift* itself: the Holy Spirit accomplishes interiorly the sanctification of the humans in whom he is poured forth. The breath, the wind, and the "tongues as of fire" are signs of this abundant sending of the Holy Spirit and of his active presence in founding and vivifying the Church. The Holy

Spirit is the *sanctifying Gift* in person, poured forth by the Father and the Son. The mission of the Son and the mission of the Holy Spirit appear in full light when one considers them in light of their personal properties.

It is necessary again to note the "parallelism" of the visible missions of the Son and the Spirit: just as the visible mission of the Son finds its completion in Christ and makes present in the world the second person of the Trinity by constituting him as Head of the Church, the visible mission of the Spirit finds its completion in the Church and brings about the formation of the mystical body of Christ.[31] "Nothing greater than the Incarnation and Pentecost will ever happen,"[32] because "God will never make a greater gift to the world than that of the Son on the day of the Incarnation, nor a greater gift to the Church than that of the Spirit on the day of Pentecost."[33] "There will never be more visible missions. Just as the Son must be incarnate once and for all, the Spirit, following the same rule, must be given once and for all. The twofold visible mission of the Son and the Spirit is irrevocable, its efficacy is unlimited in duration."[34]

The "Invisible Missions" of the Son and of the Holy Spirit

The life of the Son in our humanity and the manifestation of the Holy Spirit at Pentecost are ordered to the coming of the Son and the Holy Spirit into the heart of humans, so as to unite them to the Father. When the Son and the Holy Spirit are sent into hearts, they come in person and inseparably. The "invisible mission" of the Son and that of the Holy Spirit are distinct, but they are simultaneous and indissociable: the one is never without the other. Only the Son and the Holy Spirit are sent into hearts. The divine person is sent by the one from whom he eternally proceeds. The Father is not "sent,"

31. Charles Journet, *Oeuvres Complètes,* vol. 2 (Saint-Maurice: Éditions Saint-Augustin, 1999), 505.

32. Journet, *Entretiens sur la Trinité,* 100.

33. Ibid., 123.

34. Journet, *Oeuvres Complètes,* 2:767–68.

because he does not have a principle, but he comes with the Son and the Holy Spirit into the saints. St. Athanasius explained: "When the Spirit is in us, the Word also, who gives the Spirit, is in us, and in the Word is the Father."[35] By grace, the whole Trinity dwells in the soul of the just.[36] The "invisible mission" of the Son and of the Holy Spirit is connected to this "indwelling" of the whole Trinity, but it adds to indwelling a special note that implies a new mode of presence of the Son and of the Holy Spirit. In what consists this "invisible mission" of the Son and of the Holy Spirit?

The interior sending of the Holy Spirit and of the Son into souls consists in two aspects or two sides. The first, uncreated aspect is the divine person himself, sent in accordance with his proper mode of existence. The Son is sent by the Father, just as he is begotten by the Father; the Holy Spirit is sent by the Father and the Son insofar as he proceeds from the Father and the Son. Under this first aspect, the "invisible mission" carries in it the eternal procession of the divine person who is sent. The person sent is the *begotten* Son and the *proceeding* Holy Spirit. The Son and the Holy Spirit are sent into hearts in accordance with what they are. The second aspect that constitutes the "invisible mission" is a gift of sanctifying grace that the divine persons give to souls, a created effect by reason of which the Son and Holy Spirit are present in a new manner. When the Holy Spirit is sent, this new created effect consists in the gift of charity. Charity renders souls conformed to the Holy Spirit. And in the sending of the Son, this effect is wisdom, the gift of sanctifying knowledge of God, which renders souls conformed to the Son. The created gifts (wisdom and charity, inseparable) are *caused* by the divine persons, and they *dispose* us to receive the divine persons

35. St. Athanasius of Alexandria, *Letter to Serapion* 1.30, in *The Letters of Saint Athanasius Concerning the Holy Spirit,* trans. C. R. B. Shapland (London: Epworth Press, 1951), 142.

36. "God dwells in his temple: not the Holy Spirit alone, but also the Father and the Son. . . . The temple of God, that is, of the sublime Trinity as a whole, is the Holy Church universal, in heaven and on earth" (St. Augustine, *Enchiridion* 15.56); the translation (slightly modified) comes from St. Augustine, *Faith, Hope and Charity,* trans. Louis A. Arand (New York: Newman Press, 1947), 60.

themselves. The missions of the divine persons are, in this way, the outflowing in grace of their eternal procession.

We should take note of the gifts procured by the interior sending of the Holy Spirit and of the Son. When the Son and the Holy Spirit are sent, they imprint in souls a "seal" that bears their mark: this seal is a likeness of the Word and of Love. The seal or imprint that the Son gives to souls is wisdom, a wisdom that inspires the movement of love. This wisdom is a participation in the personal property of the Son who is the Word of the Father. Thus, the Word "is born" in the soul that receives him by grace. And the seal that the Holy Spirit imprints in souls is the charity that is a participation in his personal property of Love. This twofold imprint constitutes what above we have called the gifts of sanctifying grace—namely the gifts of wisdom and charity. Sanctifying grace, which elevates the very nature of the human being (it gives a participation in the divine nature), is the "root" of these gifts of wisdom and of charity that renew and elevate the faculties of spiritual activity (knowledge and love of God). Wisdom makes its beneficiaries like to the Son, "assimilitating" them to the Son and enabling them to *participate in the relation that the Son has with his Father.* Charity makes its beneficiaries like the Holy Spirit, "assimilating" them to the Holy Spirit and enabling them to *participate in the relation that the Holy Spirit has with the Father.* "God has sent the Spirit of his Son into our hearts, crying, 'Abba! Father!'" (Gal 4:6). The Holy Spirit procures our union with the Father by the love that he communicates when he is poured forth into our hearts.

Thus, the union of angels and of humans with God is accomplished by an "assimilation" to the personal relation that the Son and the Holy Spirit have with the Father. *The saints are grasped and transformed interiorly by the radiant power of the Son and Holy Spirit who are sent into them.* This radiant power that comes forth from the divine persons enables the just to be "conformed" to the Son and to the Holy Spirit who are sent to them; to receive the Son and Holy Spirit themselves; to "possess" them—that is to say, to enjoy the Son and the Holy Spirit who are really given; and to enter in them into the communion of the Father. Regarded in their common divinity that is the sovereign Good, the three persons are the one *ultimate End* of creatures. There is only one ultimate end: the divine Trinity. And, within this one end, the Father is the *personal term* of the economy: the Son and the Holy Spirit lead the saints to the vision of the Father.

Humans and angels who receive the "invisible" mission of the Son and Holy Spirit are not "mixed" with the Son and the Holy Spirit. They remain creatures, but they become "divinized" creatures—that is to say, new creatures who live and act for the Father in the radiant power of the Son and Holy Spirit who have visited them. Such an "invisible mission" of the Son and the Holy Spirit comes in justification by grace, in the sacraments of faith. New "invisible missions" can come often in the life of the just, each time that the visit of the Son and Holy Spirit possesses a character of newness, notably in the fruitful reception of the sacraments or by virtue of any divine initiative inspiring a new state of union with God and inspiring new acts—for example, progress in virtue, victory over temptations, the accomplishment of a difficult task by charity. In these "invisible missions," eternal life is already begun. Treating the "Second Coming" of Christ that will take place at the end of time, St. Thomas Aquinas observed that there is already a "coming" (*adventus*) in which Christ "comes daily to the Church, by visiting her spiritually, insofar as he dwells in us by faith and charity."[37]

The Divine Missions: Christ and His Spirit

The interaction of Christ and the Holy Spirit has great importance in their "missions." The Son took flesh in the Virgin Mary by the Holy Spirit: "de Spiritu Sancto," as the Church chants in her credo, signifying by this the divine origin of the human birth of Jesus. The Holy Spirit forms the human flesh of Christ. The same Holy Spirit fills to fullness the human soul of Christ, from the first instant of

---

37. St. Thomas Aquinas, *Commentary on the Sentences,* Bk. IV, dist. 47, q. 1, a. 1, qla 3, ad 2.

his conception. To his Son, the Father has given the Spirit "without measure" (cf. Jn 3:34). Christ, as man, received the Holy Spirit completely.[38] This plenitude is unique and proper to Christ, because the humanity of Christ is united to his divinity in the most profound unity (it is the unity of the very person of the incarnate Son). The human action of Jesus is animated by the movements of the Holy Spirit that "lead" Jesus (cf. Mk 1:12). The descent ("visible mission") of the Holy Spirit upon Christ, at his baptism, manifests precisely this fullness that the beloved Son received from his conception in order to communicate his grace to other humans through his teaching and through the mysteries of his life in our flesh.

When the time came for this great act of unforced generosity, which revealed in our midst the only-begotten Son, clothed with flesh on this earth, a man born of woman, in accordance with holy Scripture, God the Father gave the Spirit once again. Christ, as the first fruits of our restored nature, was the first to receive the Spirit. John the Baptist bore witness to this when he said: *I saw the Spirit coming down from heaven, and it rested on him.* . . . . Christ 'received the Spirit' in so far as he was man, and in so far as man could receive the Spirit. . . . The whole of our nature is present in Christ, in so far as he is man. So the Father can be said to give the Spirit again to the Son, though the Son possesses the Spirit as his own, in order that we may receive the Spirit in Christ. . . . The only-begotten Son receives the Spirit, but not for his own advantage, for the Spirit is his, and is given in him and through him, as we have already said. He receives it to renew our nature in its entirety and to make it whole again, for in becoming man he took our entire nature to himself. If we reason correctly, and use also the testimony of Scripture, we can see that Christ did not receive the Spirit for himself, but rather for us in him; for it is also through Christ that all gifts come down to us.[39]

The salvific value of the human action of Christ, particularly in his passion, comes from charity and the movement of the Holy

38. In his *Commentary on the Gospel of St. Matthew* 12:18 (no. 1000), St. Thomas Aquinas explained: "In Christ, [God] has not only given a part of the Spirit (*de Spiritu*), but rather he has given the whole Spirit (*totum Spiritum*)."

39. Saint Cyril of Alexandria, *On John* 7.39 (*PG* 73, col. 752–53); translation of the *Liturgy of the Hours* for the Office of Readings of Thursday after the Epiphany.

Spirit: Christ offers himself to God through the Spirit (cf. He 9:14).
In becoming incarnate, the Son imparted his own Spirit to the humanity that he assumed. Under these aspects, Christ in his humanity is the beneficiary of the Holy Spirit, for the glory of God the Father and for our salvation. Under another aspect, which we noted
above, Christ pours out the Holy Spirit with the collaboration ("instrument") of his humanity, full of grace and perfected by the Holy
Spirit. Under this second aspect, Christ in his divinity and in his humanity is the giver of the Holy Spirit. The Holy Spirit comes from
Christ to all who receive grace.

The action of the Holy Spirit is inseparable from Christ. The
work of the Holy Spirit is not different from that of the incarnate
Son, although the Holy Spirit acts in another mode. The Holy Spirit inscribes the teaching of the incarnate Son in our hearts, and he
causes us to enter into the mystery of the incarnate Son himself.
The salvific action of Christ and that of the Holy Spirit also have
the same universal extent. The universality of the action of Christ,
the Son *as incarnate,* should be considered in light of the faith professed by the Councils of Ephesus and of Chalcedon: Christ is one
person in whom the humanity is united to the divinity. By virtue of
this union, the human action of Christ is the proper and conjoined,
free and living "instrument" of the divine action. The human action
of Christ is also perfected by the gift without measure of the Holy
Spirit. The Spirit enables the humanity of Christ to work in full synergy with the divine nature. This confers on the human action of
Christ a range of action as extensive and as profound as that of his
divinity.

St. Thomas Aquinas explained in this regard: "The operation of
Christ's human nature, *as the instrument of the Godhead,* is not different from the operation of the Godhead. For the salvation by which
Christ's humanity saves us and the salvation by which his divinity
saves us are not different."[40] Thus, the human action of Christ, par-

---

40. St. Thomas Aquinas, *Summa theologiae* III, q. 19, a. 1, ad 2.

ticularly his offering to the Father on the Cross, procures a fruit of salvation that is as universal and as profound as that of his divinity. This fruit is the sanctification of humans by the sending of the Holy Spirit. There is not, on the one hand, a salvation procured by Christ as God, and on the other hand a salvation procured by Christ as man. This would divide Christ and would ruin the work of the incarnation. Neither is there, on the one side, a salvation procured by Christ, and on the other side, a salvation procured by the Holy Spirit. The same one salvation is procured in an inseparable way by Christ and his Spirit.

In sum: Christ, the incarnate Son, procures salvation *through the Spirit* that he pours out with the mediation of his holy humanity; the Holy Spirit communicates salvation *by incorporating human beings into Christ.* "Whatever is done by the Holy Spirit is also done by Christ."[41] By the united action of the Son and of the Holy Spirit, human beings are reunited to the Father: this is the Church. "Since the Word is in the Father and the Spirit is given from the Word, he wills that we should receive the Spirit, so that, when we receive him, thus having the Spirit of the Word who is in the Father, we too may be found on account of the Spirit to become one in the Word, and through him in the Father."[42]

An important passage of the Constitution *Gaudium et Spes* of the Second Vatican Council teaches: "We ought to hold that the Holy Spirit, in a manner known to God, offers to every man the possibility of being associated with the paschal mystery" (no. 22).[43] The gift of the Holy Spirit, no matter who receives it, is intrinsically connected to Christ. On the one hand, the Spirit is poured out in abun-

41. St. Thomas Aquinas, *Commentary on the Epistle to the Ephesians* 2:18 (no. 121).

42. St. Athanasius of Alexandria, *Third Discourse Against the Arians,* no. 25.

43. The dogmatic Constitution *Lumen Gentium* (no. 16) puts it thus: "Those also can attain to salvation who through no fault of their own do not know the Gospel of Christ or His Church, yet sincerely seek God and moved by grace strive by their deeds to do His will as it is known to them through the dictates of conscience. Nor does Divine Providence deny the helps necessary for salvation to those who, through no fault of their own, have not yet arrived at an explicit knowledge of God and with His grace strive to live an upright life."

dance as a result of the passion and resurrection of Christ. On the other hand, the Spirit connects his beneficiaries with Christ in his passion and resurrection. Humans who receive the sanctification of the Holy Spirit are incorporated into Christ, and thereby they are members of the Church, which is the Body of Christ. The Holy Spirit reaches his beneficiaries, whoever they might be, *through the connection that the Son established in his humanity with humans.* This fundamental truth was recalled with concision and vigor by Pope John Paul II: "No one can enter into communion with God except through Christ, by the working of the Holy Spirit."[44]

In the times before the incarnation, the gift of the Holy Spirit was already attached to the mystery of the flesh of Christ and to the one Church of Christ: the saints of the Old Testament received the grace of the Holy Spirit by faith in the Mediator. "The ancient Fathers, by observing the sacraments of the Law, were borne to Christ by the same faith and love by which we also are borne to Christ. And so the ancient Fathers belong to the same Church as we."[45] Implicitly or explicitly, faith in Christ the mediator is constitutive of the salvation procured by the gift of the Holy Spirit. "Without faith it is impossible to please him [God]" (Heb 11:6). St. Thomas Aquinas offers this commentary: "No one ever had the grace of the Holy Spirit except through faith in Christ either explicit or implicit."[46]

The Second Vatican Council specified on this subject: "Though God in ways known to himself can lead those inculpably ignorant of the Gospel to the faith without which it is impossible to please him (Heb. 11:6), yet a necessity lies upon the Church (1 Cor. 9:16), and at the same time a sacred duty, to preach the Gospel. And hence missionary activity today as always retains its power and necessity."[47] Humans receive salvation from the Father, through Christ Jesus, in the Holy Spirit. Today as on the day of Pentecost, the an-

---

44. John Paul II, Encyclical Letter *Redemptoris missio* (1990), no. 5.
45. St. Thomas Aquinas, *Summa theologiae* III, q. 8, a. 3, ad 3.
46. St. Thomas Aquinas, *Summa theologiae* I-II, 106, a. 1, ad 3.
47. Vatican II, Decree *Ad Gentes* on the mission activity of the Church, no. 7.

nouncement of faith in the Father, Son, and Holy Spirit is at the center of the mission of evangelization of the Church.

In conclusion, *the revelation of the Trinity and the gift of salvation consist in the missions of the divine persons.* The doctrine of salvation is the doctrine of the missions of the Son and of the Holy Spirit (the missions that we have called "visible" and "invisible"). This approach presents many advantages. It invites one to contemplate Christ, in his action of salvation, in his relations to the Father and to the Holy Spirit—that is to say, to regard Christ and his work in the light of Trinitarian faith. The doctrine of the missions does not separate the teaching on God and the teaching on Christ (Christology), but rather it understands them in their unity. In contemporary theology, at times one finds an opposition between "theocentrism"— that is to say, a view centered on the mystery of God—and "Christocentrism," namely an approach that places Christ at the center of all things. The doctrine of missions does not present such an opposition, and can help surmount unfruitful tensions. It also does not separate the teaching on Christ and on the Holy Spirit, but rather it regards Christ and the Holy Spirit in their unity and in their relations.

This approach shows well that salvation resides in the Trinity itself, because *the missions bear in themselves the eternal mystery of the divine persons,* the mystery of the Son begotten by the Father and the mystery of the Holy Spirit who proceeds. If one follows St. Thomas Aquinas, there is no need to reunite the economic Trinity and the immanent Trinity (after having started by distinguishing between them), because, for Aquinas, the mission or "temporal procession" of the divine person "is not essentially different from the eternal procession, but only adds a reference to a temporal effect."[48] Moreover, this approach avoids conflating the temporal work of the divine persons with the inner being of the Trinity, because it pre-

48. St. Thomas Aquinas, I *Sent.,* dist. 16, q. 1, a. 1: "Processio temporalis non est alia quam processio aeterna essentialiter, sed addit aliquem respectum ad effectum temporalem."

serves the transcendence of God in relation to the effects of his action. The mission of the divine persons thus offers a light capable of guiding all Christian theology. One could be convinced of this by considering, for example, the monumental work of Charles Cardinal Journet, *The Church of the Word Incarnate,* which is built on the doctrine of the missions of the Son and of the Holy Spirit.[49]

49. The doctrine of the missions is especially developed in the first part of the second book of this work: Charles Journet, *Oeuvres Complètes,* vol. 2, *L'Église du Verbe Incarné, Essai de théologie spéculative: Sa structure interne et son unité catholique (première partie)* (Saint-Maurice: Éditions Saint-Augustin, 1999).

By Way of Conclusion

Without repeating the various elements that constitute this book, let us briefly survey the path traversed. Our presentation of the teaching regarding God the Trinity has comprised three steps, in an investigation guided by the quest for union with God in beatitude and eternal life.

The first step is the study of the economy in which the mystery itself is manifested and given, according to the witness of Scripture: God the Father saves humans by the salvific sending of his Son and by the sanctifying effusion of the Holy Spirit. Meditation on Scripture and on the ecclesial gift of salvation by faith and the sacraments are the principal resources. We found a good example in the "soteriological" argument dear to the Fathers of the Church: by enabling us to participate in the divine life, the Son and the Holy Spirit show us their divinity; by introducing us into the communion of the Father, into the rhythm of their personal relations, they show us their distinction in unity.

In the second step, we surveyed the dogmatic teaching ("speculative," in the old sense of the word—that is to say, "contemplative") on the eternal being of the Trinity: on the divine persons, their relations and their properties, their distinct personality, and their consubstantiality. Here, in benefitting from the doctrinal deepening of Scripture accomplished by the Fathers and doctors of the Church, theology renders an account of the same mystery that the economy

manifests: the communion of three divine persons in their distinction and their unity. This is the doctrine of the Trinity "in itself"—
that is to say, of the three divine persons insofar as they are turned
toward each other in the unity of their divine being.

We have seen that the explication of Trinitarian dogma by the
Fathers and doctors of the Church was inspired by the necessity of
responding to heresies. Heresies have been the *occasion* of this explication, but they are not the most profound cause of it. This most
profound cause is the love of God, the gift of wisdom. The gift of
wisdom is the source of the intimate knowledge of the mystery of
God: this is what enabled the saints to set forth the Trinitarian mystery in such a deep manner. This is why we should say, with Charles
Cardinal Journet, "I would give all my theology for a drop of the gift
of wisdom. And the one who would not do this is not worthy to be
a theologian."[1]

Finally, the third step offered a "speculative" reflection on the
action of the divine persons in the world, by means of the insights
won in the two preceding steps. This third step proposes a doctrine of the Trinity in the economy—that is to say, of the Trinity
"turned toward creatures" in his creative and sanctifying act, the
Trinity regarded as "principle" and as "end" of creatures. This third
step is based on the first (the revelation of the mystery of the Trinity in the economy), and it also necessarily presupposes the second.
This is so because in discerning the eternal relations of the Father,
Son, and Holy Spirit, insofar as our weak understanding is capable,
we glimpsed the foundation of the paternal action of the Father, the
foundation of the filial action of the Word, and the foundation of
the gift of Love by which the Father and Son love us. In this third
step, the creative and saving act of the Trinity was contemplated in
light of the eternal mystery of the divine persons. These three steps
are unfolded in the reading of holy Scripture itself.

The quest for "the understanding of the faith" is directed toward

---

1. Charles Journet, *Les dons du Saint-Esprit* (unpublished retreat, dating from 1941).

the fulfillment of the Trinitarian economy that is the entrance of the saints into the perfect communion of the Blessed Trinity. The happiness of angels and of humans consists in the uncreated Good who is *God the Trinity himself.* The beatifying union with God resides in the vision of the Trinity "face to face" (cf. 1 Cor 13:12; 1 Jn 3:2) in that joyful communion of all the blessed in the Church of heaven, exceeding all we can conceive or desire.

In that celestial vision it will be granted to the eyes of the human mind strengthened by the light of glory, to contemplate the Father, the Son, and the Holy Spirit in an utterly ineffable manner, to assist throughout eternity at the processions of the Divine Persons, and to rejoice with a happiness like to that with which the holy and undivided Trinity is happy.[2]

2. Pius XII, Encyclical letter *Mystici Corporis* (1943), no. 80; translation from http://www.vatican.va; cf. Heinrich Denzinger, *Enchiridion symbolorum, definitionum et declarationum de rebus fidei et morum,* 37th ed., ed. Peter Hünermann (Freiburg im Breisgau: Herder, 1991), no. 3815.

Glossary

——— : ———

APPROPRIATION: attribution of an essential reality, of a divine action, or of a created effect (common to the three divine persons) to one person in a special way, by reason of the affinity of this common reality with the property of the particular person, in order to manifest better the divine persons to the mind of believers. For example, power is "appropriated" to the Father. Appropriation presupposes knowledge of the distinctive properties of the persons.

BEGOTTEN: personal property of the Son that consists in his relation of origin from the Father (filiation)—that is to say, in his mode of being relative to the Father who begets him.

COMMON AND PROPER: in Trinitarian doctrine, this twofold aspect expresses the unity of substance (common: unity of the divinity) and the distinction of persons (properties: what is proper to each person). Our knowledge of divine persons is accomplished by the "combination" of these two aspects (St. Basil of Caesarea).

CONSUBSTANTIAL, CONSUBSTANTIALITY: community of divine substance, which is one and identical in the three divine persons (identity and not merely likeness). Consubstantiality is applied to the Son in relation to the Father (Nicene faith) and to the Holy Spirit in relation to the Father and the Son, and it also qualifies the Trinity as such (Council of Constantinople II).

ECONOMY (*OIKONOMIA*): the works by which God reveals himself and communicates himself, particularly the incarnation of the Son and the gift of the Holy Spirit.

EKPOREUSIS: origin and personal property of the Holy Spirit who "proceeds." For lack of another term, one generally translates the Greek word *ekporeusis* by "procession" (taken in a special sense, this term designates distinctly the origin of the Holy Spirit and his relative personal property). Eastern Churches do not use the word *ekporeusis* with exactly the same meaning as the word *processio* has in the Latin tradition, since in the Eastern tradition the word *ekporeusis* refers to the origin of the Holy Spirit from the Father as the sole Source of the Trinity.

ESCHATOLOGY: the study of the "final realities"; what concerns the final fulfillment of the divine economy, the fulfillment of the kingdom of God.

ESSENCE: that by which a thing is what it is and is distinguished from other things. The essence of God is his very divinity (which is incomprehensible). The divine essence is one and identical in the three divine persons.

HYPOSTASIS: the substantial, concrete reality that exists through itself according to an individual mode of being, "that which is and which subsists individually through itself" (St. John Damascene). The word *hypostasis* designates what is really Three in God, that is, the *person* who subsists in a proper and distinct manner. The hypostasis is connected to a personal property.

INNASCIBLE, INNASCIBILITY, UNBEGOTTEN: property of the Father who has no origin. The Father is "not begotten" and does not come from a person: he is "without principle."

MISSION: in Trinitarian doctrine, this term designates the sending of the Son and the Holy Spirit in the economy of grace.

MODALISM: heterodox doctrine that holds the unity of the Father, Son, and Holy Spirit by denying their real personal distinction. For modalism, the names *Father, Son,* and *Holy Spirit* only describe the manners or modes according to which the same God, in himself without distinctions, acts in the world. Equivalent expressions: Sabellianism, Unitarian Monarchianism.

MODE OF EXISTENCE: proper mode that distinctly characterizes each divine person according to his relative property; distinct manner of possessing divinity.

NATURE: interior principle of the operation of a being ("principle of movement and of rest") and, by extension, the essence of a being, that by which a being is what it is. The divine nature is one and identical in the three persons.

NOTION, NOTIONAL: in the technical language of Trinitarian theology, one calls "notions" the characteristics that make known the divine persons. One counts five "notions": innascibility, paternity, filiation, spiration, and procession.

OPPOSITION: principle of formal distinction. The personal relations in the Trinity are "opposed" in the sense that the divine person who possesses one relation does not possess the corresponding relation (the Father is not the Son, the Son is not the Father: paternity and filiation are "opposed" relations).

ORDER: this term signifies the noninterchangeable relation of the persons of the Trinity, by virtue of their properties. This order excludes the confusion of persons. It is manifested by the formula of baptism and by that of the creed: Father, and Son, and Holy Spirit. This order implies no temporal interval or inferiority, but only origin, that is to say a pure relation of principle.

ORIGIN: in Trinitarian doctrine, this word designates the eternal provenance of a divine person—that is to say, the generation of the Son and the procession of the Holy Spirit.

PERICHORESIS: mutual indwelling or interpenetration of the three divine persons who are reciprocally in each other.

PERSON: the individual substance of rational nature—that is to say, the individual who subsists through himself and who possesses by nature the faculty of knowing, of willing, and of acting freely by himself. In Trinitarian doctrine, the word *person* is (despite some nuances) the equivalent of *hypostasis*. The three divine persons are distinguished by their personal properties: paternity, filiation, and procession.

PRINCIPLE: that from which a thing is produced, that from which a thing comes forth, the reality from which another proceeds. This term implies in itself no posteriority or inequality between the reality that proceeds and that from which it proceeds. In Trinitarian doctrine, the word "principle" signifies an order of origin: the Father is the principle of the Son, the Father and the Son are the principle of the Holy Spirit. The Father alone is the "principle without principle" (and, in this sense, the only "Source" of the Son and of the Holy Spirit, the unique "Source" of the deity).

PROCESSION: in its common meaning, the word "procession" designates the origin of the Son and of the Holy Spirit—that is to say, generation and procession (there are "two processions" in God the Trinity); in a special sense, the word "procession" designates distinctly the origin of the Holy Spirit and his relative personal property (see *Ekporeusis*).

PROPERTY: incommunicable characteristic of each divine person. These properties are not interchangeable: for the Father, paternity and innascibility (not begotten); for the Son, filiation (begotten); for the Holy Spirit, procession. There are three "personal properties," which are personal relations and which distinguish the divine persons: paternity, filiation, and procession.

RELATION: relationship of one thing to another, the genus or category of being that consists in the fact of being related to another thing. Traditional Catholic doctrine recognizes four real relations in the Trinity—that is to say, four relations that account for the distinction of divine persons: paternity, filiation, spiration, and procession. These relations are taken according to origin (for example, filiation, the relation of the Son, consists in his relationship to the Father who begets him), and they comprise an "opposition" (the Son is not the Father). Paternity, filiation, and procession are called "personal relations" (St. Thomas Aquinas).

SPIRATION: act of the Father and of the Son who "breathe" the Holy Spirit who proceeds; "common notion" of the Father and the Son inasmuch as they are the one principle of the Holy Spirit (that is to say: relation of the Father and of the Son to the Holy Spirit).

SUBSISTENCE: existence through oneself and in oneself; the individual substance under the aspect in which it exists through itself and not in another; what exists through itself and in itself. In Trinitarian doctrine, the word "subsistence" (in Latin: *subsistentia*) translates the Greek term *hypostasis*: three subsistences.

SUBSTANCE: what is apt to exist in itself and not in another. The "divine substance" designates the very reality of the divinity, the concrete essence, so to say, of God. The substance of the three divine persons is one and identical. To the unity of substance, the unity of power and the unity of nature are connected.

THEOLOGY (*THEOLOGIA*): the mystery of God's inmost life within the Blessed Trinity, the mystery of the three persons in the transcendent reality of their divine being.

UNBEGOTTEN: see Innascible. "Unbegotten" (a property of the Father who does not come from another person) must not be confused with "uncreated" or "not having been made" (an attribute common to all three divine persons).

VESTIGES: one calls "vestiges of the Trinity" the traces that, by his creative act, the Trinity has left of itself in the whole created universe.

Bibliography

PRIMARY SOURCES

Alberigo, Giuseppe, ed. *Corpus Christianorum: Conciliorum Oecumenicorum Generaliumque Decreta.* Vol. 1, *The Oecumenical Councils From Nicaea I to Nicaea II (325–787).* Turnhout: Brepols, 2006.

Thomas Aquinas, St. *Commentary on the Gospel of John.* Part I. Translated by James A. Weisheipl and Fabian R. Larcher. Albany, N.Y.: Magi Books, 1980.

———. *Commentary on the Gospel of John.* Part II. Translated by James A. Weisheipl and Fabian R. Larcher. Petersham, Mass.: St. Bede's Publications, 1999.

———. *In librum Beati Dionysii de divinis nominibus expositio.* Edited by Ceslas Pera. Turin and Rome: Marietti, 1950.

———. *In symbolum Apostolorum expositio.* In *Opuscula Theologica.* Vol. 2, *De re spirituali,* 193–217. Edited by Raimondo Spiazzi. Turin and Rome: Marietti, 1954.

———. *Liber de Veritate Catholicae Fidei contra errores Infidelium qui dicitur Summa contra Gentiles.* Edited by Petrus Marc, Ceslas Pera, and Petrus Caramello. 3 vols. Turin: Marietti; Paris: Lethielleux, 1961–67.

———. *Opera omnia iussu Leonis XIII. P. M. edita.* Cura et studio Fratrum Praedicatorum. Rome: Commissio Leonina, 1882–. Some recent volumes have been published by Éditions du Cerf, Paris.

———. *Quaestiones disputatae de potentia.* In *Quaestiones disputatae.* Vol. 2, *De potentia, De anima, De spiritualibus creaturis, De unione Verbi incarnati, De malo, De virtutibus in communi, De caritate, De correctione fraterna, De spe, De virtutibus cardinalibus,* edited by Pio Bazzi, Mannes Calcaterra, Tito S. Centi, Egidio Odetto, and Paulus Pession, 7–276. Turin and Rome: Marietti, 1965.

———. *Scriptum super libros Sententiarum.* Vols. 1 and 2. Edited by Pierre Mandonnet. Paris: Lethielleux, 1929.

———. *Scriptum super libros Sententiarum.* Vols. 3 and 4. Edited by Maria F. Moos. Paris: Lethielleux, 1933–1947.

———. *Summa contra Gentiles*. Translated by Anton C. Pegis, James F. Anderson, Vernon J. Bourke, and Charles J. O'Neil. 5 vols. Notre Dame, Ind.: University of Notre Dame Press, 1975.

———. *Summa theologiae*. Cura et studio Instituti Studiorum Medievalium Ottaviensis. Editio altera emendata. 5 vols. Ottawa: Harpell, 1941–45.

———. *Summa theologiae*. Latin text and English translation, with introductions, notes, appendices, and glossaries. Edited by Thomas Gilby and T. C. O'Brien. Blackfriars. 60 vols. London: Eyre and Spottiswoode; New York: McGraw-Hill, 1964–73.

———. *Summa Theologica*. Translated by Fathers of the English Dominican Province. 5 vols. New York: Benzinger, 1948.

———. *Super Epistolas S. Pauli lectura*. Edited by Raffaele Cai. 2 vols. Turin and Rome: Marietti, 1953.

———. *Super Evangelium S. Ioannis lectura*. Edited by Raffaele Cai. Turin and Rome: Marietti, 1952.

———. *Super Evangelium S. Matthaei lectura*. Edited by Raffaele Cai. Turin and Rome: Marietti, 1951.

Athanasius of Alexandria, St. *Sur l'Incarnation du Verbe*. Edited by Charles Kannengiesser. Sources Chrétiennes 199. Paris: Cerf, 1973.

———. *The Letters of Saint Athanasius Concerning the Holy Spirit*. Translated by C. R. B. Shapland. London: Epworth Press, 1951.

———. *Select Treatises*. Translated by John Henry Cardinal Newman. Vol. 1. New York: Longmans, Green, 1897.

Augustine, St. *The City of God, Books VIII–XVI*. Translated by Gerald G. Walsh and Grace Monahan. The Fathers of the Church: A New Translation 14. Washington, D.C.: The Catholic University of America Press, 1952.

———. *De Genesi ad litteram libri duodecim*. Edited by Joseph Zycha. Corpus Scriptorum Ecclesiasticorum Latinorum 28. Prague and Vienna: Bibliotheca Academiae Litterarum Caesareae Vindobonensis, 1894.

———. *De Trinitate libri XV*. Edited by W. J. Mountain. Corpus Christianorum, Series Latina 50, 50A. Turnhout: Brepols, 1968.

———. *De vera religione*. Edited by Joseph Martin, 187–260. Corpus Christianorum, Series Latina 32. Turnhout: Brepols, 1962.

———. *Faith, Hope and Charity*. Translated by Louis A. Arand. New York: Newman Press, 1947.

———. *Letters 100–155*. Translated by Roland J. Teske. The Works of Saint Augustine 2:2. Hyde Park, N.Y.: New City Press, 2003.

———. *On Genesis*. Translated by Edmund Hill, O.P. The Works of Saint Augustine 1:13. New York: New City Press, 2002.

———. *Sermons 230–272B*. Translated by Edmund Hill, O.P. The Works of Saint Augustine. 3:7. New Rochelle, N.Y.: New City Press, 1993.

———. *Sermons 51–94*. Translated by Edmund Hill, O.P. The Works of Saint Augustine 3:3. Brooklyn, N.Y.: New City Press, 1991.

———. *Sermons 94A–147A*. Translated by Edmund Hill, O.P. The Works of Saint Augustine 3: 4. Brooklyn, New York: New City Press, 1992.

———. *The Trinity*. Translated by Edmund Hill, O.P. The Works of Saint Augustine 1:5. Brooklyn: New City Press, 1991.

Basil of Caesarea, St. *Contre Eunome*. 2 vols. Edited by Bernard Sesboüé, Georges-Matthieu de Durand, and Louis Doutreleau. Sources Chrétiennes 299, 305. Paris: Cerf, 1982–1983.

———. *Letters*. Vol. 1, *Letters 1–185*. Translated by Sister Agnes Clare Way. The Fathers of the Church: A New Translation 13. Washington, D.C.: The Catholic University of America Press, 1981.

———. *Letters*. Vol. 2, *Letters 186–368*. Translated by Sister Agnes Clare Way. The Fathers of the Church: A New Translation 28. Washington, D.C.: The Catholic University of America Press, 1969.

———. *Lettres*. Vol. 3. Edited and translated by Yves Courtonne. Paris: Les Belles Lettres, 1966.

———. *On the Holy Spirit*. Translated by David Anderson. Crestwood, N.Y.: St. Vladimir's Seminary Press, 1980.

———. *Sur le Saint-Esprit*. Introduction, texte, traduction et notes par Benoît Pruche, O.P. Sources Chrétiennes 17 bis. Paris: Cerf, 1968.

Cassian. John. *Institutions cénobitiques*. Edited by Jean-Claude Guy. Sources Chrétiennes 109. Paris: Cerf, 1965.

Catechism of the Catholic Church. 2nd ed. Vatican City: Libreria Editrice Vaticana, 1997.

Cyprian of Carthage, St. *Sancti Cypriani Episcopi Opera*. Vol. 2, *De dominica oratione,* edited by C. Moreschini, 87–113. Corpus Christianorum, Series Latina 3A. Turnhout: Brepols, 1976.

———. *Letters 1–81*. Translated by Sister Rose Bernard Donna. Fathers of the Church: A New Translation 51. Washington, D.C.: The Catholic University of America Press, 1964.

Cyril of Jerusalem, St. *The Works of Saint Cyril of Jerusalem*. Vol. 2. Translated by Leo McCauley. The Fathers of the Church: A New Translation 64. Washington, D.C.: The Catholic University of America Press, 1970.

Denzinger, Heinrich. *Enchiridion symbolorum, definitionum et declarationum de rebus fidei et morum*. 37th edition. Edited by Peter Hünermann. Freiburg im Breisgau: Herder, 1991.

Early Christian Writings: The Apostolic Fathers. Translated by Maxwell Staniforth. Revised by Andrew Louth. New York: Penguin Books, 1987.

Eunomius of Cyzicus. "Apologie." In Basile de Césarée. *Contre Eunome, Volume 2,* edited by Bernard Sesboüé, Georges-Matthieu de Durand and Louis Doutreleau, 177–308. *Sources Chrétiennes* 305. Paris: Cerf, 1983.

Evagrius Ponticus. *Traité pratique*. Edited by Antoine Guillaumont and Claire Guillaumont. Sources Chrétiennes 171. Paris: Cerf, 1971.

Gregory of Nazianzus, St. *Discours 24–26*. Edited by Justin Mossay. Sources
    Chrétiennes 284. Paris: Cerf, 1981.

———. *Discours 27–31*. Edited by Paul Gallay. Sources Chrétiennes 250. Paris:
    Cerf, 1978.

———. *Discours 32–37*. Edited by Claudio Moreschini. Sources Chrétiennes 318.
    Paris: Cerf, 1985.

———. *Discours 38–41*. Edited by Claudio Moreschini. Sources Chrétiennes 358.
    Paris: Cerf, 1990.

———. *Lettres théologiques*. Edited by Paul Gallay. Sources Chrétiennes 208. Par-
    is: Cerf, 1974.

———. *On God and Christ: The Five Theological Orations and Two Letters to Cle-
    donius*. Translated by Frederick Williams and Lionel Wickham. Crestwood,
    N.Y.: St. Vladimir's Seminary Press, 2002.

Gregory of Nyssa, St. *Contra Eunomium libri, Pars Prior: Liber I et II*. Edited by
    Werner Jaeger. Gregorii Nysseni Opera 1. Leiden: Brill, 1960.

———. *That There Are Not Three Gods*. In Johannes Quasten, *Patrology*. Vol. 3.
    Westminster, Md.: Newman Press, 1960.

Hilary of Poitiers, St. *The Trinity*. Translated by Stephen McKenna. New York:
    Fathers of the Church, 1954.

Hippolytus of Rome. *La Tradition apostolique*. Edited by Bernard Botte. 2nd ed.
    Sources Chrétiennes 11 bis. Paris: Cerf: 1984.

———. *On the Apostolic Tradition*. Translated by Alistair Stewart-Sykes. Crest-
    wood, N.Y.: St. Vladimir's Seminary Press, 2001.

Holmes, Michael W., ed. and trans. *The Apostolic Fathers: Greek Texts and English
    Translations*. 3rd ed. Grand Rapids, Mich.: Baker Academic, 2007.

Ignatius of Antioch, St. *Letters*. In *The Apostolic Fathers: Greek Texts and English
    Translations*, edited and translated by Michael W. Holmes, 166–261. 3rd ed.
    Grand Rapids, Mich.: Baker Academic, 2007.

Irenaeus of Lyons, St. *Against the Heresies*. Vol. 1, *Book 1*. Translated by Dominic J.
    Unger, with further revisions by John J. Dillon. New York: Paulist Press, 1992.

Irenaeus of Lyons, St. *Contre les hérésies: Livre IV*. Edited by Adelin Rousseau,
    Louis Doutreleau, Bertrand Hemmerdinger, and Charles Mercier. 2 vols.
    Sources Chrétinnes 100. Paris: Cerf, 1965.

———. *Contre les hérésies: Livre V*. Edited by Adelin Rousseau, Louis Doutre-
    leau, and Charles Mercier. Sources Chrétiennes 153. Paris: Cerf, 1969.

———. *Contre les hérésies: Livre III*. Edited by Adelin Rousseau and Louis
    Doutreleau. Sources Chrétiennes 211. Paris: Cerf, 1974.

———. *Contre les hérésies: Livre I*. Edited by Adelin Rousseau and Louis Doutre-
    leau. Sources Chrétiennes 264. Paris: Cerf, 1979.

———. *Démonstration de la prédication apostolique*. Edited by Adelin Rousseau.
    Sources Chrétiennes 406. Paris: Cerf, 1995.

———. *On the Apostolic Preaching*. Translated by John Behr. Crestwood, N.Y.:
    St. Vladimir's Seminary Press, 1997.

Bibliography 209

John of Damascus, St. *Die Schriften des Johannes von Damaskos.* Vol. 2, *Expositio fidei.* Edited by Bonifatius Kotter. Berlin: Walter de Gruyter, 1973.

Justin Martyr, St. *Apologie pour les Chrétiens.* Edited by Charles Munier. Sources Chrétiennes 507. Paris: Cerf, 2006.

———. *Dialogue with Trypho.* Edited by Michael Slusser. Translated by Thomas B. Falls. Revised by Thomas P. Halton. Washington D.C.: The Catholic University of America Press, 2003.

———. *The First and Second Apologies.* Translated by Leslie William Barnard. *Ancient Christian Writers* 56. New York: Paulist Press, 1997.

Mansi, J. D., ed. *Sacrorum Conciliorum nova et amplissima collectio.* Vol. 11, *Ab anno DCLIII usque ad annum DCLXXXVII inclusive.* Paris: H. Welter, 1901.

Melito of Sardis. *On Pascha and Fragments: Texts and Translations.* Edited by Stuart George Hall. Oxford Early Christian Texts. Oxford: Clarendon Press, 1979.

———. *Sur la Pâque.* Edited by Othmar Perler. Sources Chrétiennes 123. Paris: Cerf, 1966.

Missale Romanum. Ex Decreto Sacrosancti Oecumenici Concilii Vaticani II Instauratum. Editio typica tertia. Vatican City: Typis Vaticanis, 2002.

Origen. *Commentaire sur Saint Jean, Livres I–IV.* Edited by Cécile Blanc. Sources Chrétiennes 120. Paris: Cerf, 1966.

———. *Traité des Principes, Livres III–IV.* Edited by Henri Crouzel and Manlio Simonetti. Sources Chrétiennes 268. Paris: Cerf, 1980.

Tanner, Norman P., ed. *Decrees of the Ecumenical Councils.* 2 vols. Washington, D.C.: Georgetown University Press, 1990.

Tertullian. *Adversus Praxean.* In *Tertullianii Opera, Pars II: Opera montanistica,*1157–1205. Edited by A. Kroymann and E. Evans. Corpus Christianorum, Series Latina 2. Turnhout: Brepols, 1954.

———. *Traité du baptême.* Edited by R. F. Refoulé and M. Drouzy. Sources Chrétiennes 35. Paris: Cerf, 1952.

SECONDARY LITERATURE

Ayo, Nicholas. *Gloria Patri: The History and Theology of the Lesser Doxology.* Notre Dame, Ind.: University of Notre Dame Press, 2007.

Ayres, Lewis. *Nicaea and Its Legacy: An Approach to Fourth-Century Trinitarian Theology.* Oxford: Oxford University Press, 2004.

Barnes, Michel René. "Irenaeus's Trinitarian Theology." *Nova et Vetera* 7 (2009): 67–106.

———. *The Power of God: 'Dunamis' in Gregory of Nyssa's Trinitarian Theology.* Washington, D.C.: The Catholic University of America Press, 2001.

Barth, Karl. *Church Dogmatics.* Vol. I, *The Doctrine of the Word of God.* Part 1, *The Word of God as the Criterion of Dogmatics: The Revelation of God.* Edited by G. W. Bromiley and T. F. Torrance. 2nd edition. Edinburgh: T. and T. Clark, 1975.

————. *Church Dogmatics.* Vol. II, *The Doctrine of God.* Part 1, *The Knowledge of God: The Reality of God.* Edited by G. W. Bromiley and T. F. Torrance. Edinburgh: T. and T. Clark, 1957.

Bauckham, Richard. *God Crucified: Monotheism and Christology in the New Testament.* Carlisle: Paternoster, 1998.

————. *Jesus and the God of Israel: "God Crucified" and Other Studies on the New Testament's Christology of Divine Identity.* Carlisle: Paternoster, 2008.

Bobrinskoy, Boris. *The Mystery of the Trinity: Trinitarian Experience and Vision in the Biblical and Patristic Tradition.* Crestwood, N.Y.: St. Vladimir's Seminary Press, 1999.

Bœspflug, François. *Dieu et ses images: Une histoire de l'Éternel dans l'art.* Montrouge: Bayard, 2008.

Brown, Raymond E. *An Introduction to New Testament Christology.* New York: Paulist Press, 1994.

Cazelles, Henri, et al. "Saint Esprit." In *Supplément au Dictionnaire de la Bible.* Vol. 11, *Safaïtique–Sarepta,* edited by Jacques Briend and Édouard Cothenet, 126–398. Paris: Letouzey et Ané, 1991.

Chevallier, Max-Alain. *Souffle de Dieu: Le Saint-Esprit dans le Nouveau Testament.* 3 vols. Paris: Beauchesne, 1978, 1990, and 1991.

Clancy, Finbarr. "*Ecclesia de Trinitate* in the Latin Fathers: Inspirational Source for Congar's Ecclesiology." In *The Mystery of the Holy Trinity in the Fathers of the Church,* edited by D. Vincent Twomey and Lewis Ayres, 161–93. Dublin: Four Courts Press, 2007.

Congar, Yves. *I Believe in the Holy Spirit.* Vol. 1, *The Holy Spirit in the 'Economy': Revelation and Experience of the Spirit.* Translated by David Smith. New York: Seabury Press, 1983.

————. *I Believe in the Holy Spirit.* Vol. 3, *The River of the Water of Life Flows in the East and in the West.* Translated by David Smith. New York: Seabury Press, 1983.

————. *La Parole et le Souffle.* Paris: Cerf, 1983.

Cothenet, Édouard. "Le Saint Esprit dans le corpus johannique." In *Supplément au Dictionnaire de la Bible.* Vol. 11. Paris, Letouzey et Ané, 1991, cols. 345–98.

Daley, Brian E. "The Persons in God and the Person of Christ in Patristic Theology: An Argument for Parallel Development." In *The Mystery of the Holy Trinity in the Fathers of the Church,* edited by D. Vincent Twomey and Lewis Ayres, 9–36. Dublin: Four Courts Press, 2007.

Davis, Stephen T., Daniel Kendall, and Gerald O'Collins, eds. *The Trinity: An Interdisciplinary Symposium on the Trinity.* Oxford: Oxford University Press, 1999.

Dixon, Philip. *"Nice and Hot Disputes": The Doctrine of the Trinity in the Seventeenth Century.* London: T. and T. Clark, 2003.

Durand, Emmanuel. *Le Père, Alpha et Oméga de la vie trinitaire: De la paternité eschatologique au Père en son mystère.* Paris: Cerf, 2008.

Edwards, Mark. *Catholicity and Heresy in the Early Church.* Farnham, UK: Ashgate, 2009.

Emery, Gilles, and Matthew Levering, eds. *The Oxford Handbook of the Trinity.* Oxford: Oxford University Press. Forthcoming.

———. *The Trinitarian Theology of Saint Thomas Aquinas.* Translated by Francesca A. Murphy. Oxford: Oxford University Press, 2007.

———. *Trinity, Church, and the Human Person: Thomistic Essays.* Naples, Fla.: Sapientia Press, 2007.

Fee, Gordon D. *God's Empowering Presence: The Holy Spirit in the Letters of Paul.* Peabody, Mass.: Hendrickson, 1994.

Gathercole, Simon J. *The Preexistent Son: Recovering the Christologies of Matthew, Mark, and Luke.* Grand Rapids, Mich.: Eerdmans, 2006.

Gavrilyuk, Paul L. *The Suffering of the Impassible God: The Dialectics of Patristic Thought.* Oxford: Oxford University Press, 2004. Reprint, 2005.

Grelot, Pierre. *La liturgie dans le Nouveau Testament.* Paris: Desclée, 1991

Harris, Murray J. *Jesus as God: The New Testament Use of Theos in Reference to Jesus.* Grand Rapids, Mich.: Eerdmans, 1992.

Hengel, Martin. "'Sit at My Right Hand!' The Enthronement of Christ at the Right Hand of God and Psalm 110:1." In *Studies in Early Christology,* 119–225. Edinburgh: T. and T. Clark, 1995.

———. *Studies in Early Christology.* Edinburgh: T. and T. Clark, 1995.

———. *The Son of God.* Philadelphia: Fortress Press, 1976.

Hildebrand, Stephen M. *The Trinitarian Theology of Basil of Caesarea.* Washington, D.C.: The Catholic University of America Press, 2007.

Hunt, Anne. *What Are They Saying About the Trinity?* New York: Paulist Press, 1998.

Hurtado, Larry W. *One God, One Lord: Early Christian Devotion and Ancient Jewish Monotheism.* 2nd ed. Edinburgh: T. and T. Clark, 1998.

John Paul II. *Lord and Giver of Life: Encyclical Letter Dominum et Vivificantem.* Washington, D.C.: Office of Publishing and Promotion Services, United States Catholic Conference, 1986.

Journet, Charles. *Entretiens sur la Trinité.* Saint-Maur: Parole et Silence, 1999.

———. *Entretiens sur le Saint-Esprit.* Saint-Maur: Parole et Silence, 1997.

———. *Oeuvres Complètes.* Vol. 2, *L'Église du Verbe Incarné, Essai de théologie spéculative: Sa structure interne et son unité catholique (première partie).* Saint-Maurice: Éditions Saint-Augustin, 1999.

Keating, Daniel A. *Deification and Grace.* Naples, Fla.: Sapientia Press, 2007.

———. *The Appropriation of Divine Life in Cyril of Alexandria.* Oxford: Oxford University Press, 2004.

Keating, James F., and Thomas Joseph White, eds. *Divine Impassibility and the Mystery of Human Suffering.* Grand Rapids, Mich.: Eerdmans, 2009.

Kelly, J. N. D. *Early Christian Creeds.* 3rd ed. New York: Longman, 1995.

La Soujeole, Benoît-Dominique de. *Introduction au mystère de l'Église.* Paris: Parole et Silence, 2006.

Levering, Matthew. *Scripture and Metaphysics: Aquinas and the Renewal of Trinitarian Theology.* Oxford: Blackwell, 2004.

Messner, Reinhard. "Was ist eine Doxologie?" In *Liturgie und Trinität,* edited by Bert Groen and Benedikt Kranemann, 129–60. Freiburg im Breisgau: Herder, 2008.

Murphy, Francis Xavier, and Polycarp Sherwood. *Constantinople II et Constantinople III.* Paris: Editions de l'Orante, 1974.

Nicolas, Jean-Hervé, *Synthèse dogmatique: De la Trinité à la Trinité.* Fribourg: Editions Universitaires; Paris: Beauchesne, 1985.

O'Collins, Gerald. *The Tripersonal God: Understanding and Interpreting the Trinity.* London: Paulist Press, 1999.

Olson, Roger E., and Christopher A. Hall. *The Trinity.* Grand Rapids, Mich.: Eerdmans, 2002.

Ortiz de Urbina, Ignacio. *Nicée et Constantinople.* Paris: Editions de l'Orante, 1963.

Phan, Peter C., ed. *The Cambridge Companion to the Trinity.* Cambridge: Cambridge University Press. Forthcoming.

Pontifical Council for Promoting Christian Unity. "Clarification on 'The Greek and Latin Traditions Regarding the Procession of the Holy Spirit,'" *L'Osservatore Romano,* Weekly Edition in English, September 20, 1995.

Quasten, Johannes. *Patrology.* Vol. 3. Westminster, Md.: Newman Press, 1960.

Rahner, Karl. *The Trinity.* Translated by Joseph Donceel. New York: Herder and Herder, 1970. Reprint, New York: Crossroad, 1997.

———. *Theological Investigations.* Vol. 4, More Recent Writings. Translated by Kevin Smyth. Baltimore: Helicon Press, 1966.

Rowe, C. Kavin. *Early Narrative Christology: The Lord in the Gospel of Luke.* Berlin: Walter de Gruyter, 2006.

Russell, Norman. *The Doctrine of Deification in the Greek Patristic Tradition.* Oxford: Oxford University Press, 2004.

Sesboüé, Bernard. *Saint Basile et la Trinité: Un acte théologique au IVᵉ siècle.* Paris: Desclée, 1998.

Sesboüé, Bernard, and Joseph Wolinski. *Histoire des dogmes.* Vol. 1, Le Dieu du salut. Paris: Desclée, 1994.

Smith, J. Warren. "The Trinity in the Fourth Century Fathers." In *The Oxford Handbook of the Trinity,* edited by Gilles Emery and Matthew Levering. Oxford: Oxford University Press. Forthcoming.

Studer, Basil. *Trinity and Incarnation: The Faith of the Early Church.* Edinburgh: T. and T. Clark, 1993.

Torrance, Thomas F. *The Trinitarian Faith: The Evangelical Theology of the Ancient Catholic Church.* Edinburgh: T. and T. Clark, 1995.

Torrell, Jean-Pierre. *Saint Thomas Aquinas.* Vol. 1, The Person and His Work. Translated by Robert Royal. Rev. ed. Washington, D.C.: The Catholic University of America Press, 2005.

Urbina, Ignacio Ortiz de. *Nicée et Constantinople.* Paris: Editions de l'Orante, 1963.

Vermeulen, Antonius J. *The Semantic Development of Gloria in Early-Christian Latin.* Nijmegen: Dekker and Van de Vegt, 1956.

Wainwright, Arthur W. *The Trinity in the New Testament.* London: S.P.C.K., 1962.

Wainwright, Geoffrey. *Doxology: The Praise of God in Worship, Doctrine and Life, A Systematic Theology.* Oxford: Oxford University Press, 1981.

Witherington, Ben, and Laura M. Ice. *The Shadow of the Almighty: Father, Son, and Spirit in Biblical Perspective.* Grand Rapids, Mich.: Eerdmans, 2002.

Index

sabellianism. *See* modalism

Sabellius, 60

sacraments, 3–4, 66–67, 182, 188, 195. *See also* baptism; Eucharist

sending. *See* missions of the Son and of the Holy Spirit

Sesboüé, Bernard, 52n2, 55n8, 85n3

Sherwood, Polycarp, 104n49

similitudes. *See* likenesses

Smith, J. Warren, 61n20

Son: as Creator, 73–74, 128–32, 168–71; as Giver of the Holy Spirit, 14, 17, 38, 41–43, 142–43, 163, 174, 180–84, 190–91; as giving wisdom, 131, 186–87; as God, 31–36, 44–46, 64–65, 68, 70, 72–73, 108, 125–26, 133; as Image of the Father, 10–11, 131–33; incarnation, 1, 2, 17–18, 58, 60, 91–92, 121n12, 125, 131–33, 159–61, 174–76, 178–80, 182, 184–85, 189–90; as Light, 70–72, 87; as Lord, 13, 31, 35–36, 52–53, 69; as making of humans children of God, 127–28, 133, 167–68, 173, 187; mode of action, 162–63, 165, 190–91; as revealing the Father, 125, 129–30, 132, 187; as sent, 178–94; as Son of the Father, 13, 16, 23–30, 34–35, 53, 69–72, 85–86, 123–31; as Word of the Father, 4, 17, 32, 128–31. *See also* Father; Holy Spirit; Jesus

Studer, Basil, 55n7

substance, 61–64, 69–70, 72–73, 81, 83, 85–87, 89, 91–92, 102–3, 106–7, 110, 126, 128, 135n34, 140, 143–44, 151

symbol of faith, 58, 67. *See also* confession of faith; creed

Tertullian, 60–61, 80n59, 101, 146

Thomas Aquinas, xiii, xvi, 3n4, 11nn18–19, 14n23, 15n25, 16nn27–28, 16n30, 31nn7–8, 43, 47–49, 79–80, 81n62, 87n10, 91, 92n23, 94, 98n38, 99n42, 100n43, 101n44, 102, 103n48, 104, 105nn52–53, 107–8, 110, 113, 115n8, 118n9, 121–22, 124–25, 130, 131n28, 132n29, 133, 136n35, 139, 142, 146–47, 150–54, 155n82, 157n84, 158n85, 159, 160, 161n3, 167, 170–71, 173n17, 178n26, 179, 182n29, 188, 189n38, 190, 191n41, 192–93, 202

Torrance, Thomas F., 134n32

Trinitarian theology, xi–xv, 20, 99–100, 153, 196

Tropikoi, 64

unbegotten, 62–64, 68, 84–85, 87, 112–13, 115, 120–23, 200, 203

unitarian monarchianism. See *modalism*

Vermeulen, Antonius J., 5n6

vestiges, 171–72, 203

vision of God, xii, xiv, 127, 138, 172–73, 177, 182, 188, 197

Wainwright, Arthur W., 22n3

Wainwright, Geoffrey, 52n1

White, Thomas Joseph, 91n21

Witherington, Ben, 22n3

Wolinski, Joseph, 52n2